To Dr. Kelly Davidson
with great respect and
deep appreciation —
4-23-2014
Gen Sam Wilson

General Sam

Lt. General Samuel V. Wilson
22nd President of Hampden-Sydney College (1992-2000)

General
Sam

A Biography of
Lieutenant General
Samuel Vaughan Wilson

Drew Prehmus
Hampden-Sydney College

Hampden-Sydney • 2011

To the men who participate in, have passed through, or supported
The Wilson Center for Leadership in the Public Interest
at Hampden-Sydney College

Printed in the United States of America

ISBN-13: 978-1484981962
ISBN-10: 1484981960

General Sam

ACKNOWLEDGEMENTS

Without General Sam's contributions, this project would not have been possible. He made time in his busy schedule during three separate semesters for weekly three-hour sessions with me while I was a student at Hampden-Sydney. Listening to General Sam talk about his life was the best academic experience of my life. In this narrative I strove to retain as much as I could of the sophisticated prose that marks his storytelling capabilities.

Without the contributions of Dr. Lowell Frye, the quality of this work would be far inferior. He sacrificed many hours to read all the chapters of this project and to offer helpful editing and writing advice.

And a special thanks to Nancy Wheeler for generously taking time to revive this project during the spring of 2012.

Projects like this one are what make Hampden-Sydney College so special. Without help from the faculty and staff and the support of alumni, there is no way this project would be completed. Thank you to everyone in the community who had a hand in making this possible and supported our efforts along the way.

TABLE OF CONTENTS

LIST OF ILLUSTRATIONS

THE PROJECT

OF ALL THE WISE MEN from the era of the Great Depression, I spent more time with my mother's father, Roger T. Bryant, than with any other. I deeply appreciated and respected Grandpa Rog's wisdom and character. When he died at the breakfast table in the arms of my mother on August 1, 2005, I realized I no longer would have the opportunity to formally record his life story as I had once planned.

An objective exploration of Grandpa Rog's life would have been difficult for me from my perspective as a loving grandson, but I had been very interested in exploring the lessons and adventures that he had experienced as a young man and how they had influenced his character throughout the rest of his life. After the death of my grandfather, I remained eager to learn by reflecting on the life history of admirable men and women.

A few weeks after Grandpa Rog passed away, I returned to Hampden-Sydney for my sophomore year, determined not to allow the death of my grandfather to prevent me from learning from his generation. My mind turned to my Leadership and Ethics Class professor, General Samuel Vaughan Wilson. For me, General Sam typified a generation of hard-working people. As he described it, life happened to give him opportunities to distinguish himself, sometimes through his own wisdom, more often by chance. His successes and triumphs, combined with his failures and mistakes, have given him a perspective and an appropriate temperament that I believed might positively mold my own personality.

After a Tuesday evening lecture in his Leadership and Ethics Seminar, I approached General Sam about the possibility of doing an independent study the following semester. I was hoping to hear more of his stories and looking to tackle a large, long-term project. At that time, General Sam had not yet organized his memoirs for posterity. We quickly discovered that the project could be mutually beneficial. I could absorb his fascinating stories and study how one successful man tackled life, and General Sam could have a regular incentive to organize his personal history. Together, we came up with our plan. Through a few anecdotes and vignettes pulled from the seemingly infinite resources of General Sam's memory, we hoped to produce an entertaining history from which readers, if they are so minded, can abstract helpful insights on productive living and leadership.

Dividing General Sam's life into simple segments cannot be done. However, for this project, General Sam and I followed a path that begins at the top of a small knoll in the Lockett District of Prince Edward County in Southside Virginia, winds around the world through varying degrees of danger, intrigue, and drama, and finally ends where it began: at a comfortable house overlooking a tranquil pond in rural Southside Virginia.

BOOK 1

EARLY LIFE

CHILDHOOD

SAMUEL VAUGHAN WILSON was born at 2300 hours on 23 September 1923 to Jasper Dennis Wilson and Helen Reed Vaughan Wilson—Cap'n Jack and Mis' Helen to all who knew them. The middle child among the five Wilson children—Virginia, William, Sam, John, and James—General Sam fondly recalls his childhood as years defined by familial love and backbreaking labor on the farm. Sammy's working life began early. He learned to milk a cow by the time he was eight years old and fondly remembers how squirting a little milk into the old barn cat's mouth earned him a loyal companion for his early morning tasks. Soon after mastering the basic chores of the barn, Sammy joined the Wilson family workforce in the fields. The everyday toil of the farm was tough, but Cap'n Jack found creative ways to enrich the lives of his family and children. His creativity and generosity to the neighborhood provided a marvelous model of unselfishness to Sammy and the other children.

Sometimes, however, Cap'n Jack's spirit had to be regulated by his wife. Mis' Helen provided a firm and exacting hand of discipline that complemented the joyful playfulness and creativity of her husband. They shared a deep love for each other and for their children. General Sam remembers the strict order Mis' Helen maintained around the household, despite the meager family income and the voracious appetites of five children, including four growing boys. Sammy's united yet distinctly different parents provided an atmosphere in which he and his siblings could learn by example or take the time to learn for themselves. His father and mother both required household chores, but they also encouraged reading, especially the Bible, and allowed the boys to wander the woods alone and encouraged them to pursue individual interests. Cap'n Jack and Mis' Helen fostered a family that valued self-discipline yet allowed time for fun and independence.

General Sam clearly cherished his mother. "Righteous," he called her, "simply saintly." She allowed him a life of blissful security as he passed through toddlerhood. When he was still quite small, she would place him with a blanket in Cap'n Jack's woodchip box near the stove so he could snuggle cozily and be near her as she attended to the daily duties of the kitchen. The wafting aromas of fresh vegetables and the heat from the wood stove blended with her soothing voice to provide daily contentment for baby Sammy. Mis' Helen loved her children very much. She scrimped and saved throughout the year to supply her children with shoes—never worn during warm weather, used begrudgingly on Sundays, but donned appreciatively during the frosty winter months—to purchase staples that supplemented the vegetables from the garden, and to provide for the needs *and* wants of a growing household.

Sammy grew to appreciate the rigid discipline Mis' Helen enforced with her children. Mis' Helen pressed her children to read and to expand their minds. Procrastination and oversleeping were sins to this woman of deep faith. She provided her family with a righteous example that was simple to understand, if perhaps more difficult to emulate. She expected to be minded closely, and when the children disobeyed or got out of line, they could invariably expect a liberal dose of "willow tea," obtained by applying a keen switch to a bare leg. Those switches, which smarted for a long time, burned a legacy of discipline in Sammy's young mind and drove Sam to a life of self-discipline. "Do right and shame the Devil" echoes in his mind.

Sammy loved his mother deeply. On one blisteringly hot August morning, she lay in bed suffering from a high fever and breathing with little short breaths. Sammy, who at the time was a barefoot, tow-headed nine-year-old, had been selected to stay home with Mis' Helen and his older sister, Virginia, while everyone else worked in the fields pulling tobacco. The two children fanned their mother and soothed her face with damp cloths.

Virginia suggested that they find some ice to help cool Mama. They went to the corn house and pulled open the trap door that led to an ice pit underneath. Down in that excavation lay chunks and chunks of ice, dug up during the winter from the nearby pond. The Wilsons had cut the ice with axes into big pieces two feet square, roughly four to six inches deep, and stacked them in the big hole under the corn house. Layers of leaves or sawdust served as insulation to keep the ice from melting during the warm spring and summer months, and the ice usually lasted until Labor Day. When Sammy and Virginia went down into the ice pit to look and scratch around for a piece of ice that morning, however, all they could find were leaves and sawdust. Frustrated, the two children agreed that Mama needed something cold and they would have to buy ice for her.

Sammy knew that Percy Trear sold ice blocks at the general store, a mile and a half away in Rice. Barefoot, and clutching his sister's quarter in a sweaty palm, Sammy took off at a run. Ten minutes later he arrived, out of breath. "Mr. Trear," he gasped, "I've got to have a twenty-five pound block of ice. Here's the money."

Percy shook his head. "Son," he said, "I'm just about sold out. All I've got left is one piece in the fifty-pound section." They walked to the back of the store, past the canned goods, farm tools, the pool table, and into the ice storeroom. Turning on the light, Sammy saw the block of ice. It was the size of two cinderblocks and a deep shade of blue. The once sharp corners had been rounded off from melting. "How are you going to carry it?" inquired Percy.

Sammy held his arms out. "You're gonna need some help before you get home," the storekeeper warned as he picked up a pair of wicked-looking ice tongs and lifted the block up.

"You'll find it's mighty hard to pick up if you drop it."

Sammy started out the screen door and headed up the dirt road. Soon he began to stagger under the weight of the ice. It was about to slip from his arms, but he did not dare change positions. He was afraid that the ice would fall to the ground. By the time the store was out of sight, he was leaving a trail of dripping ice water mingled with his perspiration. Before he was even a third of the way home, he was gasping for breath and gritting his teeth. His arms were growing numb from the cold and felt as if they were going to come out of their sockets. His knees were beginning to buckle. He stumbled once at a place where the dirt road was a little corduroyed. That scared him, but it raised his adrenaline and made the next couple hundred yards easier. As he came over a knoll and spotted home in the distance, he stumbled over a rough place in the road and fell to the ground. The ice block went scooting in the dirt.

He lay there, exhausted and wet from the ice and muddy from the dirt. After what seemed an eternity, he found a way to pick up what now had melted into a round ball of ice. Pain, cramps, and utter fatigue dogged him down the last stretch of his trip until he finally reached the porch and dropped the slippery ball of ice, which by this time had melted to half its original size. His sister came out, and together they put it into a pot and took it into the kitchen. Setting at it with an ice pick, they chopped off a few chunks and put them into an empty cloth sugar bag. Sammy beat the bag with a hammer to crush the ice into small pebbles for his mother to hold in her mouth. Pouring a dipper of water into the ice-filled cup, the triumphant children tip-toed up to Mama's room and tapped her on the shoulder. Mis' Helen rose up and took a sip of the ice water, then another. She swished it around in her mouth. "Oh my," she exclaimed as she lay back down peacefully, "that tastes so good." The children basked in her pleasure.

Sammy dug deep and discovered the ability to put one foot in front of the other, a capacity that would help him years later and in more trying circumstances. Later in his life, when he was confronted with situations that seemed impossible, he kept that memory and resolution in the back of his mind. One step—that is all that is required—except maybe also to wipe the perspiration off your hands from time to time so you can grip your gun properly.

While Mis' Helen was the disciplinarian of the family and the last court of appeal for childhood requests, Cap'n Jack balanced her influence with laughter and joy. Although he was already forty-four years old when Sammy was born, Cap'n Jack always displayed youthful energy and generosity. He loved to have a good time. He could have made more money than he did, but he was willing to sacrifice potential earnings in the fields in order to enjoy his time with his family.

Every summer, Sam helped his father and brothers dig swimming holes in the creek that ran through their property. For a farm boy toiling in the fields, mid-morning is a long way into a hot summer day of sweltering heat. On most days at mid-morning and again late in the afternoon, Cap'n Jack would delight the boys with an abrupt, "All right folks," and they would tear across the fields to the swimming hole. Late Saturday afternoons, he would again sacrifice valuable work time to take the boys fishing. Catfish, bream, crappie, and trout were all regular trophies brought back to Mis' Helen after hours spent together dangling freshly-cut hickory fishing poles over the banks of the creeping Appomattox River. During the fall and winter seasons, it would be hunting excursions that delighted the farm boys.

Cap'n Jack loved adventures with his children, but he was also a master storyteller. Field work passed almost too quickly with all the boys lost in their imaginations as they listened to one of the inventive stories their father concocted. Children from around the neighborhood appreciated Cap'n Jack's talents as well, and the generous man was often interrupted by a shaggy-haired youngster asking for a haircut and hoping for a story. Usually three or four of the boy's friends would tag along just to hear their neighbor weave his tale. The haircut would often end up taking far longer than necessary because the story had to be finished. That was the way of Sam's father.

The Wilson siblings, ca. 1933: Sam, Virginia, and James

Cap'n Jack did not hesitate to give up his own time and possessions to help others, even if it meant his own family had to tighten their belts. So it was one winter when he helped his struggling neighbor, an old black man who was down on his luck and needed some food. Cap'n Jack went out to the Wilson family storehouse and surveyed their supplies. There was not much bounty for a family of seven, but he took one of the two remaining barrels of flour and hoisted it onto the old man's mule-drawn cart. It would hold starvation at bay for the old man during the winter months that were upon them. Acts of generosity, small and large, were commonplace for Cap'n Jack. There were countless times that he gave away his prize watermelons, far and away the most delicious in the county. He could have made a good profit from their sale, but he refused to charge his neighbors.

Not only was Cap'n Jack the epitome of a generous Southern gentleman, but he was also a model in his Christian faith. Every Sunday morning he would walk the two-mile path through dense forests and fields to teach Sunday school at Jamestown Presbyterian Church. Sometimes Sammy would walk this path through the woods with his dad. The boy tried not to jabber because he knew Cap'n Jack was thinking about his lesson. Often Cap'n Jack would be quiet for minutes at a time. Sometimes he would bend over to pick up a rock, examine it, and toss it aside. He might stop to fondle a leaf, pluck a wild flower, or simply pause to gaze up through the trees at the sky. He had the keen eye of a huntsman and nature lover, and he would often spot a rabbit crouched in its bed, a squirrel flattened out against a tree limb, or the tell-tale signs of a wild turkey's feeding ground. As they crossed a branch in the creek, he'd point out to his son the schools of minnows in the pool, noting the shadows of the largest ones that hid along the rocks in eddies of deeper water below the tiny waterfall. When he arrived at the church, Cap'n Jack would have prepared a lesson that, like all his stories, held people's attention. He knew his Bible well enough to quote applicable scriptures from memory, and he inspired his children to follow in his footsteps in the church. Cap'n Jack and Mis' Helen Wilson's proudest moments were when one of their children joined Jamestown Presbyterian Church. The day that Sammy joined marked one of the few times he ever saw his father cry.

Perhaps nothing is more indicative of the standing Cap'n Jack held in his community than the respect afforded his passing. As two black boys steadily hacked at the frozen ground in the church's cemetery on a cold, bleak February day, a grizzled old black man leaned on a nearby rail fence watching them hollow out what would be the grave of Cap'n Jack. Weeping unashamedly, he admonished the gravediggers, "Dig it deep, Boys, you've never dug a hole for a better man."

Many of Sammy's boyhood heroes were men encountered in books: woodsmen, cowboys, knights, adventurers, and patriots. In the pages of the family library, Sam found exercise for the healthy imagination that his father had already been fostering. He loved the peaceful entertainment of reading about the likes of Sir Lancelot, Sir Galahad, George Washington, Abraham Lincoln, and Robert E. Lee.

Nothing pleased him more than to pass a lazy afternoon with his constant companion, Pat, a red-and-white Irish setter. Together, they would lounge on the front porch or wander through the forests looking for birds, chasing rabbits, and investigating the deep holes along the creek beds. When he was not working with his father and brothers in the fields or roaming the countryside with Pat, Sammy could be found with a guitar in his hands. He took his old six-string Gretsch everywhere with him. He loved leading group songs during recess at school or at Sunday school socials. The guitar became part of his public identity. One time an elderly distant cousin, who had come to visit the family all the way from Baton Rouge, Louisiana, saw Sammy merrily strumming his guitar and leading the group in song at a family social. On her return to Baton Rouge, the cousin wrote a thank-you letter, addressed simply "To the Boy who plays the Guitar, Rice, Virginia." Sammy was thrilled to receive the letter without any confusion in the village post office.

Sammy did not enjoy shooting a gun until much later than the other Wilson boys. He traces this aversion to gunfire back to one brisk fall morning when Cap'n Jack took Sammy and Don, a black-and-white English pointer, quail hunting. Young Sam was hardly big enough to hold a gun, but he trooped merrily along at his father's side until the dog pointed a covey. The birds flashed for safety to Cap'n Jack's left, and his gun roared. Poor Sammy was horrified by the terrific boom of the old twelve-gauge Ithaca shotgun and was so startled that he ran all the way home to avoid hearing a second shot.

Although he felt a little foolish, it made him feel better to know that Don, the English Pointer, had been equally spooked by the thunderous discharge and had arrived back at the house even before Sammy. For years afterward, Sammy blamed bad luck for the many times he trudged into the forests with his gun slung over his shoulder only to return empty-handed. In reality, he never fired a shot. Eventually, however, he became frustrated about being gun-shy. Taking the double-barreled gun to a remote place in the forest, Sammy decided to conquer his fear by forcing himself to shoot. Leaning back and pointing his gun into the sky, he grimaced and pulled, in the process accidentally pulling both triggers. As the two barrels exploded with a terrific boom, the double recoil jerked him on his back. "Well," he consoled himself, "it can't get any worse than that."

From then on, Sammy was able to fire his gun confidently, and over time, he became a proficient marksman. That talent would serve him well later in life.

Like most rural families who suffered through the Great Depression, the Wilson family faced their share of hardships, but they persevered, and young Sammy learned through their experiences to enjoy the hard work required to maintain the family's stable environment. Two loving parents formed the backbone for a powerful family and provided Sammy with the opportunity to define his own identity. Cap'n Jack and Mis' Helen were shining examples of devout love and careful order, powerful foundations that grounded young Sammy. The vestiges of his parents could be seen in the characteristics he developed: self-discipline, strong core beliefs, adept storytelling talents, and adaptive creativity. Even as he reached for the independence that he, like most young men, craved, he never forgot the righteousness by which his parents tempered their lives. "Do right and shame the devil" would be the measure for his life as well.

Jasper Wilson, Sam's father
"Cap'n Jack"

Helen Wilson, Sam's mother
Mis' Helen

INDEPENDENCE AND OPPORTUNITY

WHEREVER HE WAS, Sam loved to have fun. This trend continued throughout his life. As a farm boy in close vicinity to a women's college, he was not far into his teenage years before he realized that Farmville State Teacher's College, now Longwood University, was a ready source of entertainment and socializing. STC, as it was known to locals, became a favorite spot for dating and evening activities.

Sam hit puberty early, and into his eighties he retained the outline of the barrel-chested young man who shaved for the first time when he was eleven years old. "Lots of testosterone in me, I guess," he surmised. As a youngster he was regularly running with the older boys in town and fibbing about his age so he could date the college girls. Sammy became adept at employing what he considered a harmless pretense to disguise his age.

He had a fantastic time courting the pretty young ladies who attended STC, and during his interactions with those college girls he honed the manners and social graces that, years later, would help a rural farm boy feel comfortable at what might have been daunting social engagements. Assuming different personages to win dates with older girls was Sam's first dalliance into a talent that came into play many years later when he masqueraded under cover in the clandestine services of the Central Intelligence Agency.

Early on, his parents had instilled a deep respect for feminine purity in his heart, and while his ventures into dating "older women" were thrilling, they also retained a polite level of respect. Sam was thus quite satisfied to wait respectfully while Miss Lucy, the receptionist in the Ruffner Hall Rotunda lobby, rang up Panky, Frances, or perhaps Mary Anne to ask her if she would care to receive a call from a certain Samuel Vaughan Wilson. Young Sam was never one to pass up on a chance to impress a lady, and he always used his full name when he went calling, an introduction he figured was romantic and charming.

Usually his inquiries were met with alacrity. Girls appreciated the respect he paid them as much as he enjoyed the entertainment they provided him. He and his date would pass the evening in the recreation room happily eating popcorn, sipping milkshakes, holding hands, chatting, or testing each other's shag, swing, and jitterbug skills on the dance floor. Sam enjoyed his forays into town, but he never lost control of himself or forgot the respect that every woman deserves. He would enjoy the dancing and perhaps a goodnight kiss, but he never allowed himself to take a relationship any further. Sam had too much fun dating a different girl every night to settle on one in particular.

The fact that he did not want to get involved seriously with any individual girl did not prohibit Sam from wanting to look his best at all times. He went to great lengths to be a sharp dresser. When his older brother, Billy, who was working away from home, returned on occasion for a visit, he would leave most of his wardrobe hanging in his closet. Billy's duds were fair game, as far as Sam was concerned, for him to wear on his trips into town. Because he reached his full height of six feet early on, he was able to fit into his older brother's snappy clothes at a young age. Thus, unbeknownst to his brother, Sam made many successfully dapper appearances in pilfered outfits. On a number of occasions he even borrowed his brother's car to make the trip easier.

Unfortunately for the young masquerader, his sticky finger made for an awkward encounter when the two brothers happened to meet one night on campus after Billy had arrived back in town ahead of schedule. Sam got caught red-handed wearing Billy's best suit while Billy sported the only outfit he had been able to locate in his closet earlier that evening: his second-string combo of sports coat and trousers. No problem for Billy, however. He took it upon himself to reclaim his property, right then and there, starting to strip the suit off his younger brother and leaving his Sam, who was more than a little embarrassed, to make his way home in little more than undershirt and drawers. The cold seven-mile walk home gave Sam time to contemplate the importance of asking before borrowing important possessions. As an apology to his aggrieved older brother, he carefully polished the pair of Billy's shoes that he had managed to scramble home in.

On another occasion, General Sam brought his guitar with him to town with plans to serenade some lucky girl. Being quite a dexterous player, he contrived to perch himself on the top of a ladder he found lying behind a hedge. From there, he played and sang to his chosen girl through her open second-story dorm window while she rested her elbows on the window sill and looked appropriately appreciative. His romantic music was working its charms when his ladder suddenly stood bolt upright, away from the window and, frighteningly, away from the wall. The girl ducked from the window and dove under her covers to feign a deep sleep, while Sam looked down and in the moonlight saw two campus policemen glaring menacingly up at him. He climbed down to receive a severe chastisement for his foolish behavior and disregard for the hazards of tall ladders. But the police let him go. What breed of criminal, after all, breaks into a dorm room carrying a six-string guitar?

On Sunday, June 9, 1940, the Wilson family was enjoying an afternoon of rest following its morning at church. Mid-afternoon, Sam sat down in the front room of the farmhouse, and, as he often did, fiddled with the dials on the battery-powered farm radio. After scanning the static for a few seconds, he heard applause and a man speaking on AM-WPTF, an NBC affiliate. Although he lived in the country, he was educated enough to recognize the accent of an Englishman. Sam listened attentively to Winston Churchill conclude his speech with a moving cry, "We will fight them on the beaches, on the landing strips, in the fields, and in the hills. We will never surrender." The broadcast was a recording of Churchill's famous speech to the British House of Commons on June 4, 1940, and as Sam listened, he was awed that a man could feel such passionate patriotism. He went to sleep dreaming of the glories of defending the values of his homeland.

The next day brought rain, a drenching farmer's rain that fell straight down and methodically thrummed against the shelter of the cozy farm buildings. There would be no pulling weeds or hoeing corn in that weather. Instead they would spend time sharpening hoes, shovels, and plow points or working on farm implements in the wagon shed. Still, after the work was done, Sam had time left in the afternoon for leisure. As a part of his usual rainy afternoon routine, Sam sought the peace and quiet of the hayloft with a few of his favorite books, novels by Alger, Grey, Curwood, Twain, and London. As the steady rain tapped musically against the tin roof, Sam could not concentrate on the reading that normally enthralled him. He kept hearing the words of Churchill's passionate speech ringing in his ears.

Churchill had ignited in him a spark of patriotism that had been burning for some time. Sam knew that the United States had begun a buildup towards war and despite formal neutrality, was helping to supply its allies for the conflict that already had engulfed Europe. His mind and heart were intent on joining the effort. Just before dusk, without saying a word to anybody, Sam started at a dog-trot down the cedar-lined farm lane to the dirt road that led west seven miles toward the nearest enlistment post, the Virginia National Guard Armory in Farmville. He arrived just before the post closed. Standing six feet tall and weighing just one hundred thirty-nine pounds in his soggy tennis shoes, Sam must not have appeared to be the most desirable recruit.

He had to lie about his age by two years so he could legally be sworn in right then and there on June 10, 1940, as the company bugler for Company G of the 116th Infantry, 29th Division.

Sam's actions the night he enlisted in the National Guard demonstrated an uncharacteristic aggressiveness, but it was not a cavalier decision. He acted as he did only after giving extensive thought and consideration to his personal passion for the cause of freedom. Unlike the majority of American soldiers in World War II, Sam enlisted in the armed services before the attack on Pearl Harbor. His motivation was not one of revenge, but one of duty to the cause of world freedom, a burning stimulus that formed over the years even before the Nazi invasions.

The exact date when his patriotic commitment began to blaze, September 1, 1939, was so important to Sam that it remained etched in his memory throughout his life. On a sultry afternoon in late summer, he and his brothers were helping neighbors gather hay in a field that lay alongside the Norfolk and Western railroad tracks. In the sweltering heat, the men worked furiously to finish bringing in the hay before a looming thunderstorm reached them. Though they were exhausted, their only break that afternoon came when Sam's cousin, Polk Bondurant, drove up in his big black Chevrolet. The cotton shirts and overalls they wore for protection from the hay were sweat-soaked, but the men raised their straw hats to wipe inquisitive brows and give their attention to their neighbor's arrival.

"Germany invaded Poland today," Polk concisely reported. "The war has begun. They're at it again."

Silently and without comment, the farmers returned to pitching hay. The enormity and mystery of the European development stymied their response as they lost themselves in thought and the rhythmic lifting of heavy pitchforks. Like many other people in the United States, Sammy and the other farmers immediately felt the threat the German forces posed to their freedom. That very day, Sammy began to consider what his part needed to be in the world's struggle against Fascism. He mulled over the problem for the following nine months. He knew he had to do something, but until he heard Churchill's speech, he wavered about what action to take. Churchill's speech and Sammy's resulting march to the enlistment post were not so much the products of a child's rash behavior as they were the maturing of a brewing passion that had been stirring a young man's heart all fall, winter, and spring.

Sam's decision to act without first requesting his parents' approval contrasted strikingly with the boy's usual behavior. However, he was so firm in his belief that this was his time for patriotic service that he did not want to risk being talked out of his decision. He figured that it would work better if he enlisted, returned home, and then accepted whatever consequences his actions might bring. This occasion might have been Sam's first deliberate action in which he put himself in a situation from which he could not back down, but it would not be his last. His gambling technique would serve him successfully in numerous situations that demanded action.

However, his first no-looking-back decision left his parents quiet and reserved at the breakfast table the next morning. In truth, they could have marched Sam right back to the station to tell the enrollment officer that their son was only sixteen years old and could not legally enlist in the National Guard, but they let what had been done remain done. They never suggested changing their son's noble, if perhaps headstrong, response to the call of duty. Recognizing that Sam could not thrive if they forced him to veer from his passions, his parents accepted his entry into the service and supported him with their whole hearts.

Sam's decision to join the National Guard settled the confusing choices he had been wrestling to make about his future. His enlistment meant that he would decline an opportunity to matriculate at Hampden-Sydney College in the fall of 1940, would forego an appointment to West Point that Congressman Pat Drewry had arranged, would turn his back on the lures of the professional music business that had always attracted him, and would give up the familial comfort of another year on the farm. Sam decided to work part-time jobs while his unit trained and awaited active service.

He picked up odd jobs wherever he could. He worked as a part-time surveyor and at the farm on salary for his father, but his favorite job was as the soda jerk at Shannon's Restaurant on Main Street in downtown Farmville. His duties included serving local high school and college kids soft drinks, milkshakes, and sandwiches. The phrases he and his co-workers used for the orders were his first exposure to code words. A tables' order may have been a cherry coke, two orange Cokes, and a chocolate milk, but Sam would have to tell his cook, "Hey Ed, get me an eighty-three, kiss her once, squeeze her twice, and run one through the mud," if he wanted the kitchen to fill the order. A few months of work at the shop gave Sam his first taste of code words, an elementary prequel to an espionage career still in his distant future.

On a bright, brittle Monday morning, February 3, 1941, Sam and the other inductees in G Company all raised their right hands and solemnly repeated the oath of allegiance. Once they officially became a part of the United States active military forces, G Company spent three weeks equipping and training in Farmville. Sam had happily given up his bugling duties over Christmas and had made private first class, earning the first stripe on his sleeve. He was next appointed lead scout of a rifle squad. By the time the troops were ordered to transport to Fort Meade, Maryland, Sam had been elevated to the rank of Corporal and was second in command of his squad.

Sam's mother and sister made the trek into town before dawn to see him off as he and his comrades boarded the train for Fort Meade. He had been to the house earlier to bid farewell to his brothers and father, and the men had farm obligations which kept them from being there that morning. As he somberly waved goodbye to the two women, he desperately scanned the crowd for another girl. Bitterly, he realized that his crush had overslept and had failed to see him off on his journey. It stung both his pride and his emotions that she had not come for a final farewell, but Sam consoled himself with the realization that her absence revealed her shallowness. Later he would hear that the other soldiers' girlfriends returned to the dorm room where his girl, by then his ex-girl, was just waking up, and they told her how badly they had felt for Sam. She immediately realized that she had failed to do something important, and she wrote a long, pleading, tear-stained letter begging Sam's forgiveness. Her absence when other girls were there in abundance to see their soldiers off to war left Sam deeply saddened, but it provided him with a motivation. "I'll show her," he told himself as the ache slowly left his young heart. Although he was eventually able to forgive the girl, he could never forget what she had done to him. The young soldier stoically used her thoughtless misdeed as motivation at the beginnings of his career.

For Corporal Sam, and then by late April 1941, Sergeant Sam, arduous military rigors paled in comparison to his earlier duties on the farm. He was used to waking up before the sun rose, well acquainted with toiling all day in the heat, and able to maintain a cheerful spirit in the face of demanding discipline. Sam did not expect his days to be anything less than demanding, and that attitude gave him an advantage over his less-prepared companions. Throughout basic infantry and advanced individual training at Fort Meade, the A. P. Hill Military Reservation in Virginia, and then on maneuvers along the North Carolina-South Carolina border, Sam was well served by his superb physical condition and his adherence to strict personal discipline that his parents had helped him develop growing up on the farm.

On Sunday, December 7, 1941, Sam's unit was traveling in convoy back to Ft. Meade from South Carolina and had stopped to bivouac near South

Hill, Virginia, when they learned of the attack on Pearl Harbor. They knew that the news meant World War II had officially begun for the United States and that their lives were going to be changed forever. Shortly after the attack, the troops were convoyed to Camp Pendleton, just south of Virginia Beach, to patrol the beaches and watch for German submarines or signs of enemy infiltration into the Tidewater area. During this time, Sam and his comrades practiced defense of the beaches against amphibious assaults by the First Marine Division. Several months later, based at least in part on his leadership performance in the months of training, Sam was chosen for a leadership position over a contingent of young men awaiting assignment as students to Officer Candidate School at Fort Benning, Georgia. He proudly displayed a brassard on his sleeve, a temporary adornment for a Company First Sergeant, as he watched over the OC students waiting for classes to begin. At this point, Sam was just eighteen years old.

Sergeant Sam excelled at Officer Candidate School and graduated at the head of his class. Perhaps much of it was due to Cap'n Jack and the storytelling skills he taught his children while they worked in the fields. Sam would often remember his father's approach to telling stories as he was briefing the group about an exercise or explaining a maneuver. His ability to talk on his feet in a colorful, informative, and concise fashion soon brought him extra attention from the instructional staff at Ft. Benning. He first noticed something was afoot when he started being singled out of the crowd almost daily to brief the class of two hundred men. Even so, Sam's body went numb when Major Frank Westlake called him aside one day during a ten-minute break to invite him to teach at the school. He immediately appreciated the magnitude of the honor, and General Sam still considers this privilege one of his highest honors.

Sam joined the staff at the Infantry School in August of 1942, immediately after he graduated from OCS. The faculty of professors, playwrights, journalists, newspaper editors, bankers, stock brokers, artists, and entertainers mesmerized him with their talents. They were handpicked, the best men in the country, gathered in wartime to prepare young men to be combat leaders. Sam looked up to these people as if they were characters in his beloved childhood books. He found himself copying their expressions, walking styles, teaching postures, and reading interests. Sam tried to take advantage of every opportunity to learn from the talented constellation of men.

At just eighteen years old, he was the youngest Second Lieutenant in the army. By nineteen, he was the youngest First Lieutenant. Being invited to join the staff at Infantry School was a fitting complement to his early achievements, but Sam's success went straight to his head, and he began "living it up" far too often.

Sam enjoyed celebrating, and though he worked hard, he played awfully hard, too. Many a late night would find him drinking and dancing at a restaurant like Firm Robert's in Columbus, Georgia. Never having drunk alcohol in his boyhood, Sam soon learned how to enjoy it. The allure of the beautiful young Georgia girls and the temptations of Johnny Walker Black often kept him out of his bunk for the entire night. Although he never got staggeringly drunk, Sam did let the Scotch bring him a giddy happiness. He reveled in the opportunities to sing and dance the evenings away, occasionally on top of the piano. He frequently returned from his revels with a pounding hangover and just enough time to shave, shower, and dress himself before he met his morning class in the field.

Fort Benning had an officer's club that was notable for its attractive Spanish architectural style. The beautiful outdoor courtyard featured a large dance area lined on either side by shimmering pools. After dark, hidden lights flickered on the orchestra and the swirling dancers. One evening, Sam was dancing merrily near the edge of the swimming pool with a curvaceous and giddy blonde named Flossy. As Flossy chattered on about her delight at his dancing skills, the beauty of the night, and the pleasures of her evening, she twirled as Sammy led her but suddenly caught her heel on the edge of the tile and fell backwards into the pool, pulling Sammy in on top of her. Sam had never sobered up so quickly in his life. He could hear her shrill, plaintive complaints to him for weeks—"You let me fall . . . YOU LET ME FALL."

It took quite a while to live down the embarrassing result of his over-exuberance on the dance floor.

As a faculty member at Fort Benning, Sam taught field classes that included demonstrations on crossing shelled areas and Problem 147, "Hell's-a-Poppin'," which combined lecture with a demonstration of a rifle and weapons platoon under attack. His classes were often observed by visiting officials or high ranking officers. On one occasion even President Roosevelt, who had been visiting the Presidential retreat at nearby Warm Springs, stopped in to observe Sam's class during a tour of the base. Performing under the watchful eye of important visitors gave Sam an opportunity to distinguish himself. More than once, however, Sam drove back to the office frustrated that class had not gone as well as he hoped. He wanted to wow the observers with his abilities, and he knew when he was less than perfect even if they offered him cordial congratulations on the lesson. Even when he was not being observed, Sam despised having to award himself a B grade.

Despite his self-criticism, Sam continued to impress people with his well-polished gift for words. In the late fall of 1942, a former Russian nobleman named Serge Obolensky, who was serving as a United States Army major, brought a troop of thirty-five rough young American soldiers of Sicilian parentage, some of them with connections to the Mafia, to prepare for a behind-the-lines role in the upcoming Allied invasion of Sicily and Italy. These hard-bitten, purposeful men were talented street fighters and specialists with knives and Saturday night specials, but they were limited in their knowledge of the principles of small unit tactics.

Sam worked well with Obolensky during their three weeks of collaboration in preparing the Sicilians, and by the end of the session Obolensky was so impressed by the young man's talents that he invited him to join the Office of Strategic Services. The OSS was facetiously called the "Oh So Secret" by those in the know because of its special emphasis on total secrecy, and later called the "Oh So Social" because of the social elite who flocked to the organization. The latter group was led by Roosevelt's good friend, Wild Bill Donovan, a World War I hero and a millionaire lawyer from Manhattan. A predecessor for today's CIA, the organization soon became famous for the daring missions it performed. Sam quickly told Obolensky that he would very much like the opportunity of working with the OSS. Excited about the adventures he might encounter with this romantic group, he hitched an airplane ride from Fort Benning, Georgia, to Washington, D.C., in late July 1943, to begin his OSS training.

After his orientation, Sam was given some equipment and a training schedule, but as events developed, he never served a single mission with the OSS. A few hours before he was scheduled to depart for a training site in Western Maryland, Lieutenant Colonel Charles N. Hunter called and asked Sam to join him for dinner in Washington that evening. Hunter had been Sam's boss's superior back at Fort Benning. The Colonel, clearly one of America's outstanding young field officers, was widely regarded as an up-and-comer in the military, and Sam was awed by the man's professional pedigree, leadership abilities, and personal character. He was therefore taken aback with the invitation.

Over dinner at what is now known as the Fort McNair's Officer's Club, Hunter proposed what would become a life-altering opportunity for Sam. General George Marshall had selected Hunter to lead a special mission that

Hunter described as "strategically important to our war aims, and very, very difficult and dangerous." The mission was also said to be highly important to Roosevelt personally. Hunter invited Sam to accompany him on this mission. Sam eagerly accepted, more out of his respect for Hunter than anything else. He was only the third volunteer for the mission when he joined Hunter and a First Lieutenant named Gordon Mereness, who had been hand-picked because of his proven abilities as a logistician. After Hunter formalized the transfer by personally requesting that Sam be assigned to him, Sam received orders to return to Fort Benning and then proceed to Camp Stoneman outside San Francisco, as soon as possible.

Returning to Fort Benning, Sam met some of the other young men from the base who had also volunteered for the "difficult" mission. While the others hopped into a car for the transcontinental trip, Sam jumped into the cargo hold of a C-47 transport that took him to Meridian, Mississippi. Another C-47 flew him to San Antonio, Texas, and from there he took a train to Albuquerque, New Mexico. He completed his trip to Northern California by riding in the nose of a B-26 bomber, where he enjoyed spectacular views of the parched deserts and craggy mountains of western America and then of the Golden Gate Bridge and San Francisco Bay.

Sam's roommate that first night in San Francisco was a fellow volunteer for Lt. Col. Hunter's group, a Signals Corps officer named Charlton Ogburn, Jr. Ogburn and Sam quickly became close friends. The two men spent the night out on the town, and in the morning they taxied to Camp Stoneman to join the gathering elements of what was to become the 5307th (the "five three OOOOh seventh") Composite Unit (Provisional), later carrying the radio call sign "Galahad" and known to the world as Merrill's Marauders. From Camp Stoneman these volunteer soldiers embarked on the *SS Lurline* and sailed west across the Pacific Ocean, unaccompanied and zigzagging to avoid Japanese subs. In October of 1943, they arrived in Bombay, now Mumbai, India, still uncertain about their identity, purpose, and function.

The 5307th Composite Unit (Provisional) entered an exceedingly complex world when it joined the battle in Asia. In a campaign which by the summer of 1942 had been engaged for less than five months, the Japanese had successfully defeated British and Chinese forces and driven them out of Burma. In the process, the famous Burma Road, the only land link connecting China to India and the rest of the Allied world, lay in enemy hands. The air route from India to China led over the Himalayas—the highest and most forbidding mountains in the world—and a dangerous passage even for well-trained pilots. Further, this route was subject to continuing interdiction by Japanese fighter planes. As a result, the munitions that were necessary to keep nationalist China in the War could no longer be delivered by land and were restricted to a tiny trickle delivered by U.S. aircraft from bases in Northeast India.

Despite these seemingly insurmountable difficulties, it was vital to the Allied cause in Asia that the one million Japanese soldiers operating on Chinese soil were kept engaged and thus would remain unavailable for re-deployment to the Central and Southwest Pacific Theaters, where they could join the defense against U.S. island-hopping operations commanded by Admiral Nimitz and General MacArthur.

Of equal importance was the threat posed by Japanese forces obviously preparing for an invasion on the Indian border. India itself was in a state of seething political unrest as it sought to break away from its British masters and establish full independence as a sovereign nation. Japan had already organized the so-called "Indian Independence Army" to facilitate offensive operations on the sub-continent. Obviously, the loss of India during the peak of the War would have been a catastrophic blow to the Allied cause.

The China-Burma-India Theater, the largest Allied Theater of operations in terms of square miles and population, was lowest on the totem pole of Allied priorities after the European, Central Pacific, and Southwest Pacific Theaters. That reality added further to an already bleak situation.

The one bright spot in an otherwise gloomy picture was provided in February 1943, when an obscure and highly unconventional British Brigadier, Orde Charles Wingate, infiltrated a force of 3,000 Allied soldiers from the British-Indian Army deep into Central Burma and engaged in behind-the-lines, guerrilla-type operations—raiding supply installations, cutting rail and communications lines, blowing bridges and ambushing Japanese columns. Wingate's long-range penetration unit survived for roughly ninety days before he was forced to rearrange his men into small groups and retreat back into India. He had lost over one-third of his soldiers without achieving any significant strategic success, but he had demonstrated that the Japanese soldier was not invincible and could be thrown off schedule. Of perhaps even greater significance for the Allied forces was the badly needed boost in morale gained from Wingate's daring and innovative enterprise. Leading the applause was British Prime Minister Winston Churchill.

When Churchill attended the Quebec Conference later that year, he brought Wingate with him to brief the conferees, including President Roosevelt, on his dramatic exploits. Seeing that Roosevelt was clearly impressed, Wingate requested that, to help him put a stop to Japanese advancement along the Indian border, the Americans form a long-range penetration unit (LRPU) similar to the outfit he would be leading back into Burma during the upcoming dry season. The highly mobile LRPU would be capable of infiltrating behind enemy lines and raising hell in the jungles until the Japanese were defeated on other fronts. Convinced of the merits of Wingate's proposal, Roosevelt issued a Presidential call for volunteers to undertake "a dangerous and hazardous mission." No further details were specified. Thousands of soldiers volunteered, and that initial number was eventually winnowed down to some 3,000. It was that LRPU unit that Sam had joined.

Additional volunteers, veterans of the Guadalcanal and New Guinea campaigns, joined the American soldiers who sailed on the *S.S. Lurline* from San Francisco towards Bombay. The full complement of what was to become the 5307th Composite Unit (Provisional) had joined forces by the time the ship docked in India at the end of October. After the unit had trained under British auspices for several months, it was placed under the control of General Joseph W. Stillwell, the commanding General of the China-Burma-India Theater (CBI), who realized that he finally had a unit that could facilitate the opening of a land route from India to China. It was a small force, to be true, but it was the only American ground combat force on the continent of Asia.

The three thousand volunteers of the 5307th Composite Unit (Provisional) were brought together, trained quickly, and marched into the harsh jungles of Northern Burma with a single aim: to disrupt Japanese activity in the area. The Japanese enemy consisted of well-trained battalions that had been gaining momentum as they pushed through the defenses of a few Chinese battalions. No plans were made for the American LRPU's reinforcement, as military leadership considered the men of the unit to be expendable. Forecasters predicted that most of the soldiers would be "used up" in the process of fulfilling their mission. It took Sam years to fully realize that the entire unit had been created to buy time in a third-priority arena while the real war was fought elsewhere. It was a dire forecast, but despite overwhelming obstacles, the 5307th was expected to achieve, and eventually did achieve, spectacular military successes.

EVIL IN INDIA

TWENTY-YEAR-OLD FIRST LIEUTENANT Sam Wilson was one of the three thousand members of the 5307th Composite Unit (Provisional) who arrived in Bombay in October 1943 still uncertain about the specifics of the "dangerous and hazardous mission" for which they had volunteered. From the western Indian city, the men traveled one hundred and twenty miles northeast by local train to a permanent British military encampment near the remote town of Deolali. At that camp, the 5307th joined a British force assigned to a parallel mission and began an intensive training program. For Sam and the rest of the men in the unit, this was an introduction not only to India but also to the British-Indian Army and to the remaining vestiges of British colonial life. Existence on the arid Indian plain differed dramatically from life in the fertile fields and forests of rural America, and these U.S. soldiers initially struggled to adjust to life in such a different world.

Sam's most direct contact with the lingering British influence on the Indian social system was through his Indian bearer, a young man named Dondi Ram. Although no older than twenty, Dondi Ram looked like a shriveled old man, and his voice was piercingly high pitched. The usual routine was for Sam to spend the frigid night huddled beneath several blankets on his canvas cot and to be roused at daybreak by his faithful servant. "Tea wallah, Sahib," Dondi Ram would say in his musical voice as Sam sat up in bed.

Dondi Ram then would pull back the mosquito net and hand Sam a breakfast tray holding a cup, saucer, pot of tea, and a crumpet or two. General Sam particularly enjoyed the large-grained sugar and thick cream that Dondi Ram brought with his morning tea. While Sam breakfasted and then broke through the ice that had frozen in the wash basin to clean his face and teeth, Dondi Ram would lay out for him a clean outfit from yesterday's laundry. By the time Sam headed toward the British mess hall for the morning formation, Dondi Ram would have cleaned Sam's boots, freshened his uniform, made his bed, and swept the floors of Sam's hut.

India was a highly stratified society teeming with millions of impoverished people like Dondi Ram. British colonialism had done little to help the miserable lives of the many poor Indians, and very few locals welcomed the foreign presence. However, despite their animosity toward their occupiers, many Indians served the British army in hopes of gaining a higher standard of living. The role of native servants like Dondi Ram was to maintain the quality of life for the officers in the British army.

All too often, however, Sam observed British soldiers ungratefully exhibiting a callous and sometimes brutal attitude towards the Indians, and the situation made Sam uncomfortable. It was difficult for him to determine how to act towards his servant. He was tempted to treat Dondi Ram as an equal, but Sam knew that such treatment would never do in the land of a rigid caste system and British dominance. There are times to stand up for beliefs, and times to keep one's peace. Sam eventually resolved to do his best to respect all Indians with whom he came in contact as fellow human beings with the same right to exist and pursue their destiny as he had. Despite settling on his approach to the situation, Sam spent his entire time in India dissatisfied with the arrangement. A basic element of his soul whispered to his conscience the virtue of treating all humans equally, but ill-treatment of the natives by others was all too commonplace. Sam had to stifle his conscience and pursue his duties as best he could.

On weekends, especially on Sundays, Sam found time to bicycle through the countryside with his friends Charlton Ogburn and Phillip Weld. They visited villages, examined ancient ruins, and occasionally bought souvenirs from local bazaars. Sam and Ogburn had been friends since their first meeting in San Francisco, and Sam had met Weld in one of the classes he taught at OCS school at Fort Benning. Sam respected both men as articulate and well-educated gentlemen and would maintain correspondence with both of them for years after their adventures in Asia.

Weekdays found Sam working busily from dawn to dusk as he trained his troops. He and the other officers were intent on creating some semblance of a cohesive military unit. It was a difficult task. Many of the volunteers had not marched in formation for many months and had long ago forgotten the fine points of soldiering. The men constantly practiced saluting and close order drill: right face, left face, about face, and other parade-ground maneuvers. To an outsider, such pompous parading might have seemed pointless. However, these officers knew that learning the precision of close-order drill was the first step in molding the group into a well-trained and responsive military unit that could obey a command in unison, an imperative ability for the unit in combat. They drilled on and on to develop discipline in the volunteers.

Like most groups of volunteers, the 5307th was full of men with rebellious streaks who did not hesitate to grumble about rigorous and repetitious training. Despite the complaints of the troops, Sam and the other officers eventually succeeded in instilling a discipline that proved invaluable in the following months spent in the Burmese rainforests.

While they drilled, Sam could hear the wail of bagpipes and the muffled thumping of marching drums as the British trained nearby. The eerie music evoked a sensation in Sam that helped him vaguely understand how, since ancient times, the sound of bagpipes has inspired men to march willingly into battle.

One indelible memory from his time drilling in Deolali still vividly haunts General Sam. He remembers a shadowy, mystical embodiment of evil lurking in the streets of Nazik, a city which lies about 100 kilometers northwest of Deolali. Although outlying parts of the city were reportedly elegant and beautiful, the seedy "red light district" with which Sam was to become acquainted, was nothing less than a hell hole. That part of town seemed to thrive on the depths of human depravity. An old, dusty place, the crooked streets teemed with furtively scurrying pedestrians. Thievery, murder, and every form of debauchery dominated the neighborhood. Narrow streets reeked of curry, exotic spices, human waste, and burning trash. The scraping, one-string fiddle known as the *ektara* could be heard in the distance, and a variety of hollow-sounding flutes and pipes combined with it in a spooky orchestra that filled the night air with a grating whine. The music provided a backdrop for the steady murmur of street corner conversations. Night time was particularly dangerous, as if the curtain of darkness provided even greater incentive for demons to spread an aura of wickedness throughout this city of brothels. British officers would not dare to enter the city unless accompanied by a strong patrol. Although he went on to have many more adventures in cities around the world, Sam would never again walk the streets of a city that seemed so completely saturated with evil.

The same evils in Nazik that horrified Sam attracted wretched, civilization-starved men of both the American and British forces. Attracted by the sordid ecstasies offered in the opium dens and brothels, soldiers flocked to the ancient adobe city. Colonel Hunter and his staff worried particularly about the vulnerability of the veteran third of his contingent. These men had been isolated from civilization while in combat for many months in the South Pacific, and they were especially susceptible to the lures of such a place. Soon after his arrival in Deolali, Sam was ordered by Hunter to take an evening patrol to Nazik in an attempt to round up several soldiers who had recently gone AWOL. Sam recruited five or six soldiers, including a British Lance Corporal to act as a guide, and they jumped into two armored jeeps, arriving at Nazik just as the sun was setting. The group was careful to stay together as they went from house to house checking for soldiers. Each man felt very distant from home and vulnerable in the filthy buildings they entered.

The patrol quickly realized that the most likely place to find their wayward comrades would be inside the brothels. These brothels were of simple design. A man would enter the brick, one-story building, select from the collection of prostitutes, and take her behind a thin curtain to one of the simply furnished stalls that lined the wall. Although the nicer places might have an oriental rug providing color for the sparsely decorated room, none of them were the kind of places to linger in comfort. Nearly every establishment had some sort of discordant musical ensemble, and all the brothels were suffused by a peculiar odor. When Sam asked the Lance Corporal about the smell, the man cheerfully replied, "Oh, that's opium, Old Boy."

The Brit repeated "Old Boy" quite often as he led the Americans around a circuit of seedy establishments and pointed out particular oddities in the brothels they searched. The Lance Corporal would whack on a door with his swagger stick, push open the rough wooden entryway, lead the group inside, and in most instances be greeted by name by the Madam of the house. After inquiring if any Americans were present, the men would ignore the immediate denial and ask to check for themselves. Sam's men pulled aside the curtains and peered in each stall while looking for their men. The Madams eyed them furiously for interfering with their business, but they were helpless to deny the searches. After a few failed house checks, the face of a 5307th volunteer stared back at Sam as he pulled back the curtain. Sam quickly put a hand on his shoulder and yanked him out of the stall. Furious, the soldier came after Sam like a raging bear and knocked him across the room in his anger. He growled, shrieked, and roared like a wild beast in his rage. It took three of Sam's companions to subdue the man, who grudgingly joined the patrol when it returned with four or five other AWOL soldiers.

As Sam was rendering his report of the evening patrol back at the Deolali base, he stated that he did not wish to press charges for the soldier's attacking him, but he did want the fact to be known. As he related his tale to the debriefing officer, Colonel Hunter overheard the adventure.

"Sammy, Sammy, Sammy . . . " said Hunter thoughtfully, "if you'd only let him finish, he would have come along like a lamb." Sam had been in no mood to wait for the man to "finish" while he and his recruits combed the evil city for misbehaving soldiers.

After three weeks of training in Deolali, the 5307th Composite Unit (Provisional) boarded a train for Jakhlan Station in the central plains of India. For two days and three nights the train car crept along the tracks, swarmed by pleading beggars at every station it passed. Some of these beggars had been deliberately crippled as small children in order to improve their chances for getting a handout, and they were all desperate. If one of the soldiers made the mistake of dropping *baksheesh* (Hindi for "small change") into an outstretched hand, the tangled rush to his window by the other vagabonds would soon make him regret his generosity. The troops eventually made it to Jakhlan Station, and from there, they marched about five miles to Deogarh, an ancient Indian village near the eastern banks of the Betwa River, in whose vicinity a well-designed tent encampment had been constructed by the British for use by the 5307th.

At Deogarh, the senior leaders of the 5307th were finally told that their mission would be to infiltrate behind Japanese lines in North Burma. Their assignment was to harass and distract the Japanese with raids, ambushes, and trail blocks so that the jungle warriors could not gather to invade India, a frightening prospect since India might conceivably take the Japanese side. While the 5307th was distracting the Japanese, its men also would have the mission of helping to reopen the Burma Road between India and China, which would provide a strategic connection for moving provisions, supplies, and materials necessary to keep China in the war. As agreed between the Americans and British at the Quebec Conference in 1943, the 5307th had been placed under the military command of British Brigadier Orde Charles Wingate, one of the most romantic and colorful military leaders of the twentieth century.

While readying his Anglo-American forces for their campaign, Wingate brilliantly reorganized Sam and his fellow soldiers to fit his model for a "Long Range Penetration Group" (LRPG). The LRPG was a novel and highly imaginative concept of waging war behind enemy lines while being supported solely from the air. Once again, the 5307th was thrown into momentary confusion as fast-forming friendships were broken off and a new organizational structure was implemented. The 5307th was still a Composite Unit (Provisional) but was now structured as a Long Range Penetration Group, British style.

When the unit was reorganized at Deogarh, Sam was given a new responsibility. He and a fellow officer, Logan Weston, were each ordered to form their own Intelligence and Reconnaissance platoons for highly dangerous advance work in the jungles. They were both told that they could get any willing men in the entire unit for their platoons, as long as those who volunteered knew that they were going to be on the point more than any others. Both men set out to form units that could staunchly perform their duties in the face of startling danger and fear.

Logan Weston was a deeply religious man. He had been studying at divinity school before he left for the war, and he still considered himself to be a preacher. When forming his I and R platoon, he recruited men of similarly deep religious conviction. He sought men for whom death was not an end but a beginning. While considering different candidates, he would both interview and pray with the soldier. The final product of his selection was a platoon that achieved phenomenal combat success. He found men who could stare death in the face without flinching.

Sam used a very different technique for selecting his men. Although he too was a man of deeply rooted faith, he chose instead to visit the guardhouse prisoners to find his volunteers. Upon reaching the guardhouse, which was actually nothing more than a collection of tents behind barbed wire, Sam had the prisoners line up in rank for him. He slowly made his way down the line, speaking separately to each man, trying to size him up and sense what sort of person he was. Sam especially relied on the quality of each man's handshake, his salute, and his overall bearing as he made his decisions. He offered the best men a chance to volunteer for an independent mission of compounded danger. One of the men he selected happened to be the same one who had ferociously attacked him back at the brothel in Nazik. Since the man had barely been able to mask his disgust for Sam since that incident, Sam worried that the man still held a grudge and might fantasize about finding an opportunity to extract revenge on Sam somewhere in the Burmese jungle. However, once the man accepted Sam's offer to join the I and R platoon, he proved to be dependable and courageous. In fact, before they had completed their mission, the soldier had distinguished himself by winning a citation for heroism in battle. Not surprisingly, most of the rest of the prisoners were eager to join as well. Although Sam found that his group of daredevil, rebellious, independent men was difficult to lead at times, the platoon enjoyed success equal to that of Weston's group.

Some weeks later, Sam's friend and fellow officer, Charlton Ogburn (later to be the author of the definitive book entitled *The Marauders,* which details the heroics of the 5307th), asked the Battalion Commander, William Lloyd Osborne, which of the two types of groups would do better in battle. Osborne replied that it does not make a difference what kinds of men are in the group. What matters is the sort of leadership they are given. Looking back, General Sam observes that the two groups, seemingly different in temperament, were actually quite similar in their potential. Both religious men and rebellious men are less attracted to things of this world than their more conventionally minded friends, and, therefore, both types can face death with less apprehension.

At first, the men of the unit volunteered for what they had understood to be a three-month mission, after which they assumed that most of them would be allowed to return to the States without having to serve combat duty again. It did not take long for all of the men to see that they were probably not going home any time soon, certainly not after just three months. The same rebelliousness that made them excellent recruits for an undefined, dangerous campaign was at work when a contingent of the men, disappointed at the extended duty they saw before them, hijacked a train at Jakhlan Station and took it across the subcontinent to Calcutta for a brief period of unrestricted pleasure. The men could not help but feel that the military owed them a chance to enjoy themselves since they had already been constrained in the army for well over their allotted duty periods, and there was no end in sight.

After their fun, the AWOL soldiers returned the train to Jakhlan Station and sauntered back to camp at Deogarh. Even though their pay would be docked and they might have to spend a few nights in the guardhouse as punishment, for them, the excitement was worth the price. Perhaps the military administration understood the mindset of these men. They declined to mete out severe punishments.

Lieutenant Sam Wilson valued the rebellious spirit of his platoon, but he realized that it was his challenge to prepare the recruits for the unknown, but certain to be daunting, challenges of combat. He intended to create the most effective Intel and Recon outfit ever assembled. As a youngster, he had studied the Civil War in detail and had been especially impressed with General Stonewall Jackson's ability to move his forces with unbelievable speed. It was this speed which allowed Jackson to surprise the Union Army, appearing in places where no one expected him to be and gaining advantage through surprise. His men moved with such speed that they became known as "Stonewall Jackson's foot cavalry." Sam, who became a great believer in speed marches, set out to create a unit that mimicked Jackson's forces.

He himself was young and sinewy and could march tirelessly for days, and it was not unusual for him to set out with his troops and spend an entire day at a high-paced, shambling walk-trot through the Indian countryside. The focus was on pushing himself and his unit to their maximum capacity, and he and the quickest men often kept moving, not waiting for the slower men to catch up. As the day progressed, the unit would be strung out along several miles of the march, with the slower men always struggling to catch up to the lead and sometimes having to march all day long to complete the route. Some men simply could not handle the pace, as was the case for a man named Robinson, one of the older members of the platoon. The wear on his body proved too difficult, and one afternoon, after particularly arduous maneuvers under the glaring summer sun, he approached Sam to say that he could not continue. Sam allowed him to return to the 5307th headquarters where he assumed his old position with the S-2 (Intelligence) staff section and worked under the supervision of a man named Billy Laffin. Interestingly, before the 5307th launched their official campaign into Burma, Robinson voluntarily returned to Sam's platoon.

Those who remained with Sam's I and R platoon gradually became accustomed to the harsh rigors of the long speed marches. They took pride in trying to outmarch everyone else in the 5307th, and they knew that these miserable, grueling, and torturous training runs were honing their physical strength and endurance for the mission ahead. Sam's boys, affectionately known as "The Galloping I and R," achieved a masterful level of physical preparedness.

But physical preparedness was only one aspect of the training that Sam initiated for his platoon. In conjunction with Major Caifson Johnson, a combat team commander, Sam devised modified treasure hunts for his men. Johnson, a big Swede from Minnesota, had been a college football player and a professional wrestler before he joined the army, and he was no physical lightweight himself. He and Sam launched their joint missions by secreting a series of messages around a designated plot of land. As the platoon found the messages throughout the day, they would carry out the stated tasks and then continue to the next pickup point. The troops learned to problem-solve in the field and to handle the unexpected circumstances that threatened their success. Upon returning from each exercise, Sam gained valuable experience briefing Johnson on what had transpired and what had been learned.

On one such mission, the platoon was crossing the Betwa River just after sunrise. Normally the river was about a hundred yards across, but at this particular point, the clear, cold current rushed through an area of less than half that width. The men drove posts deep into the ground on both sides of the river and rigged up a rope stretching across the water so that the platoon members could safely shimmy across with their rifle wrapped tightly and pack secured from the deep and rushing water. With about two-thirds of the men safely on the opposite shore, a simple-minded giant of a solider began to make his way across the line. He was half way across the raging current when, someone foolishly cried out, "It's breaking, it's breaking!"

The huge man panicked, his fear of the water causing him to lunge on the rope. Under the profound stress, the rope indeed did snap. He plunged into the icy water and sank like a stone. Despite desperate diving by the platoon, they could not find their comrade. Eventually, Sam had no choice but to write a report of the tragic incident and continue the mission towards completion. While the platoon kept marching, they were morosely subdued by the loss, and Sam was unsuccessful in rallying interest in their exercise.

Sometime after midnight, they paused for a half-hour break, and while the men sprawled, exhausted on the ground, rumblings of mutiny came to Sam's ears. As soon as he heard the talk, he knew immediate action would be necessary to maintain order in the group. Masking his trepidation with a confident, forceful edge to his voice, he boldly ordered, "Cut that talk right now."

He described to the platoon a shady glade about eight miles away where they could have some time off, catch fish, shoot game, and relax for a bit after the distressing morning. Confidently, he called the order, "On your feet."

He held his breath, hoping desperately that the men would follow his lead. Relief washed over him as every single man stood up, shouldered his pack, and set off down the trail behind him.

Sometimes Sam's intelligence and reconnaissance troops would train with a squad of Ghurka warriors. The Ghurka tribes, who hailed from central Nepal, had earned a reputation for perseverance, single-minded loyalty, and courage. Their self-discipline and respect for authority awed Sam, and he marveled at their adeptness in handling their famous Ghurka knives. Ghurka knives are a foot of sharp-tipped, sneering steel, and they were never pulled from their sheaths unless the intention was to draw blood. So deep-set was this tradition that if no enemy presented himself after the knife was drawn, the warrior would ceremoniously prick his own finger. With their patience and strict adherence to orders, these Ghurka warriors proved highly valuable to the 5307th.

On one afternoon training exercise, Sam and his platoon practiced setting up an ambush with a detachment of Ghurkas. Sam carefully placed his men, and then set a Ghurka soldier with a British automatic rifle at the head of a small valley. After tapping the man on the shoulder, Sam let him know that he would come for him when the exercise was over. That evening, around ten o'clock, with the drill successfully completed and the participating troops already asleep back at the base, Sam remembered that he had left the Ghurka soldier at his post. He immediately hopped into his jeep and hurried back to the site of the exercise. He found the man exactly as he had left him, crouching in his firing position. Once they returned to camp, Sam rewarded the young warrior with an extra shot of rum. There was no complaining or sulking, and Sam could only feel entirely humbled by the young Ghurka's display of stoic discipline.

In January 1944, the 5307th was surprised to learn that they were no longer under British command. Rather, they were considered a part of the American Theatre under the direction of General Joseph W. Stilwell. The troops also learned that, contrary to earlier information that they would be dropped by gliders behind Japanese lines in central Burma, new orders mandated that they infiltrate behind enemy lines by marching across the mountains in the far northern part of Burma. From there, Stilwell would use them as a wedge to force the stalled, American-trained Chinese divisions to advance their positions. On the heels of this news came the arrival of an energetic and smiling Brigadier General Frank D. Merrill. At just thirty-eight years old, Merrill assumed command of the 5307th from Colonel Charles N. Hunter, his former West Point classmate, class of 1929. Hunter, who until this transition had commanded the unit, thus became second in command, and the 5307th became known as "Merrill's Marauders."

Shortly after Merrill took command of the 5307th, the outfit broke camp at Deogarh and began a rail and river journey eastward across India. First, they journeyed by train for several days until they reached Calcutta, and they made their way from there by steamboat slowly up the Brahmaputra River northeast to Ledo. The three-day steamboat ride up the muddy waters of the Brahmaputra allowed the men idle time to ponder their pending introduction to battle. To the east of Led, a small town tucked away in the western foothills of the Naga Mountains in the Assam Province, a new road was being carved through the jungle and mountains just behind the Allied advance into northern Burma. The eventual objective of the 5307th was to connect the new road with the famous Burma Road.

As the broader purpose of their platoon began to emerge with greater clarity to the American volunteer force, Logan Weston, the leader of the men of deep religious faith, told Sam that he took comfort in John 19:41. "At the place where Jesus was crucified, there was a garden, and in the garden a new tomb, in which no one had ever been laid" (NIV).

Sam worried whether or not he would be able to face violent combat resolutely. During the nights spent on the old Indian paddleboat, as he lay on the open deck and stared up into the starry Indian sky, Sam recalled Shakespearian passages. In one excerpt from *Henry IV,* Feeble the Taylor proclaimed that " . . . by my troth I care not . . . .a man can die but once . . . we each owe God a death, and he who dies this year is quit for the next." Sam also read and reread the prologue in his paperback edition of Ernest Hemingway's *Men at War* to remind himself that others had been in his position before. No death is crueler than those that have already been suffered, and no fate is more miserable than those that have already been endured. Glumly hoping that if those before him had been able to fight valiantly, so too would he, Sam steeled himself for pending misery.

From Ledo, Sam's I and R platoon was the first unit of the 5307th to begin the weary march one hundred and forty miles over two mountain ranges toward the valley of the Chinwin River in northern Burma. For Sam, the most memorable sight of this long march was the day they passed through the Pangsau Pass. As the men looked north, the staggeringly majestic Himalayas glittered in the far distancelike jeweled necklaces, piled one on top of the other. Just beyond this pass, Sam caught his first glimpse of General Stilwell, the Theatre Commander.

The men of the 5307th had long wondered why Stilwell had never visited them during their arduous and seemingly never-ending training, but they were finally given a chance to look at the old man as he sat next to a Chinese driver in his jeep. Holding a carbine between his legs and wearing a Chinese soldier's duckbilled cap on his head, Stilwell peered through the windshield at the small, spread-out column. No one slowed his marching pace, but one man, a mule skinner, paused long enough to remark, "Well, God damn! Duck hunters way up here!"

Humor seemed a small relief to the men as they moved ever closer to the distant thundering artillery of the battlefront, for as the men drew nearer to the Japanese, the eastern breezes began to carry growling rumbles from distant explosions that made the hair on Sam's neck prickle. The men assumed a heightened degree of wariness with each day's progress.

As the exhausted men finally made their way into the Ningbyen camp on the Tarung River, a Chinwin tributary, they received a welcome sight, their first supply drop. This would be one of many supply drops the men would receive, for the 5307th would become the only major unit in World War II that was maintained completely by provisions dropped to them by air.

As the men enjoyed their first rations that the C 47 transports dropped from the sky, General Stilwell visited the First Battalion's bivouac area. After delivering an encouraging speech to the assembled officers, Stilwell had taken the time to shake hands with each officer in the battalion. He then lingered long enough for a brief conversation with Merrill. Sam found an unobtrusive place from which he could observe the two men as they talked. He was startled when he saw Merrill's thumb point in his direction and shocked when he lip-read Merrill saying, "Sammy's the youngest First Lieutenant in the Army. I expect great things from him."

Suddenly, and for the first time, Sam felt a tremendous burden that ensued from his recognition that high-ranking people were watching him and that he had better not let them down.

THE FIRST BURMA MISSION

AFTER MARCHING ON THE LEDO ROAD until it narrowed and dwindled into nothing more than a jungle trail, the 5307th Composite Unit (Provisional), a.k.a. Merrill's Marauders, assembled for a few days of rest on a small island in the Tarung Hka, a major tributary of the Chinwin River. By that point, the Marauders were forced to rely exclusively on their radio for messages from the outside world, and they waited for the order to move deeper into the jungle. Meanwhile, they rested. The march into Burma had been grueling, and they slept deeply, even in the oppressive heat that would be a constant companion during their mission. They dipped into the rations they had procured from their first aerial supply drop, and they prepared to move into the nearly impenetrable tangle of jungle growth that lay around them.

The Marauders were on the precipice of the Burmese jungle, inside which lurked Japan's Eighteenth Imperial Guards Division, one of the crack divisions in the Japanese army. Led by Lieutenant General Tanaka, the Eighteenth Division had already earned decisive victories at Singapore and Rangoon. Subsequently, it had spearheaded the Japanese advance northward through Burma and toward India. This division's outposts marked the extent of the Japanese Empire westward in the Asian Theatre.

Originally, Allied forces had placed two American-trained Chinese divisions opposite the Japanese advance, but the Chinese resistance had soon stalled against the well ensconced and better equipped Japanese. General Stilwell, the commander of Allied operations in the Theater, planned to use the Marauders to prod the recalcitrant Chinese into moving again. His strategy was to infiltrate the Americans to positions well behind the Japanese, and then to have the Chinese break through Japanese lines to link with the Americans. It was a "hammer and anvil" technique, using the Chinese as the hammer and Merrill's Marauders as the anvil.

In response to Stilwell's strategy, Merrill began hatching a plan to maneuver his troops around Tanaka's east flank. Once he could establish blocking positions on the Japanese main supply line, the Kamaing Road, which approached the Japanese position from the south, the Japanese forces would be caught with the Chinese at their front and Galahad (the Army's code name for Merrill's Marauders) in their rear, both forces cutting off their supply route.

To find a way past the Japanese lines, Merrill dispatched three I and R platoons, one from each of his three battalions. The platoons were to move to the east along a well-traveled native track which ran parallel to the Japanese front. Each platoon had orders to cut south at a specified location and probe for gaps in the Japanese lines. Logan Weston's 3rd Battalion I and R platoon was to turn south after eighteen miles; Lieutenant William Grissom's 2nd Battalion platoon was to do the same thing about seven miles farther on; and Sam's I and R 1st Battalion platoon was to continue east for another ten miles or so before they turned south in the direction of a Kachin village called Tanja Ga, situated just north of the Tawang River. All told, Sam and his men were assigned to march through a total of forty miles of dense, Japanese-patrolled jungle.

Sam's "Galloping I and R" set off at 2:00 a.m. For the first few miles, the men trotted confidently through relatively safe territory. As they neared the potentially more hostile areas, they gradually slowed their pace. At dusk, after nearly seventeen hours of steady marching, they pulled off the trail and set up defensive positions so the men could bed down and sleep. A hundred yards down the trail they had traveled, Sam posted two sentries, and he assigned another two men to guard a spot that was a hundred yards in the opposite direction. As an added precaution, he laid booby-traps along the trail ahead of the sentries. At dawn, the men awoke and turned south, away from the main trail, and towards Tanja Ga, known enemy territory.

All morning the troops moved rapidly ahead in single file. Sam had organized a system where his men, spaced at fifteen-foot intervals along the column, would peer into the forest in specified directions. The first man was responsible to observe straight ahead, the second watched the forest on the right, the third covered the left, the fourth scanned the trees, and the fifth soldier watched the rear. The system started with the lead scout, continued back through Sam's position (third in line), and finished at the fifty-man column's rear with Sam's platoon sergeant, Technical Sergeant Ed Ammons. As Sam marched, he could hear nothing more than the sounds of jungle boots softly thudding on the forest trail, sometimes a stifled cough, and the occasional rattling from the packs on the trail horses. The men were totally alert and concentrated, and the air was charged with suspense.

The platoon continued southward into enemy-controlled territory until mid-afternoon, when the sharp and sudden sounds of small arms fire, grenades, and blasts of Japanese mortars broke the jungle silence. The platoon froze in place, a number of the men dropping to one knee with weapons at the ready. The firing, although loud, was some distance off to the platoon's right.

After a short pause, Sam signaled with his hand, and the platoon continued onward. Clearly, one of the other I and R platoons had run up against a Japanese trail block. Apprehension escalated. Tension increased. About an hour later, they heard the outbreak of the other I and R platoon in a firefight with the Japanese. Sam's platoon froze in position again, the men practically holding their breath. The prolonged firefight quit abruptly, and a long silence ensued. Sergeant Ammons came up from the rear. Shifting his tobacco chew, he warned Sam to keep a sharp eye and moved back to his position in the platoon's rear. The men continued on their course, suspense becoming more and more intense. Every curve in the trail brought a heightened sense of danger as the men pondered what was around the next bend, and the next, and the next.

By late afternoon, the men reached a break in the jungle. In the hazy sunshine, a few bamboo-walled, thatch-roofed huts on the far side of the clearing betrayed no enemy movement. After sending out scouts to reconnoiter both sides of the open area, Sam sent two men to investigate the village. A few tense minutes elapsed, and then the men reappeared to give the all-clear sign. Tanja Ga was unoccupied. They had reached their destination.

The rest of the platoon cautiously approached and established themselves in what had clearly been a Japanese outpost, and which only recently had been abandoned. In the well-trodden mud, Sam identified the split-toed tracks of the special shoes that Japanese snipers wore to shimmy up trees and the hobnailed imprints from regular Japanese military footwear. Following a thorough check of the surrounding area, Sam placed outposts on the three separate trails leading out of the village and ordered the rest of the men to unload the mules, feed the pack animals, get some chow themselves, and then stretch out for some well-earned rest.

While the men were bedding down, it was becoming evident to Sam that he had penetrated beyond the extremity of the enemy's right flank and established himself behind the Japanese front line. Apparently, the large Japanese patrol that had been stationed at Tanja Ga had pulled out to the west toward the Japanese main body in response to the same firefights that had earlier made Sam's patrol so nervous. If the main battalions of the Marauders were to move rapidly, following the trail that his platoon had blazed, they might be able to outflank the Japanese with minimal resistance. Sam knew that Merrill needed this intelligence as quickly as possible, before the Japanese could respond to his platoon's maneuver. The mule-packed radio was quickly set up, and at 9:00 p.m., the scheduled contact time, Sam's patrol made preliminary radio contact with the main force, some forty miles away. After brief contact, communication went dead and could not be restored.

It was imperative that Merrill have this critical intelligence as soon as possible, and since radio communications were down, Sam decided that his only option would be to race the thirty-odd miles on horseback and let his commander know the situation. Sam climbed aboard his beloved steed, a powerful horse named Pride-and-Joy, and set out at 10:00 p.m. for the Marauder's main camp. One other man, John Epperson, volunteered to go with him. They agreed that the safest way to travel the treacherous path would be for Sam to lead sixty or seventy yards ahead of Epperson. If Sam encountered any Japanese, Epperson would halt and maintain the interval, thus standing clear of any fracas. If Sam made it through the enemy trail block safely, he would fire twice to signal that he was free and on the other side. When Epperson heard the shots in spaced succession, he would know to return to Tanja Ga since the Japanese would be on full alert, and at that point Sam would continuing the ride solo. If Sam failed to fire two shots after an encounter with the Japanese, Epperson would know he had to find another way to get the intelligence to Merrill.

Pride-and-Joy had such a smooth, loping canter that Sam felt as if he were sitting in a rocking chair as they sped back along the trail his platoon had followed earlier that afternoon. On the open stretches, Sam let Pride-and-Joy out to a gallop, for they had a great deal of territory to cover. Whenever Pride-and-Joy galloped across the open clearings, Sam could look back and see Epperson and his big roan trailing behind him in the shadows. In the darkness of the jungle night, there was no way for the two men to sneak their way back to Merrill. There simply was not enough time. They had to count on speed over stealth and hope that they could ride through any danger before the Japanese along the trail became fully aware of their presence.

In the wee hours of the morning the trail dipped sharply into a ravine. As Pride-and-Joy scrambled up the far bank, Sam's saddle twisted to the left and he was thrown nearly to the ground. At that instant, two huge jungle cats bounded out of the forest fifty yards up the trail. His left foot in the stirrup, his right foot on the ground, Sam dangled precariously for a moment before he could shake himself free. As he scrambled to gain his footing, the cats began a cacophony of thunderous roars, growls, and hisses. Terror crept through Sam's body as Pride-and-Joy began rearing, beset with fear. In the back of his mind, Sam remembered hearing that predatory animals could sometimes be distracted by the human voice. Unable to come up with any other plan, Sam began yelling at the savage beasts. "You don't want to eat me, you crazy cats. I'm too sinewy and full of bones. I'd break your teeth!"

He slid his carbine from its scabbard and pointed it in the air, firing three quick shots. As the shots echoed in the forest, the cats stopped their hideous noise and sprang off the path and into the jungle. After quieting Pride-and-Joy, Sam straightened his saddle and tightened the girth, frustrated with himself for not checking it more thoroughly earlier. He shook a sugar lump from his pocket and offered it to his brave horse, but for the first time ever Pride-and-Joy was not interested in sweets.

Sam pulled himself up into the saddle and glanced back to find Epperson. Suddenly he realized he had fired three times. If Epperson had not counted carefully, he might retreat after he heard those shots. The weight of the mission sank onto his shoulders as he considered that he might be bearing it alone. Determined to complete the mission safely, Sam put Pride-and-Joy into a fast gallop for the next few miles. Soon he came to a long clearing in the jungle, and glancing back in the pale moonlight, he could see the dark blur that was Epperson on Big Red. Wonder of wonders . . . Epperson had figured out what had happened from the noise of the cats and was still riding with him.

Just as the misty dawn was beginning to break, a low branch knocked Sam's helmet off at the edge of a small clearing. Dismounting to pick up his headgear, Sam started across the foggy clearing on foot. His heart stopped when, just as he was almost across, he found himself staring down the menacing barrel of a .45 caliber pistol. A white-faced American soldier, quite frightened and seemingly hostile, tensely requested, "Get out of the clearing, please."

Sam moved through the positions of what he soon discovered to be Second Battalion's Lieutenant Grissom's I and R platoon. In a brief discussion with Grissom, he discovered that they had encountered the Japanese, had lost their lead scout to enemy fire, and had then pulled back to set up a position near the junction of their southern track with the main east-west trail. Armed with this additional information, Sam continued on five or six miles to Third Battalion's Lieutenant Weston's well-organized defenses. With his pulpit-worthy voice, Weston pointed out to Sam his well-dispersed men and carefully established defenses. Weston's platoon had suffered one slight wound, a bullet-creased cheek, in its encounter with a Japanese trail block, but they had killed at least one enemy.

A few miles farther on, Sam rode through the main body of the First Battalion, which was already in a marching column along the trail, and soon after, he came upon Merrill's command group. Sam stumbled off Pride-and-Joy, handed the reins to an equally exhausted Epperson, and immediately relayed his information to Merrill. After Sam and the two commanders carefully reviewed maps and details, Merrill thanked him for his initiative and energy. The intelligence would enable Merrill to act decisively. Sam was told to get back to his platoon as soon as possible and reconnoiter for crossings of the Tawang River to the south.

Moving with deliberate speed, Sam and Epperson safely made the return trip to their apprehensive platoon. They arrived at camp just before sundown, and as Sam pulled his saddle off, he noticed that when he had retightened the saddle girth, he had wrinkled the saddle blanket in such a way that it had rubbed a deep sore the size of a lemon high on Pride-and-Joy's left shoulder. Immediately he summoned the medic: "Doc Anderson, we've got a wounded soldier here." Sam put Pride-and-Joy's saddle on a mule pack while Anderson applied sulfur to the wound.

As soon as he paused, Sam realized the depth of his exhaustion. The ordeal of the past three days had depleted his store of strength. He made a quick check of his own security outposts and then ordered the rest of the men to get another good night of sleep and a full meal. Their task, at first light, would be to reconnoiter for suitable crossings on the Tawang River. Then, with a deep sigh, he sat down to munch on a fruit bar. He fell asleep before he could finish the first bite.

Meanwhile, Merrill realized that he could use the intelligence that Sam had brought him to gain a strong advantage. With dispatch, Merrill force-marched his entire unit deep in the rear of the Japanese force and established his troops for battle on grounds of his own choosing, near the village of Walawbum. There, they would wait for the Japanese advance.

Sam was directed to lead a lightly armed, twenty-five man patrol north to the Japanese rear to gain information on how the Japanese were responding to Chinese pressure that had ensued. Sam's men advanced slowly, creeping on tiptoe along a trail next to the small Numpyek Kha River. He had just led his men through a small glade when Sam heard the danger signal, "Pssst."

His eyes followed the pointing fingers of his rear soldiers and spotted a large roan horse swishing his tail on the riverbank. One of the men thought he recognized the horse as that of Colonel Still, and Sam, somewhat relieved, started across the glade, carbine cradled across his left arm, to investigate.

Some sixty feet from the river's edge, all hell broke loose. A machine gunner and three riflemen cut down on him. He dove for cover. A grenade flew by, within inches of his face, and Sam flipped it away with his hand, just in time to divert it about ten feet away. The explosion ripped into his pack and, for a moment, stunned him. Quickly recovering, his eyes trained on a man jumping onto the roan horse. In his nervous excitement, he emptied all fifteen rounds of his carbine into the man's body. The next thing he knew, a huge soldier, the largest Asiatic man he had ever seen, leapt towards him with his bayonet aimed at Sam. Taking aim with his own gun, Sam heard the telling click that revealed his carbine was empty. Just at that second, Staff Sergeant Branscomb, stood up and poured three shots into the man's chest. The Japanese soldier fell dead, right on top of Sam. The skirmish was over.

The American patrol had killed two Japanese soldiers and wounded three others who managed to flee. Sam's men had escaped unscathed except for one man who had had a bullet crease his left side and Sam, whose ears still rang from the grenade explosion that had come so close to killing him. Not only had it left him with ringing ears, it had also given him a nose bleed and had deposited a few fragments of shrapnel in his right leg.

Rummaging through the belongings of their enemies for possible military information, Sam and his men confirmed that the man Sam had shot off the horse had been a Major. Sam cut off his insignia and went through his saddle bags, finding some maps, three or four reports in Japanese, and a few personal papers and photos. The pictures showed a doll-like Japanese lady, clearly the man's wife, and two little, round-faced children. Sam could not choke back the emotion of the moment. The photographs gave his enemy a persona, and Sam realized that there were people who would mourn the man's death. Sobered by the events of the day, the patrol returned to Merrill and the rest of Galahad in time to help prepare a defense against the impending Japanese attack.

The battle at Walawbum was a slaughter. One of the Marauders' combat teams of four hundred men had trained thirty-nine automatic weapons on a stretch of river that the Japanese would have to cross in order to attack the Americans. Resolutely, the Japanese made desperate banzai charges across the two hundred yards of flat, open ground that lay before the river. Then, they plunged into the water, determined to overrun the U.S. forces on the eastern bank. After a series of unsuccessful tries, the Japanese gave up.

Sam was a little frightened, more for the safety of Pride-and-Joy than for his own health, when the Japanese began a covering artillery fire. However, the pack train soldiers had cautiously hidden the best animals in a deep gully, so while many of the exposed animals were killed, Pride-and-Joy was able to escape unharmed. As Sam turned his attention back to the river, he noted the Japanese dead littering the banks on either side. His companions estimated that they had killed just under a thousand Japanese, while Galahad suffered five dead and thirty-nine wounded. After the defeat, the Japanese folded their troops around Galahad's position and set up a new front about twenty miles further south, while the American-trained Chinese divisions moved forward to occupy the former Japanese defense positions.

After the battle, the Marauders desperately needed to rest, re-equip, and recuperate in a quiet area. Sam's I and R platoon returned to the control of the First Battalion. Lieutenant Colonel Osborne, the battalion commander, directed Sam to guide the unit to a good location upstream of Walawbum. Sam was not sure where there might be a good location for the troops to rest, but he followed a trail upstream in hope of finding one. Within a couple of miles, the trail abruptly ended. Thinking that the trail might continue on the western bank, Sam led the entire outfit across the river, right into a dense jungle. Before they had gone far, Sam realized that he was a lost man. He thought it best to keep his dilemma to himself. After more than an hour of wandering, he blundered suddenly into a beautiful, abandoned village right on the river's edge. It was so picturesque that it seemed as if they had stumbled onto a movie set. Sam chuckled silently when Osborne complimented his decision to lead the troops to that spot. An old saying of Cap'n Jack's came back to him, "Sometimes I'd rather be lucky than smart."

Once camp was set up, Sam settled himself for some badly needed rest and did not stir again until sunrise, when he awoke and considered rising, shaving, and getting ready for the day. But, convincing himself that he needed more sleep, he rolled over, exhausted. Shortly afterwards, he was waked by Battalion Commander Osborne. Osborne, Hunter, and Merrill were headed to meet General Stilwell in a nearby village where they would discuss the d etails of the Marauders' success. They wanted Sam to join them. Osborne was in a hurry, and since Sam had not shaved or dressed, he would meet a trail guide at an intermediate village, and the guide would take him the rest of the way to the meeting. Sam lost little time in getting started, but when he arrived as the designated village, the sentry was nowhere to be found. Frustrated, Sam turned back.

When Commander Osborne returned, he apologized. The man posted to wait for Sam had fallen asleep. Relaying the events of the meeting, Commander Osborn reported that General Stillwell had been highly impressed at the reports of Sam's work and had ordered that, in recognition of his courage and initiative, a citation for the Distinguished Service Cross be written. Sam lamented that by snatching a little extra sleep he had missed a rare chance to enjoy the praise of a higher ranking officer. He resolved to be better prepared in the future.

THE SECOND BURMA MISSION

AFTER THE BATTLE AT WALAWBUM, the men of Merrill's Marauders went into what they anticipated to be an extended bivouac. They had fought hard and well. They had trudged through dense jungle and crossed rushing rivers. They had braved the elements with little to comfort them and had lived on the barest of rations. They were weary of Burma. Furthermore, General Stilwell's Chinese divisions had shaken off their lethargy and were beginning to advance against the Japanese. Most of the Americans expected they would soon be relieved of their miserable duties in the jungle swamps of northern Burma and would have an opportunity to recover, recuperate, and reorganize before they returned for more combat.

However, the success of the Marauders at Walawbum prompted General Stillwell to see an opportunity to further decimate the Japanese line. Rather than ordering R & R for the Marauders, the General ordered a second mission on the heels of the first. He wanted to repeat the success of the first mission by dividing his battalions and again skirting the eastern Japanese flank. For this second mission, he sent the First Battalion on another loop, like the one they had just traversed, with the eventual goal of returning to the Kamaing Road at the town of Shaduzup, about twenty miles behind the enemy front and fifty miles from their interim location. The Second and Third Battalions were ordered to make a wider arc and engage the Japanese on the road about fifteen miles deeper into Japanese territory. Sam's I and R platoon, part of the shallower run, was again assigned to reconnoiter the route for the rest of the battalion.

The second mission was even more challenging than the first, and from the moment it began, Sam and his men felt the heightened adrenalin that comes with fear. They were entrapped in constant, high level danger from every side, 360 degrees of possible threats, for every minute of every hour of every day. Fear gnawed at them and would not go away. They lived on edge, knowing that circumstances could change at any moment and their lives would be at stake.

Sam was not immune to the overwhelming force of fear. He never forgot the vivid impression that fear left, as though it would suck his guts out and shrivel him up. He was all too aware that it could paralyze men who did not brace against it.

Whenever fear was most overpowering Sam relied strongly on his relationship with his Maker. Armed with faith in the Eternal, he could cope with that fear. Months later, when Sam found his way out of the hell of combat, he felt the grip of fear loosening its hold. The feeling was so strong that he felt an overwhelming desire to run around, jump up and down, flop in the grass, kick his heels and do silly things. He wanted to shout, "It's gone!" The absence of overwhelming fear became a delicious lightness of being, and he could appreciate the luxury of feeling secure more fully than ever before. As General George Patton stated, "Freedom has a taste for those that have fought for it, a sweet taste the protected will never know."

Long after he left Burma, Sam could still taste that sweetness.

Years later when he reflected on the miseries of the terror he had felt in battle, Sam realized that in order to persevere in combat, a man needs three things. First, he needs enough to eat. At times in the jungle, Sam was starving, but when he found enough food to generate some energy, he could begin to face his problems. Second, a man requires some kind of shelter, a source of warmth and protection from the elements. Whether it was a depression in the side of a mountain, an abandoned native hut, or a thick bamboo grove, Sam needed some place to gain sufficient rest once he had found enough to eat. Third, a man has to believe that no one is going to be shooting at him. A whirling canopy of bullets can destroy any hope, however firm the courage in a man's soul. In conversations with his good friends, Charlton Ogburn and Phil Weld, Sam found that other men had come to similar conclusions.

But these musings would come later. There was no time for reflection as Sam and his men marched steadily from Walawbum towards Shaduzup. After two days at the head of the battalion, Sam and his patrol began to encounter fresh signs of enemy activity. The lead scout, John Sukup, began spotting Japanese boot prints that were still filling in with water in the soggy creek beds. Sukup was Sam's best scout, despite being partially deaf. As is often the case with people who suffer minimization of one of their senses, Sukup's other faculties were extraordinarily well-developed. He possessed keen eyesight and a remarkable sense of smell.

The hearts of the men in the patrol froze when they heard several rounds spit from Sukup's Tommy gun. They leaped into combat positions and opened fire at the flitting Japanese figures who, from the jungle shadows, were feeling out the American platoon's flanks. As Sam crouched under some bamboo stalks, scanning the dense jungle, a bullet hit a bamboo stalk just a foot above his head. Water stored in the hollow of the shoot began to flow from the stalk, as a reminder of how close Sam and his companions really were to the reality of death.

Lying there during the first moments of the Japanese attack, Sam's mind raced. Somehow the danger seemed unreal. There was no way that they could really be in the midst of yet another firefight. Yet, at the same time, he knew that somebody was going to suffer; they could not all emerge unscathed. He hoped he would not be an unlucky one. All of Sam's years of training had prepared him for just such a situation. He hoped that the rest of the platoon would remember their training as well. They were all struggling with a desperate desire to burrow down into the ground and let the bullets fly over their heads until the Japanese stopped firing.

Sam knew he had to be careful that his men did not freeze in their positions. He had to dispel the paralyzing sensation of fear that could so easily overtake them, and to do that, he needed to get his men moving aggressively. His tactic was to have each of them drop back and fan out in a horseshoe-shaped defense position while they waited for the lead elements of the main battalion to arrive. The job of the I and R was to find the enemy, not to fight him. Upon the arrival of the first friendly combat units, Sam's patrol unit folded back behind the main body of the First Battalion. They waited in the rear for the combat teams to clear the path for their next scouting mission.

Over the next twenty-four hours, the First Battalion skirmished with the Japanese on nineteen separate occasions, all of them more or less similar to that first contact. Each time it appeared to Sam that the Japanese were adding forces. It became increasingly difficult to push them back. Battalion Commander Osborne was also becoming acutely aware of this difficulty, so he sent Sam's reconnaissance platoon out to the left of the column to see if they could find a trail that would allow the First Battalion to skirt this stubborn Japanese resistance.

As Sam's platoon returned from their reconnaissance of territory to the east of the column, they came upon the First Battalion's Red Combat Team, a force of about four hundred men, situated on a hill overlooking the ravine of a stream called Tingkrung Hka. On the ridge at the far side of the stream the Japanese had surrounded two of the Combat Team's platoons. The Team leader was in a state of near panic and was preparing to abandon the men on the other side of the creek as Sam approached. In a heated argument,

Sam demanded that the seventy men on the other side of the stream not be abandoned. When the terrified Team leader would not give sway, a heated altercation ensued. Sam's view prevailed, however.

Sam directed the mortar units of the Red Combat Team to provide him with a rolling barrage box covering both flanks so that he could get through the encircling Japanese forces. Led by the deadly fire of the accurate gunmen, Sam and his radioman proceeded to cross the stream and mount the opposite ridge, penetrating the Japanese siege line as they went. Gathering the two platoons, who had been stoutly defending themselves from the Japanese offensive for the better part of the day, Sam ordered them to fall back, bringing with them the wounded and as much of their munitions as they could manage. Three men from the besieged platoons, including Lieutenant Billy Lepore, helped Sam carry two dead soldiers across the stream and safely back to the American-occupied ridge. By the time the rescuers returned, the Red Column Team leader and his troops were gone, leaving Sam and his patrol to bury the dead in the hard, rocky soil. Using a pack shovel, Sam and Lepore were able to scratch out shallow graves. They hung a dog tag on each of the bamboo crosses which two others from the patrol had cut, and then each of them said a prayer over the fallen soldiers. Presbyterian Sam quietly eulogized, "The Lord giveth and the Lord taketh away, blessed be the name of the Lord," while Billy, a Catholic, crossed himself and added, "May the Lord have mercy on their souls."

The following day, First Battalion Commander Osborne boldly decided that by cutting a track eastward through the mountains, they could elude the pestering Japanese trail blocks that were hindering progress on the main trail. The Marauders were forced to hack their way with machetes through the virgin jungle, a process that took several days of sweltering cutting and chopping as they attempted once more to get around the Japanese right flank.

The exhausted nerves of all the soldiers were put to a demanding test when Osborne, in his effort to get around the Japanese right flank, decided finally to come down from the mountains through a gorge cut by the Chengun River. A huge gamble, this maneuver left the entire unit potentially exposed and boxed in should the Japanese discover what they were doing. The men were very much aware of the predicament they would face if the Japanese caught them descending the mountains down the deep Chengun defile. There would be practically no way for the First Battalion to defend itself. They steeled themselves for the arduous trek and hardly dared to pause as they made their way down the steep slopes and past the rushing water of tumbling waterfalls.

The Chengun gorge spat the First Battalion out just across the Mogaung River from what Osborne's officers calculated to be the village of Shaduzup, the battalion's intended destination. As the men from Galahad stealthily spread out and prepared themselves for battle with the forces on the far side of the river, they could hear the sounds from the Japanese camp across the way. American scouts could make out the hollow "pong" of an axe cutting bamboo for firewood and the deep "thung" of a grenade exploding underwater somewhere upstream, probably a Japanese detachment fishing for dinner. The men, still breathing heavily after their long ordeal in the mountains, could smell wafting wood smoke as their enemies prepared an evening meal. Concealed on the river's edge with Sam, Commander Osborne wondered aloud what was over there on the other side of the river. Was the camp indeed Shaduzup? Sam responded, "Why don't I go see?"

After a brief pause, Commander Osborne said, "Yes, why don't you?"

Sam gathered his I and R platoon and started upstream along the near bank to find a suitable place to cross the river. Locating a crossing that was partially concealed from Japanese observation by a sharp bend in the river, he turned to his platoon, "I've got to go across. Who'd like to go with me?"

A long silence ensued. He looked into the faces of his men and they stared back at him. For the first time ever, no one stepped forward. They had simply had enough. Sam thought to himself that the only thing more stupid than volunteering was asking for volunteers. Sam asked his men to cover him from the near bank while he made his way across the water. As he set out, one other man, Perlee Tintary, stepped forward to accompany him. Sam carried two grenades, his OSS knife, and his favorite carbine with extra ammo. He and Tintary half-waded, half-swam the seventy-five yards across the cold waters of the stream. As the pair, drenched to their chins, neared the opposite bank, they heard desperate "Psst . . . PSST . . . " warnings coming across the water from their patrol. Doubling their speed, they rushed into the cover of the jungle on the far shore just in time to hide from a patrol of three Japanese coming along the far bank. Sam and Perlee spent about forty minutes on the Japanese side of the Mogaung. During this tense time, they snuck around and through the enemy camp, practically under the nose of the unsuspecting Japanese soldiers. They were able to positively identify the Kamaing Road, the main enemy supply line up from the south, and the locations of stockpiled ammunition and supplies. Stealthily, the two made their way to the river and slid back into the stream. Once again when they reached shore, they had to lunge out of the stream and hide, just as a large patrol marched along the opposite bank. Panting from the exertion, Sam made sure that his men were all accounted for and well positioned in locations that allowed them to observe the Japanese movements. He then went to report to Commander Osborne.

Sam gave Commander Osborne an account of the Japanese activity he had observed. He was shaking as he spoke. There was blood spattered on the side of his still-soaking wet uniform. In response to Commander Osborne's query about if he had been wounded while on the mission, Sam responded, "It's not my blood, sir." Commander Osborne looked hard at his exhausted lieutenant. "That's all for you for this operation, Sammy," he ordered.

Sam suggested he be allowed to remain in his current position with his platoon and keep an eye to the north in the direction of the main enemy force. He then hastened to rejoin his troops, who were already dug in on the side of the hill overlooking the Mogaung. The sun was setting as Sam came back to his men. They were chowing down and putting finishing touches on their hasty entrenchments. In the evening darkness, one man, known as Young Allen, who often paired with another soldier called Old Allen, began to argue irrationally with Sam to allow the platoon to move to the back side of the hill where they would be less exposed to enemy fire. Sheer fear showed in Young Allen's eyes as Sam permitted the men to reconnoiter for a fallback position but refused to let the men move for the night.

In the small hours of the following morning, the First Battalion waded quietly across the river and swept through the Japanese bivouac at Shaduzup at dawn. The Marauders were able to take the Japanese camp by complete surprise and managed to ambush trucks coming up the Kamaing Road from the south as well, but the violent firefight lasted all day. During the night the Japanese brought up artillery and began shooting at anything that moved on the American side. The first barrage screamed over the heads of Sam's platoon, frightening but not harming them. During the second barrage, Sam heard the desperate screaming of a dying man. When the dust cleared, he heard someone calling that Old Allen was dead and Young Allen badly hurt in their foxhole. As he dropped down into the hole to try to help the young man, he stepped on a severed part of human debris torn by the shell that had mutilated both Allens.

In Sam's mind he could hear Young Allen's insistent plea earlier that night that the platoon be moved to a safer place. He ordered the rest of the platoon to a spot they had reconnoitered, but he stayed behind with Sergeant Ammons and the Medic, Andy Anderson. Together, the three men spent the rest of the night comforting and trying to aid a dying Young Allen. They also wanted to ensure the Japanese were not crossing the river. Hunkered down beside their dying comrade, the three men endured the heaviest artillery barrage that Sam would ever experience.

Dawn came suddenly the next morning, as if God just flipped a switch. The booming enemy artillery and mortars from across the river suddenly stopped. After the thunderous clamor of the night's attack, an eerie silence lay like a canopy over the valley. Sam's every sense had been magnified from the shock of the prolonged Japanese bombardment. Patches of a crystal blue sky peeked through the jungle foliage, somehow deeper and darker than it had been the previous days. The surviving jungle flowers bloomed in brilliant colors, stimulated by the heat of the night's barrage and highlighted by the charred remains left by the explosions. The flowers were so bright that they hurt his eyes.

Then suddenly, the morning's tranquility was broken by a roaring American fighter plane, zooming by overhead on its way to strafe the Japanese camp. Sam and his buddies jumped up and down with joy, yelling with glee that finally they were being relieved. From a distance behind the American position, Chinese artillery began zeroing in on the Japanese camp. Soon an even greater joy arrived. A Chinese infantry division, relieving the worn-out Marauders, came to take over ensuing operations for the Shaduzup region.

The exhausted and nearly starving troops of the First Battalion backed out from their positions at Shaduzup via the Chengun Gorge. It would not be until two days later that they received a badly needed aerial supply drop. While the men relaxed briefly in their bivouac, Lieutenant Charlton Ogburn, Sam's friend and the First Battalion's communications officer, got the radio operating again and received a message that the Second and Third Battalions had not fared as well as the First.

The rest of the Marauders urgently needed Commander Osborne's men to help them fight off superior numbers of Japanese who had surrounded the Second Battalion at a village called Nhpum Ga. A speedy response was urgent because the Japanese were threatening to destroy the entire force. The First Battalion gathered themselves together and quickly began the race to aid their brothers in arms.

If their endurance had been tested before, it was savagely challenged during the grueling week-long march the First Battalion completed through the dense jungle to reach their comrades. First Battalion arrived to find that Allied air support and imrovised artillery had already severely mauled the

Japanese, thereby allowing the Third Battalion to break the Japanese siege and get through to the encircled Second Battalion. The First Battalion began the gruesome task of burying the dead and burning the rotting carcasses of pack animals.

Merrill's Marauders had completed their second mission. They had fought with determination and resolve, and they had accomplished great things for the Allied forces in the Asian Theater of operations. But the cost had been high. The end of the second mission found the three battalions of Merrill's Marauders reduced to half their original numbers. Merrill had suffered a heart attack, and the surviving troops were physically and emotionally worn from weeks of continuously fighting. All the men now felt they needed to recover, reorganize, and retrain, and they deserved to do so in an area far removed from the devastation in Northern Burma.

But a shocking surprise awaited them.

THE THIRD BURMA MISSION

THE MEN OF MERRILL'S MARAUDERS recovered quickly from the stress and strain of the unit's first mission, which had ended with outstanding success at Walawbum, but after the much more arduous and bloody mixed results of the second mission, the Marauders desperately needed time to rest and regain strength. All three battalions were now at less than half their original size. Most of the remaining men were in weakened physical condition. Sam was beginning to suffer from amœbic dysentery and early stages of malaria. Grenade fragments in his right leg from the firefight during the first mission were festering and beginning to bother him more and more. Any feeling of invincibility that he might have felt early in the deployment had long splintered and been replaced by the constant irritation of physical ailments and the traumatic effects of the constant savage fighting.

Other men suffered similarly or worse. Some had been overseas in combat for more than two years and were worn out. It was time for even the most stoic veterans to get some respite from the strain of continuous combat. Everyone in the 5307th knew the group had done more than had been expected of them, and all were ready for time in India to recover and to relax. Once more, however, the duties of freedom called them into action.

In a face-to-face meeting in April 1944, shortly after the battle for Nhpum Ga, General Stillwell told Merrill of his intent to seize the Japanese airstrip at Myitkyina before the start of the monsoon season. The town commanded the northernmost terminus on the Japanese-controlled railroad running from the south, as well as traffic on the strategic Irrawaddy River. Japanese fighter planes based at the Myitkyina airstrip constantly harassed and interdicted Allied supply aircraft traveling from India to China over the Himalayas. Myitkyina was thus a pivotal location for the war in Asia. Sam and his comrades groaned aloud as they picked up their packs for a third time and set out in on a one-hundred-fifty-mile journey across two mountain ranges.

There could be no stealth in this mission, for the Japanese were fully aware of the Marauder's presence in their territory. The 5307th could only rely on other advantages. Their ability to march rapidly enabled them to disappear and reappear at unexpected places. Also, the indigenous Kachin people of Northern Burma had cast their lot with the Allies and willingly rendered various kinds of useful support.

By the time they set out, the help of the Kachin became especially important to the Marauders marching to Nhpum Ga. The Japanese were blocking all known trails leading to Myitkyina, and Merrill decided to rely on the Kachin people to help his troops move along native paths and elephant trails. Galahad was still trying to do the unexpected. Merrill divided his American volunteers into three combat teams, two of which were to be followed by a Chinese regiment. The First Battalion, with which Sam and his I and R continued to march, and the Chinese force it spearheaded, were controlled by Colonel Hunter and referred to as "H-Force." In "K-Force," Colonel Kenneson led the Third Battalion and the other Chinese regiment. Merrill's "M-Force" followed behind with the remnants of the Second Battalion, some Kachin rangers trained by the Office of Strategic Services, and a few Gurkha troops.

During the march from Nhpum Ga, Sam became especially close to his young Kachin sidekick, Pom Ya Tu. Pom Ya Tu was the fifteen-year-old son of a Kachin village headman and had already become an OSS ranger. His father had insisted that he accompany Sam, and was holding Sam personally responsible for ensuring that nothing bad happened to the boy. Sam picked up a smattering of the Kachin language while he and Pom Ya Tu ranged through the deep forests, jungles, and mountains of Northern Burma. The two became buddies.

One night, Sam and his patrol were holed up in a Kachin village high in the mountains and far away from the Japanese down in the valley. Sam was sleeping peacefully, warmed by a small fire in the center of the hut, when he was awakened by the sound of someone stirring the fire. Pom Ya Tu crouched over the flame with a thoughtful expression on his Oriental face.

"What's up, Little Buddy?" inquired Sam.

"Duwa," Pom Ya Tu asked Sam, "why are you here? What are you fighting for?"

Man, what a bad time to ask this, Sam thought to himself as Pom Ya Tu continued. "Your home is far away, far across the great water, which is far wider than all our rivers and lakes combined. Then one day, you come to our land. The Japanese had come earlier and been cruel to us. They molested, burned, stole, and forced us to flee and hide in the hills. We hate the Japanese. But you are very kind to us. Your noisy machines fly over and drop mushroom shaped supplies. You share food with us. Your doctors treat our sick people.

You protect us, and you defend us against the Japanese. But why?"

In the middle of the night, in his broken Kachin, Sam tried to explain to Pom Ya Tu how his people had decided to fight the Japanese, so that they could not do to the Americans what they had done to the Kachin. Frustrated with the continued perplexity in the boy's face, Sam tried a different tack. "Pom Ya Tu, you know Duwa Stuart?"

Sam referred to the renowned Irish Catholic priest who had been serving as a missionary to the Kachins since 1936, ministering to the Kachins and gaining their highest respect.

Pom Ya Tu told Sam that he did know Duwa Stuart and that he was the greatest man the Kachin knew. Sam continued, "You know what Duwa Stuart says about loving God and our fellow man, and living in peace, freedom, and security? Duwa Stuart is talking about the things we fight for."

"I understand. That is very simple. What took you so long to explain?" Pom Ya Tu bluntly replied as he returned to stirring the embers of his fire.

In the days following Sam's discussion with Pom Ya Tu, the men in Sam's patrol noted a perceptible upsurge in the efforts of the Kachin. During one march deep in the Kumon Mountain Range, the men had been dragging for three days without food. Passing through a Kachin village, however, they saw local villagers eagerly pointing down the trail. As the column passed through a ravine, they were greeted by a Kachin ranger who directed the men each to take one of the packages lying there on the slope. Arranged in green banana leaves, the wrapping paper of the jungle, were heaping portions of the most succulent rice and chicken curry that the men had ever smelled. The column hurried to a suitable place to take a break and began to gulp down the delicious gift. Almost immediately, their empty stomachs sent the rich food right back up. But the men did not care. It had it tasted so wonderful and felt so good going down their throats.

The Kumon Range is a long finger of mountains extending south from the Himalayas, and it lay directly in the path of the Marauders as they marched towards Myitkyina. With their manpower diminished even further, down to barely more than one third of the original outfit, fewer than four hundred men for the First Battalion, Sam and his buddies began the grueling work of crossing the mountain ranges on unused and crumbling trails that ran along precipitous cliffs. Their first goal was to reach Naura Kyet Pass safely, but as the men approached the beginning of their ascent on the first day's march, a brooding fog turned to mist and then rain fell in earnest. In the best of weather, the mountain path was dangerous, but as the rain beat against the mountains, the dusty trail turned to mud and the rocks that peppered the surface grew slick. Unstable footing became more and more treacherous.

As he led the column along the trace of the ancient Kachin trail, winding around the steep slopes in the driving rain, Sam worried about his faithful horse, Pride-and-Joy, as well as his men. In some places, the trail had crumbled away entirely, leaving thousand-foot drops down to jagged rocks at the base of the cliffs. The column advanced slowly, but occasionally, one of the pack horses would slip, and the echoes of the falling steed sent a chill over the unit. For a time, everyone seemed to hold his breath in cautious horror. Finally, Sam sent to the back of the column for his horse to be brought forward, and he halted the progress of the entire column until he held Pride-and-Joy's reins. Sam hugged the beast's neck and fed him a few sugar cubes before he gradually began to work his way, with Pride-and-Joy in tow, around the steep mountainside. The trail began to narrow around a bend, and the two inched their way forward, but suddenly, the path behind him began to crumble under the weight of the horse. Sam glanced back and saw Pride-and-Joy's hind legs dangling over the precipice as the steed struggled to regain his footing. Sam reached for a little bush as he clung to his horse's bridle, but the trail suddenly gave way. Pride-and-Joy slapped his front hooves onto the solid ground once, straining to climb to safety, but the bush that Sam had been holding began coming out by the roots. Sam was forced to release the reins, and Pride-and-Joy tumbled a thousand feet down the sheer mountainside, screaming a heart-rending cry as he fell. With a sickening thud, Pride-and-Joy smashed into the jagged rocks below. Sam's anguished pain at his loss choked him. For a minute, he did not believe he could continue, but he knew that he had no choice but to trudge on, one precarious step after another.

That night, the column straggled into the Naura Kyet Pass, a cold, windswept plateau high in the Kumon Range. A heavy fog hung between Galahad and the valley below and safely obscured the group's fires from the watchful eyes of the Japanese. The men unpacked the radio, which had previously been christened "Becky," off the mule's back and arranged the antennae to pick up short wave radio broadcasts. Radio Manila, Radio Free Rangoon, Radio Free Calcutta, Radio Australia, and the BBC were all audible that night as the radiomen scanned the dials. Among the international call signs was one with the strange words *"Govorit Moskva,* Moscow calling." Sam had his radioman stop on that station. One of his men, a mule skinner of Russian parentage, interpreted the Russian broadcast for him. Sam listened to battle communications being broadcast to Soviet citizenry. They described the advances of the Red Army against the Fascists over their two-thousand-mile front. As Sam listened to the Russian broadcast, tales of the mighty and terrible battles fought at Stalingrad and elsewhere along the front were confirmed. It became clear that as bad as things were for the United States' forces in Burma, the war on the Soviet-German front was taking place on a far greater scope and scale, and it was causing human casualties and devastation to a degree that was scarcely imaginable. As the Russian broadcast began to fade into static, Sam turned to the little band that had accumulated by the fire and said, "When this is all over, I'm going to go home and study Russian. Then I'm going to go to Moscow as an assistant military attaché, and I'm going to find out why these people fight so bravely and for so long in the face of such terrible odds." Several years later, motivated by his epiphany on the lonely slopes of the Naura Kyet Pass in Northern Burma, that is exactly what Sam would do.

On the evening of May 16, 1944, General Sam and his comrades in H-Force slipped by a defending Japanese force, with which K-Force had become heavily engaged, and they stealthily made their way to the outskirts of the landing strip at Myitkyina. During that night, one of Sam's I and R subordinate commanders, Sergeant Clearance E. Branscomb, led a patrol to reconnoiter the airstrip under the cover of darkness and returned with the intelligence needed for a successful attack. Using Branscomb's intelligence, H-Force assaulted the Myitkyina airstrip early on the morning of May 17th. Within less than an hour, American planes and gliders were landing on the airstrip.

Merrill's brilliant tactical maneuver became the subject of instant headlines back in the United States. *Time* magazine labeled it the "culmination of Merrill's epic march." But the troops of the 5307th were too exhausted to celebrate their own victory. They stumbled around like figures in a dream, expecting planes to bring relief troops and to carry them out. Most men figured they would be flown to hospitals in India immediately after they had captured the airstrip. Once again, however, the cause of freedom demanded that they remain behind. This time the Marauders were retained at Myitkyina to hold the airstrip and subsequently to besiege the city. They were aided by no more than a trickle of untrained reinforcements.

Following the seizure of the airfield at Myitkyina and the beginning of a steady flow of aerial resupply, Sam was instructed to take a reconnaissance patrol southeast of the city to a place on the map marked Zyguyn Ferry. His orders were to secure the ferry and then to cross the river and reconnoiter the eastern bank of the Irrawaddy River. Taking a patrol of about twenty-five men with him, Sam reached the ferry uneventfully. After leaving part of his force to keep the ferry secure, he proceeded with the remainder of his men to cross the river and visit the Indian village along the far banks. No one spoke English in the village, and there were no Burmese or Hindu speakers in Sam's patrol. Clearly, however, the villagers were friendly as they offered water to the parched soldiers and let them know by gestures that they were thrilled to see them. They had not fared well under Japanese domination. The natives expressed their gratitude to the patrol by gathering rice and a couple of gaunt chickens to offer the soldiers a meal. Sam and his men accepted the meal gratefully and headed upstream about two miles to a small grove by a rice paddy to prepare the chickens and rice.

Sam's patrol was tending the cooking fires when two American P51s appeared in the sky and zoomed over the village that Sam and his men had just left, strafing it mercilessly. Mouth agape, Sam watched as machine gun bullets pummeled the village and incendiary bullets set a number of the thatched roofs aflame. The men were quickly pulled out of their horrified stupor when they saw that the planes had spotted them and were heading right in their direction. They dove headfirst into a nearby irrigation ditch and clawed their way into the earth, pressing as hard as they could into the near side of the ditch to avoid the thudding bullets showered over them during three or four passes. After the planes flew away, Sam and his patrol abandoned their much-needed dinner and scrambled back to the village.

Tribesmen were just emerging from the sheltering pits and caves they had dug under their huts. The village headman came running up to Sam and threw himself screaming on the ground. He grabbed Sam by the arm and half-dragged him to a demolished hut. The headman called down into the dugout cellar, from which came the muffled sound of a woman's voice. His wife emerged from the shadows holding up the body of their eighteen-month-old child, struck in the abdomen by a twenty-millimeter round from a strafing aircraft. The bullet had exited the spine and blown off half the child's back. The woman was screaming as she held the child over her head, intestines dangling from the frail child's now lifeless figure. In that moment, Sam began to understand what war was really all about.

They could not linger, so Sam and his men hurried back over the Irrawaddy and rejoined the guard waiting on the western bank. Sam was handed a day-old radio message urging their return to the airstrip command post where he was to report to the unit intelligence officer (S2) as quickly as possible.

The exhausted men practically jogged the three miles back. Out of breath, they flopped to the ground just short of the runway. Sam wanted to catch his breath before reporting to the intelligence officer. He dropped to the ground with his back against a small mound and took a deep breath. As he did, he noticed something shiny hanging just out of the range of his peripheral vision. Looking more carefully, he realized it was a dog tag hanging by a tiny chain to a cross. It read: "Captain William A. Laffin," the same intelligence officer to whom Sam was expecting to make his report.

Sam had worked very closely with Laffin since the Marauders had sailed from San Francisco. He had come to know Laffin, whose mother was Japanese, as a well-educated, highly cultured man. Again, Sam leaned his back against the mound, the fresh grave of his colleague. In the command post, Sam learned that Laffin had been aloft in a small American reconnaissance plane over the city of Myitkyina when Japanese Zeroes spotted him and shot him down. For some reason—perhaps it was the half-starved, feverish, fatigued state that he had been in for weeks, or perhaps it was the recent memory of the dismembered child—the knowledge that Billy Laffin had been killed was especially hard for Sam to take.

A half-hour later, Sam was at the command post of the First Battalion, rendering his report through chattering teeth. The battalion medical officer stood nearby and waited until the report was complete, then he pulled Sam to one side and tied a medical evacuation tag to his fatigues. "I don't even have to take your temperature," he said.

As Sam stumbled out of the post to collect his belongings, he remembers one of his men calling, "Sammy, can I have your Tommy gun?"

The siege would continue on without Sam for roughly three months, until finally, on August 3, 1944, the city of Myitkyina fell to the combined American and Chinese forces. On August 10th orders were made to demobilize Galahad, a.k.a. the 5307th, a.k.a. Merrill's Marauders, as a fighting unit. Sadly, it was nothing more than a formality. Galahad had already ceased to exist. The energy, hope, and too many lives of its men had been sacrificed in a valiant crusade to preserve freedom.

SAM'S RETURN TO VIRGINIA

SAMMY LAY ON HIS BACK, strapped down in an evacuation transport plane flying away from Myitkyina. He was too exhausted to keep himself from falling to the floor, thus the straps, and he was too depleted to support himself on his own. His gallant efforts in leading the intelligence and reconnaissance platoon for the First Battalion of Merrill's Marauders had left him incapable of putting another foot forward on his own. He was finally felled by an attack of mite typhus, but only after many weeks of suffering from amoebic dysentery, malaria, and minor shrapnel wounds from the early grenade explosion. Flying over the Burmese jungle, he lay helpless on a stretcher, a high fever making him almost delirious. Despite his deep fatigue and illness throughout the campaign, Sam's mind had been branded with stark pictures that would remain embedded in his memory for the rest of his life. As an evening rain jostled the C-47 aircraft on its way back to India, Sam entered a period that he would never remember with the same clarity with which he recalled almost every day of the long march from Ledo to Myitkyina.

He was immediately hospitalized in the Twentieth General Hospital in Ledo, where he and the other invalids from his transport were placed in the anteroom in front of the hospital ward. The first English-speaking female voices he had heard in months murmured quietly as a nurse inserted a metallic instrument into Sam's mouth and held it there briefly checking his temperature.

She glanced at the thermometer, and then shouted, "My God, bring me some wet blankets, fast!"

Sam woke up several hours later in the back of a ward with five other men, all very ill, all with raging fevers from typhus. He was the only one, however, with additional complications. For the next several days, the medics struggled to keep the men hydrated.

Sam recalls the medics trying desperately to bring his temperature down by wrapping him in wet blankets. Around the middle of the third night, Sam vaguely heard a commotion in the bed next to his own. People with flashlights and medical paraphernalia tried in vain to revive the patient as Sam drifted back into sleep. Next morning, an empty void was all that remained where his friend's bed had been. No one, neither patients nor doctors, ever mentioned the incident, not even when the same trauma repeated itself time after time in the ward. Even in the delirium of his fever, Sam realized that eventually he was the only patient still alive. Five of his comrades had died, all of whom had less serious infections than his own. The vague thought began to take hold in his fever-worn mind: perhaps the Lord was saving him for something.

It was weeks before Sam had recovered enough to walk around the ward. He ventured up to the Red Cross area for donuts and coffee in the morning. He especially enjoyed sitting at the piano and playing his favorite songs. One day, as Sam was sitting at the foot of his bed, Father James Stuart walked into the ward. Father Stuart was the same legendary Catholic missionary in Northern Burma that Sam's Kachin friend, Pom Ya Tu, had loved so much, and he had been evacuated from Myitkyina alongside Sam. Father Stuart complained that he was getting an itchy foot after sitting around in the hospital for so long and that he wanted to go south. He proposed that Sam and he visit the OSS Detachment 101 headquarters in India's tea district. Sam willingly agreed.

Strapping two five-gallon cans of gasoline on the back of a jeep, the two men cheerfully set off on the four-hour drive to a huge tea plantation in Nazrah that Lieutenant Colonel William Ray Peers had secured as his headquarters for OSS Detachment 101. Peers had been charged with the tasking of arming and training the Kachin scouts who recovered downed U.S. pilots. His scouts also provided intelligence about the enemy and aided Allied units like Merrill's Marauders against the Japanese in the north Burmese valleys.

It was well after dark when Sam and Father Stuart arrived in Nazrah, and Sam's delight at being out of the hospital had turned to a fatigue that was so consuming he could hardly step out of the jeep. Peers, a vigorous and athletic chap, prematurely grey and with a nose that had been rearranged during his football days at UCLA, came out to meet the men. He lifted Sam from the jeep and half-carried him to a seat on the veranda. He then offered him gin and grapefruit juice, the first cold drink Sam had tasted in months. Sam and Father Stuart spent most of the next month relaxing and recovering in the main house on the British-run, Indian tea plantation. It was perhaps the most enjoyable vacation of Sam's entire life. The three weeks passed quickly, and on a stormy Sunday afternoon in early July, Sam flew back to Ledo in a small L-4 airplane. Almost as soon as Sam signed back into rear headquarters of the

5307th, he began to shake with fever as a recurring case of malaria took hold. It was a harbinger of the recurring nightmare to come over the next eighteen months, when Sam experienced nineteen bouts of malaria, each one requiring hospitalization and each one debilitating.

Between bouts of malaria, Sam passed his time checking on the men from his platoon who were in neighboring hospitals in the towns of Ledo, Margarita, or Chabua. He also was always on standby as a volunteer to carry the mail pouch to Colonel Hunter, by then the Commander of American forces participating in the siege at Myitkyina. The commanders at headquarters always seemed glad to see Sam when he came with deliveries, and sometimes they allowed him to stay overnight. They flatly refused to let him talk about rejoining the fight, however. It had become a nasty and dirty brawl, they said, and they did not want him to be one of the many good men killed for nothing.

One of the men from the OSS Detachment 101 tea plantation had given Sam an Australian bush hat, and during the summer of 1944, Sam decided to put his new captain's bars on the front of his hat. He wore it proudly. One day, as Sam was coming by the main command post (CP) at the Myitkyina airstrip, returning from Colonel Hunter's CP, the then-commander of the entire siege, Brigadier General Tommy Arms, was exiting a tent. General Arms screwed his face up into an ugly frown as he turned abruptly towards Sam. "Captain, are you in the U.S. Army?" Arms growled.

"Yes sir," replied a startled Sam.

"Then get rid of that goddamn hat." Sam snatched the hat off his head and, faster than the old man could furrow his sun-stretched brow, he sailed it like a Frisbee across the rice paddy.

"What's your name?" the imposing general inquired. When Sam told him, the old man paused. "So you're Sammy Wilson?" he drew a raspy breath. "Son, go get your hat."

Sam felt the compliment deeply. He was beginning to realize that tales of his escapades in the jungles had traveled far beyond his own platoon.

It was not until August 3, 1944, that Myitkyina fell to the Allied siege. The end of the Japanese hold on the city was accompanied by the end of the existence of the 5307th Composite Unit (Provisional) as a combat unit. Eligible members of Galahad were returned to the United States based on accrued points from combat. Those lacking enough points (from time served, acts of valor, and the like) became part of the newly formed 475th Regiment of the MARS Task Force, the unit that succeeded the Marauders. The

475th was commanded by newly appointed Colonel Lloyd Osborne, Sam's commander in the First Battalion of the 5307th.

Sam began taking steps to rejoin the fight as the commander of one of the 475th's rifle companies when the dry season came. As he was preparing for the new campaign in central Burma, however, General Stillwell, still in charge of Allied operations in the Theater, received news that Sam would be offered a fifth consecutive appointment to the Academy at West Point. The General took interest in young Sammy and decided to invest in him for the long range future of the U.S. Army. He put Sam on orders to return to the United States immediately.

Overnight, Sam flew back to the Theater headquarters in Delhi. He brought with him letters of introduction to United Press Reporter Darrell Berrigan from First Lieutenant Phil Weld, one of Sam's closest friends in the 5307th. Berrigan warmly accepted Sam into his comfortable lodgings as a house guest, and in the big city, Sam began to receive attention for his heroics in Burma, especially for his midnight ride with Pride-and-Joy. Numerous senior military folks and local movie stars invited him to be their dinner guest and were thrilled by his tales of the war in Burma. Sam's head began to swell as he became the object of attention among the rear echelon's social scene.

One afternoon, however, Berrigan, who had been observing Sam's struggle with newfound cockiness, took young Sammy aside. The two were driving out from Delhi to tap Berrigan's contraband gin source when a powerful storm approached. The rainstorm was so severe that they were forced to pull to the side of the road. As the men settled down to wait out the rain shower, Berrigan began a story.

Berrigan had been successful as a college student in southern California, and had been a much-sought-after social leader on campus. He had begun to think that he was something special. One evening, a favorite professor invited him to dinner. Afterwards they drove up a nearby mountain and looked down together at Los Angeles sprawling in the valley below. The professor and Berrigan took turns pointing out to each other the glowing lights of significant landmarks and prominent locations. Eventually, the professor pointed out the college, a tiny square speck, so far away that you could not see the many people walking across the lawns between the buildings. "Sort of cuts you down to size," commented the professor, "doesn't it, Berry?"

And it did. Berrigan realized that he had not been keeping his own worth in perspective.

"Berry, don't forget to climb that hill once in a while," the professor finally advised.

On the morning Sam flew out of Delhi on his first leg home, Berrigan gave him a bound volume of the complete works of William Shakespeare. On the fly leaf was the inscription, "Sambo: don't forget to climb that hill once in a while."

Sam kept that book with him from that day forward. The pages turned musty and yellow with time, but the message never faded.

From Delhi, Sam made his way by air through a number of overnight stops to Casablanca, where he was disappointed to have his carbine confiscated. It was the same one which he had carried with him throughout the Galahad campaign, and he had hoped to smuggle home. While he waited in Casablanca for a flight to the Azores, he encountered a beautiful and celebrated Hollywood actress who was on her way to the front to parade her beauty on stage and give the boys "a little touch of home." Sam was struck by the ridiculous disconnect that would make this brunette think that, with her sculpted face and gorgeous eyes, she could be considered a touch of home for the soldiers. She was removed from their reality, whether they were overseas or at home. Regardless, the actress spotted Sam in his cavalry boots, riding britches, and British bush jacket, and casually began a conversation with him.

Sam remembers her leaping to the conclusion that an officer this young and healthy belonged at the front. He deduced a haughty arrogance mingled with a self-centered righteousness in her attitude as she scolded him for not being with the men who were still fighting. Clearly, she could not read the medals on Sam's tunic which proved he had done exactly the opposite of running away, but had rather run forward under fire. Sam almost opened his mouth to defend himself, but decided that silence would be the more valiant course of action.

He took the tongue-lashing and boarded the next plane, but he was stung to the quick by her hyper-critical attitude. A lasting distaste for the haughty attitude of the pampered and deified increased his newly acquired focus on humility. The world might be full of arrogant people, but Sam was determined not to be one of them.

As soon as the big cargo doors had slammed shut on the runway in Delhi, the sensation of going home perceptively increased its thrill. Many of the guys with whom he had fought were not as fortunate as he was. Some were still over there fighting, and some of them were resting quietly on remote hills under bamboo crosses. Exultation mingled with melancholy when he thought of the enormity of their sacrifice. Still, from Delhi on, with every place he stopped—Karachi, Basra, Cairo, Tunis, Casablanca—the rising expectation of how it was going to feel when he got home began to overwhelm Sam.

Three years earlier he had left home, and now he was returning from war. He was going to see his mother, father, sister, whichever brothers were still home, and his German Shepherd, Mike. He would share meals at his mother's dinner table and go to church with friends and kinfolk. He was almost dizzy with anticipation. The last several stops—Westover, New York, Washington, and Richmond—became a blur. When he arrived at the Richmond airport, there was no fanfare or ceremony. He made his way to the bus station to buy a ticket to Farmville, where he had to wait the longest hour of his life to board a bus. As the morning began to gray, Sam was rolling through Powhatan and Cumberland counties, tantalizingly close to home. He wiped the frosted window with his handkerchief and looked out at the first cedar trees he had seen in months. The bus seemed to be crawling at a snail's pace.

Finally arriving in Farmville, Sam stuffed his suitcase and big barracks bag into the backseat of the only available taxi and rode up front with the driver as they rolled home. When they turned onto the cedar-lined farm lane leading up to the Wilson farmhouse, Sam saw smoke in the kitchen chimney. His mother was fixing breakfast. He paid an exorbitant ten dollar fee to the taxi driver and lugged his suitcase and barracks bag to the porch. As he slowly pushed open the door on that gray Sunday morning, he saw his mother halfway across the hall. She looked up, paused, and in her wonderful and unperturbed way said, "Now, look who's here."

Sam hurried to her and gave her a big hug. His father came out from the kitchen, grabbed him, and began to sob a little bit, unable to control his emotions. The rest of the family converged on him from all directions—a welcoming and joyous homecoming. The Wilson family had been caught by surprise with Sam's return, and their joy was boundless. Sam showed them a few things he had brought with him in his suitcase and then enjoyed a hearty breakfast with his folks.

He became so absorbed in the happiness of being with his family that he lost track of time and was late for church. He quickly washed his face, and without changing out of his travel-stained uniform, he drove down the lane to Jamestown Church. Still feeling as though he were in a dream, he parked the car and walked up the front steps of the church into the anteroom. Not wanting to walk in while someone was praying, he cracked the swinging doors so that he could peep in and listen. He quickly recognized the voice of his uncle Will Vaughan praying. All of a sudden, it hit him. He heard his name and realized that Uncle Will was praying for him and his safe return from the war. He had to release his grip on the handle and let the swinging door close as he moved back slightly. Regaining control of his emotions, Sam walked through the swinging doors and into the church sanctuary, capping what was easily one of the most dramatic moments of his life.

The first phase of his life was over. Sam had come home. Hearing his uncle praying for him seemed to be more than just a coincidence. The timing was more than he could explain. Clearly, to Sam, someone above was watching out for him, and he could not help but be grateful.

BOOK 2

MILITARY LIFE

REORIENTATION AND REFOCUSING

IN THE FALL OF 1944, twenty-one-year-old Sam Wilson returned home to Virginia. His body still suffered from the injuries and diseases he had contracted during his time with Merrill's Marauders, and his mind was still shaken from the trauma of combat, but a wave of unreal relief washed over him the first morning he woke in the safety of his family home. He no longer had to reach above his pillow to see if his dagger were still there. Though he was still haunted in recurring nightmares by blood-curdling screams, visions of blood and dismembered bodies, ear-shattering explosions, and an overall sense of panic, Sam gradually relaxed. His nerves slowly adjusted to the safe environment of a home where there was enough food to eat and pastoral safety. He spent most of his first days with his family trying to calm his overwrought nerves, and he passed the time aimlessly wandering the neighborhood, catching up with old friends and regaling them with tales of his adventures.

One evening, he attended the fall cotillion at Farmville State Teachers College with a young lady he had met while giving a talk about his war adventures to her students at a local high school. In preparation for the evening, Sam meticulously laundered and starched his military uniform, then carefully arranging his medals and ribbons so that he could appear as dashing as possible. The party vastly improved for Sam when he ran into his former girlfriend, the one who had failed to see him off at the train depot that early morning so long ago. She greeted him excitedly, but Sam kept himself distant from her affection. He had moved beyond his love for her and on to a broader stage, or so he had convinced himself. Still, his mind was torn in two directions throughout the night. One half looked to enjoy this small, belated victory over a girl who had scarred his heart, while the other half looked to rise above the pettiness of revenge.

Another evening soon after his return, Sam was given the honor of being invited to dinner by two local citizens of prominence. Over the meal, the two men proposed that Sam seriously consider taking advantage of the reputation he had gained in the war by entering politics. The suggestion inflamed Sam's imagination and stoked his already swelling ego. When he returned home late that night, he eagerly woke up his parents to tell them about the proposal. Cap'n Jack did not let Sam wallow in his pride for long. Early next morning, he roused his son to suggest that he was still young, immature, wet behind the ears, and in danger of letting all the attention he had been receiving go to his head. General Sam still remembers Cap'n Jack warning him that, "As long as you know you're green, you'll grow. But when you think you're ripe, you're already beginning to rot." That advice quickly dissolved Sam's giddy dream, and he began to realize how, in spite of the advice Darrell Berrigan had given him in Delhi, he had been letting the attention from newspapers and local citizens inflate his ego.

Although, outwardly, Sam seemed to have avoided psychological war trauma, he inwardly struggled to establish and retain any purposeful direction or continuity in the peaceful world. The years following his return to the States were littered with false starts and disconnected activity. His actions mirrored his damaged mental state, which most likely was a case of post-traumatic stress syndrome, but that condition had not even been identified in 1944, and treatment would be decades in the making. Despite his disoriented mind, disconnected pursuits, and regular relapses of malaria, the years following Sam's return were still full of endeavors that helped shape the young soldier's career and complete his preparation for more significant leadership positions down the road.

At the end of October 1944, after spending several in the comfort of his family's home, Sam headed north to Massachusetts to participate in Amherst College's U.S. Military Academy Preparatory Program (USMAP), a prerequisite to his accepting an appointment to West Point. Upon his arrival, he found the picturesque New England town in the embrace of its first real snowfall of the season. He spent the remainder of a very rigorous semester studying at the highly regarded college. Although he excelled in English, history, and political science, mathematics proved to be quite a challenge. The schedule was demanding for the pre-cadets. Six to seven hours in class followed by four hours of study left only the weekends open for entertainment. However, diligent adherence to the study hours on his hall allowed Sam to perform satisfactorily. He was motivated to work exceptionally hard by a latent sensation of running scared. He always felt that his contemporaries were getting ahead of him and that he needed to run faster.

While all the pre-cadets living on Sam's hall were officers, most of USMAP was comprised of fresh volunteers. For the first time in his career, Sam found himself to be the oldest and most senior member of his military group. The other members of USMAP were mostly privates or corporals, while Sam was the only captain. Although he wanted to be a friendly and considerate buddy with the other guys in the program, he knew that it would not be appropriate for an officer of his rank to fraternize on an intimate basis with juniors. His social interactions at Amherst were marked by the tension of maintaining a balance between friendship and military order with his peers.

While Sam was attending classes at Amherst, his second Silver Star arrived in the mail at the office of the USMAP Commander Lieutenant Colonel James P. Jervey, a fellow Virginian from Cumberland County. When Sam's combat decorations from the Burma campaign caught up with him in rural Massachusetts, Jervey asked whether Sam wanted an award ceremony. Sam decided against it, preferring simply to stop by Jervey's office to pick up the citation. This oddity of receiving awards for service at his subsequent posts would be repeated about five times, an indication of both Sam's extraordinary service and of his frequently shifting assignments.

Sam's main diversions from the rigors of the academic world were his weekend visits with Margaret "Peg" Johnson at her off-campus house. The distinguished grey-haired widow of a world-renowned *National Geographic* South Seas explorer was herself a traveler, and she regarded the weekend as party time. She opened her house to the college boys and delighted them by showing selections from her collection of thousands of exotic photographs. As she regaled the boys with tales of her adventures in the South Pacific, she liked to have Sam improvise Hawaiian music on his guitar as an accompaniment. The pairing worked well, and Peg grew to enjoy Sam's music so much that she would postpone her evening talks until Sam arrived to strum background tunes.

Over Christmas break, Sam returned home to Rice. However, Sam's delight at visiting his family for a leisurely holiday was tainted by a feeling of guilt that he was safely enjoying the company of friends and family at home while many of his contemporaries were still posted around the world, embroiled in bitter conflict. He felt especially guilty sitting in front of the fire sipping wine while he listened to radio newscasts about the Germans' breakthrough at the Battle of the Bulge. Sam could not overcome a sensation that he had abandoned his brother soldiers while they still needed him. His sense of guilt continued after the Christmas break and proved to be such a burden to his conscience that he was prompted to act.

To ascertain if his physical condition would allow him to be admitted to West Point after the spring semester of the USMAP program, Sam requested an off-record physical exam. He failed miserably, and the doctor advised him not to go near an official physical for at least a year. Repeated malaria attacks as well as with the residual effects of his severe bout with mite typhus had worn down his body. He could not withstand the physical demands of life at the military academy.

Upon learning that he could not pass the West Point entrance physical exam, Sam immediately took steps to quit the USMAP program at Amherst. He called his old boss, Brigadier General "Daddy" Weems, the Assistant Commandant of the Infantry School at Fort Benning, and asked his former superior if he could resume his former job of teaching prospective infantry commanders. General Weems seemed pleased to hear from Sam and requested that he be placed on orders to withdraw from Amherst and be reassigned to Fort Benning.

"Benning School for Boys" had not changed much since Sam left it for the jungles of Southeast Asia. He found it hard to believe that he had been away for a year and a half. But upon his arrival, he learned that while the school had remained unaltered, his assignment as an instructor had changed. Instead of teaching classes, Sam was to command a company of West Point candidates gathered from programs at several colleges around the U.S. Ironically, Sam was given responsibility over some of the same men he had just left at the USMAP detachment at Amherst.

Within a couple of weeks, he was given charge of a second company as well. These soldiers were a more experienced group of lieutenant colonels and colonels who were at Benning to be transformed from non-combat to infantry officers. Sam operated well with the senior officers, mostly because they were already well-trained and required little supervision, but the company of pre-cadets bound for West Point proved to be more difficult for him. Sam's mind was preoccupied with recovering from his traumatic overseas experience, and he lacked the energy to focus on haircuts, improperly shined shoes, and other minutiae that were necessary to keep the pre-cadet company in order.

While Sam was working at Benning, he started receiving requests from local churches in Columbus, Georgia, to speak about his war experiences. One Sunday at a local Methodist Church, he took a back pew seat to enjoy a morning service before he delivered that evening's presentation. As he sat there, a lovely young woman with brown eyes stood up and sang the Lord's Prayer in a clear, bell-like voice that completely enthralled him. After he spoke that evening, he was able to meet the soloist and his positive reaction to her only increased. He was immediately smitten by Frances "Brenda" Downing.

She was the daughter of an old-line Southern family of lawyers, judges, and landowners. Though born in Columbus, on the Georgia side of the border, she lived on her family's estate a few miles away across the Chattahoochee River in Alabama. Sam asked if Brenda would mind if he called on her, and she said she would be happy to see him. Sam returned to his military quarters exultant and began spending all his free time courting the beautiful young girl from the Methodist church.

During the following weeks, Sam was hospitalized three more times for recurring malaria attacks. Towards the end of the third bout, his regimental commander visited him on his sickbed. The Colonel offered to arrange for two, consecutive, thirty-day sick leaves so that Sam could have an opportunity to shake off the residual effects of the North Burma campaign, especially the malaria attacks. He even offered to make reservations for Sam at a vacation resort in Lake Placid, New York. The Colonel also counseled Sam against immediate marriage and stated his hope that sixty days of sick leave in pleasant surroundings and away from the distractions of a girlfriend would work to cool down his ardor and rebuild his health.

Against the expressed wishes of his commander and following his own feelings instead, Sam married Brenda on June 25, 1945. He used his sixty days of sick leave for a honeymoon visit to the Wilson family farm in Southside Virginia, where Brenda met his relatives and the two of them relaxed in the quiet countryside. The time away from Fort Benning provided a badly needed opportunity for Sam to slow down and let life catch up to his emotions and memories. Conveniently for Sam, when he returned to Fort Benning his mentor had been reassigned, and Sam did not have to justify his decision to choose marriage over a peaceful but solitary recuperation.

Sam and Brenda enjoyed being together and having time to set up their first house at Fort Benning. Sam considered every day with his bride to be a treasure. He felt privileged to be an audience of one when she played the piano for him. He especially enjoyed her renditions of Broadway musicals as well as famous melodies from movies starring Jeannette McDonald and Nelson Eddy. But, in reality, it was the girl playing the music that captured his heart. The pair was truly in love.

With her family living just a few miles away from the base where the Wilsons made their home, the newlyweds were able to spend time at Brenda's home in the Alabama countryside. Her family's nearness proved to be especially helpful once Samuel Vaughan Wilson, Jr. was born on August 19, 1946. The Downings eagerly helped Sam and Brenda take care of the new baby and welcomed their daughter's family whenever they could visit the homeplace.

Some of Sam's fondest memories of these years are of fishing on the Chattahoochee River with Brenda's father, Lemuel T. Downing, whom Sam called "Pa Lem." The Downings were financially comfortable and enjoyed passing their time playing cards, hunting, and fishing on the estate. Although Sam enjoyed their carefree lifestyle, it starkly contrasted to the strict habits that he needed to maintain in order to be successful in his military career. His work demanded that he keep long hours and, even at the end of lengthy workdays, he regularly brought assignments home for completion. To a family of Southern aristocrats, such intensity seemed unnecessary.

On his return from his sixty-day leave, Sam was assigned once again to teach the small unit tactics classes that he had supervised before he went off to war. He was just beginning to fall into a rhythm with his courses when he was called into the office of one of his superiors and told that he was to assume the responsibility of teaching some of the school's military leadership courses. A previous instructor had suffered a serious heart attack, and all his files were to be turned over to Sam so that he could begin immediately.

The assignment proved to be one of the most challenging tasks of his life. Sam strongly felt his inadequacies in assuming the position. He lacked his predecessor's panache, his ability to draw on his own heroic record to illustrate military tactics, and his maturity—which was highlighted by a dazzling shock of white hair—all of which had mesmerized students at the school for years. The old man had been famous for captivating his students with poignant lessons from his heroic adventures during World War I. Sam would have to find a different approach to teach the class successfully. He began to develop his course by seeking out anyone at the college who had had a successful leadership experience and asking them what had worked for them. From his interviews with dozens of individuals, including many military heroes, Sam helped devise a refocused leadership program for the school.

In early 1947, with most of the finishing touches of his leadership lessons completed, Sam applied for a commission in the regular Army. Until then, he had been a temporary, non-tenured captain, but he wanted a permanent rank to ensure that the Army would find a job for him in case it had to downsize. Some confusion arose during the interview process when he had to produce his birth certificate, which of revealed what Sam had known all along, that his age was wrong on his official records. His lie from his day of enlistment had finally caught up with him. Although the military men laughed at the revelation, Sam was frustrated that the legal date of obtaining rank as a Second Lieutenant in the regular Army would have to be his twenty-first birthday, even though he had been promoted to the rank of Captain in combat while he was just twenty years old. At least, when he accepted his regular Army commission, he was not stripped of the promotion to Captain, even though, strictly speaking, his age should have disqualified him.

Later that spring, Sam applied for and was accepted into a new program designed to assist young regular Army officers in completing educational requirements for a college degree. The program consisted of two full years of academic work with all tuition paid by the government, during which time the officer could still receive his military salary. Unfortunately, program funding for the 1947-48 academic year had already been expended when Sam completed his application, so he was unable to follow the plan he had developed, to get his degree from Hampden-Sydney College.

Still eager to pursue a college degree, Sam then applied to the Army's new Foreign Area Specialist Training program (FAST). Initially, he considered entering the Chinese program at Yale because he retained a smattering of the Chinese he had learned while associated with elements of the Chinese army in the Southeast Asian Theater. He also gave consideration to the program in Arabic. He eventually settled on applying for the Russian program. His application was accepted, and Sam prepared to enter the Russian program at Columbia University. His ultimate decision to focus on the Russian program fulfilled the promise he had made to his men at that campfire high in the mountains of Burma in the spring of 1944. He now looked forward to years of serving the American military as a Russian linguist and as a trained specialist in Soviet matters. Sam's goals were once again falling into place, and he was beginning to feel a new sense of purpose and direction.

BECOMING A RUSSIAN IN AMERICA

AS SOON AS THE ARMY INFORMED SAM that he had been accepted into the Russian program at Columbia University, he packed up his family and headed north from Fort Benning. He wanted to take advantage of the few days between the end of his duties in Georgia and the start of the fall academic semester in New York by squeezing in a short visit to his parents' farm in Virginia. Though still in his early twenties, Sam had been developing a growing feeling of disquiet and guilt that he was not spending enough time with his parents. Cap'n Jack and Mis' Helen were growing older and more feeble, and with their children all grown and moved away, Sam knew that they were lonely. Even though he sent money to them every month, he could seldom escape the duties of his career to spend time at home. Not that his parents ever complained, because they did not, but Sam still felt that after all his parents had done for him, he should be able to do more for them in their old age.

All too soon, after only a few days in Prince Edward County, Sam hugged his parents, kissed his wife and baby boy goodbye, and traveled north to his new assignment in New York City. They had originally planned for Brenda and little Sam to spend the autumn months with Cap'n Jack and Mis' Helen, but at the last minute, Brenda decided that she would prefer to spend the time with her own family. A few weeks after Sam left for New York, she boarded a train for her family's home in Alabama. From there, Brenda would maintain regular mail correspondence with Sam until he established himself in New York and could bring her up to join him.

Sam arrived at Columbia University in New York City in early September 1947, ready to start his graduate level Russian language and area study. It had been more than seven years since his graduation from Rice High School, one of only eleven students in his class. Since then he had received limited formal education. Now he was assigned to tackle graduate work in a language he knew nothing about at one of the most prestigious universities in the nation.

The Russian Institute of Columbia's School of International Affairs proudly supported the Army's new language and area training program.

Distinguished professors who knew Russia and the Soviet Union better than anyone else in America lectured the group of ten hand-picked Army and Air Force officers. Students ranged in rank from Colonel down to Captain, Sam's rank at the time. Many already held graduate degrees from other institutions and were well on their way to becoming proficient in the Russian language. The program included intense language study accompanied by relevant Russian history, political science, economics, and literature courses. Sam, working with nothing more than a high school degree, was the youngest of the group and labored under a staggering workload to keep up with his more advanced colleagues.

Distinguishing himself academically at Columbia proved to be a steep, uphill climb for Sam. Continued restlessness, which stemmed from his still incomplete adaptation to stateside life, kept him from settling down to his tasks and added to his already ponderous workload. He found it difficult to sit and study for sustained periods of time, and often he found himself playing his guitar instead of hitting the books. One of his good buddies at the time, an older soldier and a West Point graduate, Lieutenant Colonel Monk Mazlowski, added to Sam's distractions with his regular visits. Since Monk was already fluent in Russian and a quick study in the other classes, he had time to kill and enjoyed trying to entice Sam to play the guitar or join him for a show on Broadway. Sam was easily tempted. The big city offered many evening entertainment opportunities for a country boy.

On weekends, another pleasant distraction for Sam came from his brother Billy's brother-in-law, Dick Aranow. Dick had been a Naval officer in the Pacific and was badly wounded during the closing months of World War II by a Japanese kamikaze attack just offshore from Okinawa. Dick and Helen Aranow lived comfortably on his family's lavish estate, Wonara Lodge, in the suburbs of Springdale, Connecticut, and Dick was a law student at Yale. He would often invite Sam to his home for the weekend or to a Saturday afternoon Ivy League football game. These and other invitations generally had Sam returning to his studies in New York very late on Sunday afternoons. Despite the countless attractive diversions around him and the difficulty of the Russian language, Sam somehow maintained *a solid B average* in the classroom.

Near the end of his first semester, final exams loomed like a thundercloud over Sam's spirits, as he realized that he had lollygagged and played his guitar too much and was unprepared for his exams. His only solution was to cram late into the night all during the week prior to finals. Already fatigued, Sam knew he needed to energize himself for some serious studying. He walked across the street to the Chock Fulla' Nuts all-night coffee shop and bought himself a decanter of black coffee and a package of Pall Mall king-sized cigarettes. Returning to his room, he poured himself a steaming cup of coffee and lit up one of the cigarettes and inhaled deeply. In his exhausted state, Sam could feel the effects of the two stimulants all the way down to his toes. That moment marked the beginning of a thirty-eight-year cigarette habit for Sam.

As the need for cramming and the need for sleep simultaneously increased, the exhausted student went out again in search of stimulants to keep himself awake. This time he dragged himself into the local drugstore to buy a pack of Dexedrine, which at that time was an over-the-counter pep pill. Two days later, Sam completed his first semester exams, and he was confident that he had earned decent grades. But he was at the limit of his endurance, and when he put his pen down and turned in the last of his exams, exhaustion overcame him. He walked out the doors of his examination building, stumbled across Broadway to a green park overlooking the Hudson River, and collapsed into a deep slumber under the unseasonably warm late-afternoon sun. When he awoke, a violent thunderstorm was crashing around him, and a torrent of warm rain had soaked him through. Sam decided right then and there that he would never revisit his undisciplined habits of that fall semester.

Two days later, Sam's best buddy at the school, Major Jim Reitz, also finished his exams. Reitz dropped by Sam's apartment late that afternoon, and the two of them proceeded to hit just about every beer joint from Sam's apartment on 116th Street to the Battery, several miles away at the tip of Manhattan Island. By midnight, the pair was wrapping up their shenanigans with a stop at a hot dog joint. Sam carelessly put too much hot mustard on his oversized dog, and when he squeezed down for a first bite, it squirted his tonsils. Reitz rolled around in hysterics as Sam attempted to regain his composure after the choking shock to his throat. Finally, the two made their way to the nearest subway station, but finding only a dime between them, half the fare, they looked at each other momentarily, then slammed through the turnstile together, lockstep, and slipped into the rail car just as it was leaving the station. Their train sped away into the night before anyone could accost them for their two-for-one antic.

With the Christmas holiday upon him, Sam drove south to Alabama where Brenda, his son, and her family greeted him. After the stressful end to the semester, he reveled in the contrast of the leisurely, fun-loving atmosphere in the Downing household. The Christmas tree, pine wreaths, holiday feasts, deer and quail hunting, winter fishing, and card playing—all designed for relaxed pleasure—were exactly the tonic Sam needed to revitalize his spirits. After Christmas, Sam, Brenda, and Sam, Jr. headed back to New York to begin their life together in the big city. Until they could secure permanent housing elsewhere, the couple moved into visiting officers' quarters on Governors Island, just off the tip of Manhattan. Their first several weeks were spent recovering from a violent influenza attack which hit each of them. Once they recovered, they were able to leave Governor's Island and move to a suitable quarters in a renovated World War II military building at Camp Shanks, located on the Hudson River near Orangeburg, New York. The new home's location left Sam with an hour-long commute in his old Jeep every morning and evening, but he did not mind. He was happy to have his wife and son with him in New York.

Their Jeep provided many wonderful excursions for the young married couple. Sam bought the navy blue, canvas-topped, open-sided vehicle for about five hundred dollars shortly after Brenda and he returned to New York together, and in it Sam and his family made multiple excursions from their new home to the countryside for picnics and walks through the forest. On rare occasions, Brenda and Sam would hire a babysitter to look after their son, and they would drive to Manhattan to attend concerts or musicals on Broadway. Excursions were always exciting for both husband and wife. Sam's high-stress studying left little time for the couple to relax together, and they appreciated the occasional escapes they could share.

On one particular morning that spring, Sam was racing to get to school on time. Reasoning that paying a parking fee would be a lesser penalty than arriving late to class, he parked his Jeep illegally by the sidewalk next to his old apartment on 116th Street. He was rushing down the sidewalk on Morningside Drive when a figure came out of the university president's quarters. Even in civilian clothes, Sam recognized the figure of retired General Dwight D. Eisenhower, then President of Columbia University. Two years earlier while at Fort Benning, Sam had served as fishing guide for Eisenhower, who was quietly visiting the Fort at the time. Sam would never forget how gracious Eisenhower had been to him on that outing. On this day, Sam executed a snappy salute as the great man approached him on the sidewalk. Just as the two men passed each other, Sam heard Eisenhower put on the brakes and inquire, "Son, how's fishing?" After a brief exchange of pleasantries the two went their separate ways, but for Sam the chance encounter was a ray of bright fortune.

Sam enjoyed the spring with his wife and child, and he was beginning to hit his stride academically. Increasingly, however, he realized that there were parts of the program that were not ideal, and although he was not as vocal as some of his fellow students in criticizing the Russian Institute, he was not entirely satisfied with the program's structure. He believed that some of the required subjects were irrelevant, and he was frustrated by some of the professors who extolled the virtues of the Soviet Communist system. One, in particular, delivered an hour-long dissertation on how much water each pound of Russian black bread contained. Sam believed that he was learning meaningless details. He also hated the required reading in published, Soviet propaganda periodicals that praised the virtues of collective farming, five-year plans, and the overall goals of the Communists. Finally, Sam felt that the program's dependence on lectures, a single paper, and a final exam left much to be desired. Without real room for discussion, there was very little give and take, very few chances for students to raise questions, and no probing into current political or economic developments. Sam believed the program should be emphasizing Soviet foreign policy, goals and objectives, and the appropriate U.S. responses.

Sam also knew that politics in Eastern Europe shift quickly. Never was this lesson clearer than the day after Dr. Philip Mosley, one of his favorite professors, gave a lecture praising republican Czechoslovakia as a ray of hope in the Red Communist sea that was engulfing Eastern Europe. Ironically, at the very time Dr. Mosley was speaking, Czechoslovakia was being overrun by Soviet Communists. The professor entered class the next morning with a rueful face, apologetic that he had been unknowingly extolling the democratic virtues of a nation that was at that very moment collapsing. Despite his frustrations, Sam refused to join the others in the group when they went to the Pentagon to complain about their program to the officer in charge. To him, the educational opportunity was pure gold, one not available to many young men. He could not complain about free education with all expenses paid and a full salary to boot.

In 1948, after a long week of arduous Russian study, one of Sam's classmates, a Senior Lieutenant Colonel who had graduated from West Point in 1936, offered to take Sam to see the military academy. The day proved to be Sam's first look at the institution that he had hoped to attend after USMAP at Amherst three years earlier. With a steely feeling of irony and disappointment that he had not been able to continue his road to West Point, Sam gazed at the massive stone buildings and spreading parade grounds overlooking the Hudson. At the same time, he was comforted by the feeling that he had established a positive direction for his life even without West Point.

After completing three semesters at Columbia, Sam and the other military students in the Russian Institute were ready for the European phase of their education. On a bleak, rainy afternoon in mid-October 1948, Sam, Brenda, and Sam, Jr. embarked from Brooklyn on the *USS General Taylor* destined for Bremerhaven, Germany, and the final portion of area studies and language training. Standing there at the railing of the renovated World War II Army transport, with one arm around his beloved Brenda and the other cradling his son, Sam listened to a small Army band playing farewell songs in the gently falling rain. His pretty wife looked up at him, brown eyes full of trepidation, and squeezed his hand. The couple had begun a journey into an uncertain future, and Sam prayed to God that he would be able to care for his little family and protect them from harm.

LEARNING TO THINK LIKE A RUSSIAN
FOR THE AMERICAN MILITARY

SAM WAS PROUD of the direction his career was taking, but as the unimposing Army transport, the *USS General Taylor,* wallowed in the wake of the luxurious *SS Queen Elizabeth* cruise liner passing through New York harbor, Sam became acutely aware that he was twenty-five years old and still situated rather low on society's totem pole. A desire to escape the feeling of second-class citizenship stirred him to resolve that he would work hard enough to become a person of note, a man who rode a bigger ship. Ten stormy days of seasickness on the North Atlantic did nothing to lessen his resolve, and Sam stepped off the *General Taylor* onto European soil in the dark of an early morning in Bremerhaven, Germany, determined to make the most of this opportunity to advance his education and career.

The transition from shipside to passenger train took place without delay, and soon the Wilsons were speeding through post-war Germany in a southeasterly direction. Outside the train window, the pastoral countryside they passed poignantly contrasted with the rubble of German cities and towns still recovering from World War II bombings. The family ended its journey late that evening in the picturesque Bavarian town of Garmisch-Partenkirchen, nestled cozily beneath snowcapped mountains. Because of its isolation, the town had remained relatively untouched during the war and now supported a thriving tourism industry. A culture of fun and recreation had resumed after the Nazis had been driven from the region, and the people were recovering from losses that had been inflicted on their families and their nation. Bells dangling from horse-drawn sleighs jingled and chimed as Bavarian mountaineers decked out in Tyrolean hats, embroidered vests, lederhosen britches, and thick knee-length socks drove tourists down snowy cobblestone streets. As they carted customers around the town, the splendidly appareled drivers thrilled visitors with their whistling and yodeling. At every turn, the charms of Garmisch-Partenkirchen delighted Sam and Brenda, and every morning they awoke in their hotel suite with the feeling that they were living in a real-life picture postcard.

For Sam, however, the business at hand quickly resumed. The U.S. military institution to which Sam and his language and area training group belonged was known simply as "Detachment R," and the men of Detachment R met daily in the nearby mountain village of Oberammergau. The first phase of language and area training, completed at Columbia University, had consisted of intense Russian language training, supplemented by continued graduate work which emphasized studies of the Union of Soviet Socialist Republics. In Germany, Phase Two was designed to build on that base by immersing students in the Russian language, and maintaining the study of relevant topics in Russian culture, history, geography, and economics. From the time they entered the school buildings in the early morning until the hour they departed in the evening, members of Detachment R were not allowed to speak a word of English. Everything transpired in Russian, including oral examinations, written tests, papers, and the eventual program thesis. The penalty for being caught speaking English, even if it were to a wife on the telephone over lunch break, was buying drinks for the house that night at the local bar. The threat of that expenditure kept Sam and his buddies very attentive to their language use.

The course load at Detachment R was even more demanding to Sam than his studies were at Columbia. He spent about sixteen hours a day focused on his work, eight hours in class and eight of studying. Sensitive to his limited previous education, Sam felt that to master the material he had to work harder outside class than his colleagues. The time in class was equally intense, as a proportionally large faculty worked with only a few students. In a few classes, teachers actually outnumbered their students. Nearly twenty full-time teachers facilitated the education of about a dozen students, and an additional nucleus of talented tutors periodically visited the program to offer new perspectives. The teachers were a brilliant group of intelligent and successful people who came from rich and varied professional backgrounds. They were all highly qualified to teach about Russia and the Soviet Communist world. Most had been born and educated in Russia or in other Soviet satellite countries, and all had reached positions of responsibility and importance in society. Several ex-Soviet military officers, members of the Soviet Academy of Sciences, including a renowned expert on the Soviet Arctic, journalists, ministerial-level officials, and ambassadors from East European satellite countries were members of Detachment R's faculty. The diverse group had one thing in common: as stateless expatriates, they all had serious reasons for hating Communism.

Out of this group of highly distinguished and talented people, one individual stood out. Sam knew him as "Aldan," the name the man used when they first met in 1948, though that was not his real name. While hiding in post-World War II Europe, he chose to take on the name of the river on whose banks he had been born early in the 1900s in Russian Siberia. His real name was Andrei Georgievich Neryanin. Over the years of their relationship, Sam came to recognize the Russian as one of the most capable intellects that he had ever encountered and as a tremendous conversationalist who had an endless reserve of interesting stories. At the same time, Aldan was one of the most deeply philosophical and highly moral men that Sam had ever known.

Aldan was about fifteen years old when the Russian Revolution began, and while he was still a teenager, he joined the Bolshevik army. He served with distinction throughout the civil war and was cited for courage and bravery in combat several times. After the conflict ended, Aldan remained in the Red Army. He served as a cadre officer in a variety of posts and capacities over the 1920s and 1930s and remained devoutly Communist. He carefully avoided the purges and snares of the Communist system and graduated as a full Colonel from the Voroshilov General Staff Academy on the eve of World War II. He immediately deployed to the European front as the Chief of Staff of a Soviet field army. In the winter of 1942-1943, at the same time that orders issued by the Red Army promoting him to Major General were en-route to his camp, he was captured by the Germans and impounded in a German prisoner of war camp. Languishing in the German POW camp with a number of other Soviet officers, he became starkly aware, far more than ever before, of the hideous evils inherent in the Communist system. He had maintained tunnel vision as he served his country and had not worried about what was happening economically, politically, or morally in the society around him. His great awakening occurred to him only after he was away from that system. Once he understood the reality of the Soviet system that he had been fighting to support, he banged his head with his hand and said, "I'm a fool." From that point on, he became a dedicated anti-Communist activist.

As the number of German troops fighting the Russians on the Eastern Front began to dwindle, the Germans organized their POWs, many of whom had become disillusioned with their native government, into an all-Russian army of four divisions who could fight alongside them against the Soviets. This formation came to be known as the Russian Liberation Army, with its acronym in Russian being "ROA". Its commander was Lieutenant General Vlasov, who, like Aldan, was captured on the Soviet-German front. By this time, Aldan was totally disenchanted with the Soviet version of Communism, and in exchange for the chance to fight against the Soviet government, he willingly accepted an assignment as Chief of Operations of Vlasov's army. Aldan believed that Stalin, the Soviet Communist leader, was a paranoid megalomaniac who needed to be deposed, and like many of his fellow Russian POWs, he joined the ROA in hopes of first eliminating Stalin and then tackling Hitler afterwards.

At the end of the war, the victorious Allies interned Aldan and many of his fellow POWs in American prison camps to wait for their scheduled repatriation back to the Soviet Union. Tales of Stalin's vengeful and indiscriminate punishment of Soviet POWs, both those who were loyal to him and those who eyed him with disfavor, leaked westward from the Soviet Union. Several of Aldan's close friends who had returned home had already disappeared at the hands of Stalin's secret police, so Aldan knew that his return to Russia would bring certain death. Further rumors circulated around his camp of a Russian POW repatriation group of about 30,000 men who had been systematically mowed down by Stalin's machine guns as soon as they stepped on Soviet soil. The Russians were brutal to countrymen who abandoned Soviet ideologies during the war, and they did not mind killing loyalists along with dissenters.

A return to Russia was out of the question, so Aldan developed a plan to escape his camp. He shaved his head and eyebrows so he could not be recognized. Then, the night before his scheduled repatriation, he pretended to have extreme diarrhea. The latrine was close to the outer fence and some distance from the shacks in which the POW's lived, so he had to be accompanied by a guard every time he complained of his irregular bowel movements. The guard would stand just outside while Aldan groaned and grunted in an effort to simulate the appropriate symptoms of his condition.

About the third time he asked for permission to visit the latrine, his escort removed himself a considerable distance away from the facility so he did not have to hear Aldan's horrible moans. Under that cover of distance, Aldan slit a hole in the canvas wall and slipped out the back as fast as he could. He cut a hole in the fence, crawled about a hundred yards to get beyond the search lights, pulled out a compass he had been able to steal, and moved as quickly as he could to the railroad tracks in the distance. He could hear the search party after him with dogs barking, and he could see the spotlights scanning the undergrowth. Realizing he was trapped, he saw that his only way to escape the search party was to leap into a nearby stream. Jumping into the stream, he immediately discovered it was an open sewer. But it was too late to turn around. He waded and swam for about two miles in the sewer before scrambling up the opposite bank. He did his best to scrape off the waste, but he could do nothing about the putrid, lingering stench. He had shaken the immediate threat of his followers, and covered by damp, smelly rags and shivering in the cold February wind, he continued down the railway tracks until he got to a station where a train headed to Frankfurt was loading. He sneaked into a packed third-class car, aware that all the passengers in the coach were retreating with disgust from his horrible odor. As he huddled in a corner, trying to warm himself, a new threat arose. The conductor was slowly making his way through the car and validating tickets. Of course, Aldan had no ticket. Providentially, the train came to a sudden stop and he was able to avoid discovery by ducking into a car that the conductor had already checked.

By stealth and wits, he had finally reached Frankfurt. Half-starved, he pilfered a loaf of bread and washed the meal down with a drink from a street puddle. This meager meal, his first since his escape, provided him with enough strength to make the rail journey to Munich, where he knew the address of an old friend. Exhausted from his journey and desperate to see a friendly face, Aldan arrived at the door of his old friend, who, when he recognized Aldan, slammed the door in his face. Aldan was devastated that his friend was too frightened to help. He passed the rest of the night wandering the streets of Munich until he stumbled to the gate of an outpost of the local U.S. military headquarters. The on-duty officer of the watch glared at him, telling him to leave. At that point, Aldan did not care. Utterly exhausted and depleted, Aldan could only mutter, "I am Major General Aldan . . . you may have the body . . . " before he collapsed.

There, the unfortunate story of Aldan would have ended had not a Russian-speaking U.S. Army Captain come by in a jeep and noticed him moaning and muttering there on the ground in front of the gate. The captain recognized several names that Aldan was incoherently muttering as high-ranking officials of the Soviet government. He was able to persuade local authorities to take the exhausted man to a bed and revive him. By that time, Aldan had a raging fever that reached 105° and did not break for six days. He woke to see the Captain sitting by his bed. As soon as he realized where he was, he asked the Captain what the Americans would do with him. A pencil and pad of paper were shoved into his lap. "Start writing" was the order.

Aldan's duty to the American military eventually led him to accept a position as one of the professors at Detachment R, where he educated students like Sam Wilson about Soviet culture, especially its military. Sam quickly

Sam Wilson in 1949, in a portrait
painted while he was in Germany
studying Russian.

discovered that very few other professors at Detachment R could approach Aldan in his overall knowledge of the Soviet system.

For his part, Aldan and the other Detachment R professors appreciated that their pupils were a handpicked group of young American military officers who showed the potential to rise to high levels of responsibility not only in the American armed forces, but also in the greater society as well. They respected their students and worked hard to ensure that the men achieved maximum benefit from the program. As Sam surveyed this elite group of teachers who had at one time held positions of power in the Soviet Union or one of its satellites, he recognized that he was involved in a once-in-a-lifetime opportunity for learning, and he was determined not to squander the opportunity. He redoubled his determination to give his utmost effort to his studies. He paid close attention to his professors as they taught him how to speak, think, and see the world like a Russian. He even had a class dissecting Soviet vulgarity, and from that he learned how English profanity cannot even begin to match the richness of Russian cursing. The lessons about Russian culture that Sam learned while at Oberammergau would prove incalculably valuable during subsequent career assignments.

In the second week of December 1948, after spending the latter part of the fall at Oberammergau, Detachment R's entire administrative staff, faculty, and all its students relocated north to Regensburg, a city of around 100,000 citizens on the Danube River and one that was widely accepted as the cultural center of southern Germany. It would be home to the U.S. Army's Russian language and area program until 1954, when the school (Detachment R) would be relocated back to Garmisch-Partenkirchen. While military installations and factories on its outskirts had been struck heavily during World War II bomb raids, Allied attacks had spared the medieval city's downtown of winding streets and cobblestone alleyways. The twin spires of the huge Gothic cathedral still dominated the horizon for miles. Sam came to love the atmosphere and beauty of the historic city and often roamed its streets to soak in its sights, sounds, and symbols of the past.

Detachment R was housed in what had formerly been the local Nazi party headquarters, a three-story gray stone building in a walled caserne on the southern outskirts of the city. Sam commuted to school via streetcar, which took him to within a block of the rear wall of the caserne. From there, he habitually took a shortcut to his classrooms. Instead of walking almost a mile to the main entrance of the compound, he approached the gate in the rear wall and, employing the ranger wall-climbing technique he had learned at Fort Benning, he would half-climb, half-vault himself over the locked twelve-foot-high iron gate, thus putting himself with a few yards of the entrance to his school building. One day the Detachment R Commandant spotted the young captain practically flying over the wall of the caserne and suggested that this was not a dignified way to begin the school day. Thereafter, Sam allotted a few extra minutes to his commute so he could take the more generally accepted, circuitous route into the compound through the main gate.

When Sam's studies at Detachment R took him to Regensburg, Brenda, Sam, Jr., and their newly arrived daughter, Susan, went with him. The post-war advantages of the American occupation in Germany allowed them to live a life they could not have afforded back in the U.S. After staying in a two-room hotel suite for several months in Garmisch-Partenkirchen, they appreciated the opportunity to live in a nice house with a front yard, a garden, and an iron-gated entrance. A housekeeper, a yardman, and a maid helped Brenda run the house, maintain the yard, and take care of Sam, Jr. and their infant daughter. Even with the domestic help, Brenda had her hands full adjusting to life in the new city and caring for Susan, who was born on August 19, 1949, and Sam, Jr., who was just three years old.

Despite the busy activity in the house, she agreed to Sam's inviting an instructor and his wife to stay free of charge in their third floor apartment so Sam could practice speaking Russian in the evenings. She fully supported her husband's intention to become fluent in the language, and she made countless selfless sacrifices to help Sam as he immersed himself in his studies. She worked hard to ensure that Sam came home to a bustling but orderly household after his long days spent working to expand his Russian language and area expertise. Sam realized that, without her support, he could not successfully master "all things Russian," and he appreciated her willingness to facilitate his education in so many ways.

One of the most important parts of the Detachment R experience was its extracurricular programs. These mission-based activities varied in duration from a few weeks to several months, and one of the duties Sam undertook in conjunction with his studies was to serve as a liaison officer to Soviet forces in Eastern Austria and in East Germany. In addition to the opportunity to speak idiomatic Russian, these assignments provided unparalleled insights into the psyche of Russian soldiers.

Part of Sam's responsibilities involved serving as an escort officer for the U.S. to the Soviet Repatriation Mission in Salzburg, Austria. More than five million Russians refused to go back to the Soviet Union after World War II ended, and their mass refusal to return to their homeland stingingly blighted Stalin's pride. In response to their stubbornness, the Soviet government had organized special teams to persuade the expatriates to come home. On occasion, Sam traveled with the Soviet Repatriation Mission teams to displaced persons' camps (DPs) in Western Austria and West Germany. In addition to scheduling such visits and making necessary administrative and logistical arrangements, he helped the Russians set up 16mm projectors for displaying Soviet propaganda films, and then he would formally introduce his Soviet counterparts to their audiences of erstwhile countrymen. It was not a pleasant duty.

During his time with the Soviet repatriation teams, Sam listened to countless entreaties for the exiles to return to the Soviet Union. Using smooth blandishments, the Soviets hoped to convince their countrymen that Russia had somehow turned into a land flowing with milk and honey. For a young language and area officer, it was clearly a blatant propaganda exercise in which he was an uncomfortable participant, but it provided practice in the spoken language and taught Sam how to recognize an absurd Soviet sales pitch as he developed his ability to manage local crises.

From time to time, irate Soviet émigrés would erupt against the smooth-talking ambassadors from Moscow and try to harm them physically. One night Sam learned through his own intelligence sources that a group of ex-Soviet citizens had rolled a large rock down a railway track and had positioned it teetering dangerously on the edge of an overpass through which he and the Soviet representatives were scheduled to pass that night. He had no choice but to cancel that evening's presentation, but when he informed the Soviet officer in charge of the repatriation committee, the Colonel insisted that they not cancel. In what became Sam's first face-to-face confrontation with our Communist enemies of the Cold War, the young Captain adamantly refused to allow the mission to proceed, and the team did not make the trip.

All the Russians who were a part of Sam's repatriation team were heavy social drinkers. Like many of their countrymen, they enjoyed laughing, singing, and toasting to everything. They also enjoyed getting their American guests drunk. When he was working with them, public drinking of vodka became a real hazard for Sam because his Russian companions would collaborate in schemes to try to get him drunk while they themselves avoided full inebriation. At any given party, multiple men would separately approach Sam and propose toasts to him that he could not politely refuse. Since the Russians insisted that each participant drain his glass on every toast, Sam, if he were not careful to thwart their repeated compliments, could easily end up drunk from the endless stream of toasts to his health, the health of his father, his mother, his wife, the United States, and Russian-American friendship in general.

On the final night of one of his assignments with a Soviet repatriation team in Linz, Austria, Sam proposed that the officer in charge of the team, Colonel Kirov, bring the entire Soviet repatriation team to his suite in the Hotel Goldener Kroner for an evening of farewell drinks. Sam disliked vodka at that time, so he supplied his guests with a left-over case of Canadian Club whiskey. Sam diluted his glasses with water throughout the evening to slow the alcohol's effects, but the Russians drank it straight. He managed to further ensure his own safety from their tag-team attempts to get him drunk by making sure that the entire group of seventeen Russians drank to every proposed toast with him. That way, they all would be consuming the same amount of alcohol. After only a couple of hours, they had finished off his Canadian Club.

"Bring in the vodka," cried Kirov, and soon numerous bottles appeared to reinvigorate the partying. Sam tried to continue mixing water with his vodka, but the Russians would not allow it. They did, however, permit him to chase his vodka with a glass of water. To ensure his own safety, Sam employed a trick where he could take advantage of the similar appearance of the two liquids. He managed to shuffle the drinks so that he drank water for the rest of the night. Only once did he slip and swallow a full glass of vodka, an accident that briefly caused him to gag as tears streamed down his face. By the end of the night, only two of the Russians remained on their feet. His scheme had worked. At four the next morning, Kirov's blood-red eyes bulged as Sam finished off the last of the vodka, and the colonel stumbled off to his room to get some much-needed sleep. The rest of the team lay passed out where they had fallen.

Sam's train left that morning at 6:30, and, shortly beforehand, he dragged himself out of bed, exhausted but sober, and beat on the Colonel's door, requesting that Kirov have his team see him off at the train station. The Russians seemed far more fatigued from the evening's activities than Sam. The farewell salutes Sam observed that morning from that worn, bedraggled group of Soviet soldiers satisfied him as much as any salutes he ever received. From then on, Sam found ways to kill a lot of hotel and ballroom plants with tossed vodka during social evenings with his Russian compatriots.

Another one of Sam's extracurricular activities for Detachment R was performing the duties of a U.S. diplomatic courier. As a diplomatic courier, Sam carried locked pouches of diplomatic mail to and from the Paris office of the U.S. Diplomatic Pouch and Courier Service. This assignment gave him an opportunity to visit a number of American diplomatic installations, including those in the Soviet Union, East European satellite countries, and a number of other countries generally peripheral to the Soviet Union. Sam rather freely interpreted his courier assignment that gave him freedom "to travel along the periphery of the Soviet Union from any direction." While performing these diplomatic duties, Sam wandered as far afield as Tokyo, Manila, Hong Kong, Jakarta, Rangoon, New Delhi, Kabul, Baghdad, Damascus, Amman, Cairo, and Johannesburg, and he journeyed on one occasion across the Atlantic to Buenos Aires and to several other prominent South American cities. The way he figured it, all these places were "peripheral" to the Soviet Union, and these trips were extraordinarily interesting and truly beneficial to Sam's studies.

After several weeks of studying under the tutelage of a former diplomat of an Eastern European country that lay behind the Iron Curtain, Sam made a practice of taking his diplomatic passport and setting out via train or plane to the country he had just been studying. These excursions gave him an opportunity to view firsthand all the cathedrals, parks, libraries, and other significant places described to him only days earlier by his professor. From time to time, a nostalgic professor would request that Sam take pictures of his old home or office building. Whenever Sam returned from a mission with pictures and descriptions of a professor's home or workplace, the older man's dormant affection for his home country always sparked a touching gush of memories. Although the Detachment R professors hated the Soviets and what the Communists had done to their countries, they maintained a vibrant passion for their oppressed homelands.

Early on one Monday morning, 26 June 1950, while on a diplomatic courier run which had taken him from Paris to Rome, Athens, Jerusalem, Damascus, and finally Baghdad, Sam learned that just the previous day the North Koreans had invaded South Korea across the 38th Parallel. From his location, climbing around the ruins of ancient Babylon, the skimpy news reports which were available left him unsure whether World War III might have started. He immediately began to worry about his family back in Regensburg, less than fifty miles from the Soviet/Czech border.

Returning home, he found his wife deeply concerned and anxious to return to the security of the family hearth in Alabama. In mid-August, Brenda and the two children climbed aboard a British Overseas Airways flight in Munich and flew back to the U.S., leaving Sam staring at the plane as it disappeared on the horizon. He would be without the support of his wife and children for a full year while he remained in Germany to complete the Detachment R program. He somberly moved into bachelor's quarters in the Park Maximilian Hotel in downtown Regensburg, his operations base for the remaining year as a Language and Area student in Europe. Although their departure gave him greater flexibility in his travel schedules, the absence his family left Sam very lonely for his final year of studies.

Sam enjoyed the jobs provided for him by the Language and Area specialist program, but his favorite operation was not related to Detachment R. While living with his family in Regensburg, Sam had come to know some of the local case officers of the CIA. Two of them had actually occupied the upstairs apartment of the Wilsons' house for a few months. Gradually, Sam became aware of their interest in his diplomatic access to areas denied to them, and before long, he was performing favors for the case workers and their superiors. These favors began as simple requests such as surveying a given area within an Eastern European or Soviet city, describing traffic into and out of a certain office address, observing the types of people frequenting a particular workman's pub, or noting the fare for a specific streetcar ride.

As these duties were accomplished successfully, the requests became more substantial and sophisticated in nature. Sometimes, Sam surreptitiously left small packages in the corner of a city park at a hiding place, or "dead letter drop" as it was referred to in the clandestine, tradecraft language. Other times he fastened a small parcel with a magnetic clip to the undercarriage of a railway car traveling east from Warsaw to Prague, a "moving dead letter drop." Of course he would also be required to report the name and serial number of the rail car to his CIA buddies upon his return to Regensburg. Other times, CIA officers would request that Sam attempt to establish an acquaintance with certain persons and then to describe fully the physical appearance and personality of each one.

Engaging in such activities totally contradicted Sam's instructions from his superiors at Detachment R, as well as his official orders from the U.S. Diplomatic Pouch and Courier Service. Detection by enemy intelligence of Sam's clandestine operations would have unleashed a propaganda exposé by the Communists that could have ended Sam's military career and provided significant embarrassment to the U.S. Army and the U.S. government. Despite the strong incentives to avoid such activity, Sam felt that he could occasionally take a chance if he knew his calculated risks would help his country gain an advantage over the Soviets.

In spite of all his efforts to remain anonymous to enemy intelligence organizations, Sam gradually noticed that he was beginning to attract more surveillance than a normal diplomatic courier would require. He frequently had to dismiss alluring young women who stopped by his train compartment and asked him for the time, and rarely was he able to walk around a city without having someone follow him. But the increased hostile attention failed to stop him from completing his assigned tasks. Instead, Sam rather enjoyed the opportunity to put into practice the counter-surveillance lessons he had learned during World War II while training for operations behind enemy lines in Southeast Asia. In the Cold War years, he could practice handling enemy surveillance in a different venue.

On occasion, Sam admittedly dealt with his surveillance assignment a little recklessly. With his proficiency in the Russian language and a rudimentary knowledge of Soviet secret police tactics, learned from his Detachment R professors, he would boldly approach the man assigned to tail him inconspicuously for the day and ask if he wanted to join him for tea and a cigarette. Other days he would pull out one of the tricks he had learned from his professors and give his tail the slip. Sam quickly learned, however, that if he got away one day, he could be sure that enemy surveillance would be swarming around him the next. The best way to handle surveillance, Sam found, was to lollygag along and keep relaxed. As long as he made the job easy for his trackers, they would unknowingly give him freedom to complete his missions. Sam's success with his tasks endeared him to CIA officers in the field, and later, it resulted in a warm and sincere invitation to join CIA's clandestine services and to play the spy game on a long-term basis.

For the majority of Sam's time at the Detachment R campus in Regensburg, his studies centered on an independent research project. He spent three years preparing a paper devoted to a survey of Soviet émigré political organizations and their potential relationship with the United States as they opposed Russia. The professors supported his research and occasionally excused him from class to pursue it further. School officials provided him with financial support for research trips because they felt Sam's project was a valuable and applicable learning experience.

Most of Sam's inspiration for his project had come from observations he had made while accompanying the Soviet repatriation teams. There were over five million Soviet émigrés in the West after World War II ended. These people had been uprooted by the war, had wound up in the West, and somehow had managed to avoid being returned to the Soviet Union after the armistice. From this population, political parties of various stripes and colors sprouted, and they began developing plans for their role in the re-conquest of Mother Russia. The parties ranged from ultraliberal, Trotsky-like organizations to hyper-conservative Fascists. There were Russian nationalist organizations, and then there were political parties representing the interests of peoples from the Ukraine, the Baltic States, and Central Asia. Some were merely debating clubs, but others were active units working to infiltrate spies into the Soviet Union with hopes of establishing revolutionary organizations on the inside. All shared a common desire to return to the Motherland and release her from Stalinist control. They dreamed of the day they could go home and be a part of the political process in a liberated Russia.

Time spent with these émigrés convinced Sam that the U.S. shared their vision for a free Russia, and he believed there should be a way for America to work with these organizations to further their collective interests. After subsequent research, Sam proposed several plans that could promote the interest of these émigré groups. One of Sam's recommendations was conceived in collaboration with a couple of former Soviet officers who were instructors at Detachment R. Together, they researched how Stalin's regime had imprisoned sixteen to twenty million "political dissidents" in Siberian labor camps. Given proper leadership and supplies, Sam and his friends suggested that these prisoners, many of whom were totally innocent of any crime, could provide a powerful revolutionary force to work against the Soviet Communist regime. Sam developed the idea as a proposal and fed it back to the CIA.

The research Sam conducted proved sufficiently valuable to the CIA that he was called upon several times to present findings of his survey at different headquarters, including CIA's primary headquarters in Western Europe. But the project provided an unpleasant outcome for Sam back at Detachment R, where Sam's classmates grew resentful of his irregular attendance. They were envious that he was on wild adventures while they were stuck in class. Despite the School Commandant's assurance of his support for any ideas of equal promise, Sam became ostracized by some of the students. Later, when these same students who hardly spoke to him for a long time because of this dispute worked for him in D.C., Sam tried to forget their ill-will toward him.

The years in Europe with Detachment R ended all too soon for Sam. He would come to regard this "truly golden era" as the most rewarding and personally satisfying educational experience of his life. In August 1951, when he was handed his academic transcript and a certificate for successful completion of the program, Sam reluctantly departed Europe for his new assignment as a general staff officer in Army intelligence at the Pentagon. Sam had thoroughly enjoyed being a full time student, unencumbered by command or staff duties, and with the freedom that came from simply being a student roaming Europe, he had matured and blossomed. When he returned to the States, he was a man who was idiomatically fluent in Russian, proficient in German and French, and well versed about life in Russia and how Russians think. Sam knew that he had been incredibly fortunate to land such a rewarding assignment.

INTELLIGENCE AND SPECIAL OPERATIONS
IN WASHINGTON

AFTER FOUR YEARS OF STUDYING the Russian language and culture, and forays around the world delivering mail as a diplomatic courier, liaison service with the Soviet Armed Forces, and an unofficial but effective adjunct for CIA friends, Sam realized that his had been a most unusual experience. The intense education in all things Russian, peppered with secret assignments that put him squarely in the midst of excitement and danger, were rare opportunities that suited his inquisitive, restless, and creative personality. It would be hard to sit in an office in Washington, but Sam had family obligations as well as professional ones, and in August 1951, just shy of his twenty-eighth birthday, he accepted his diploma and journeyed home.

Any hesitation he had about returning to America was immediately forgotten when he saw the beaming smile on his wife's face and heard the joyful squeals from Sam, Jr. and baby Susan. Since their return from Europe at the start of the Korean War, the family had been staying at Brenda's family home in Alabama, and it was there that Sam joined them for a brief vacation before he resumed his duties. In September, they moved to Washington, where Sam began his new assignment at the Pentagon as a general staff officer in Army intelligence.

Sam's first assignment required that he sit all day with other officers in cramped cubicles, not unlike the desk jobs of a junior reporter in the press room of a major newspaper. Their responsibility was to research and draft manuals on Soviet military doctrines and tactics and on the organization, arms and equipment of Soviet forces. Sam primarily used materials that American military attachés had been able to smuggle out of the Soviet Union, as he wrote about the Soviet military and the tactical doctrine of Soviet ground forces, especially at the small unit level. The manuals they wrote were published by the Army Department of Intelligence and distributed to Allied ground forces as preparation for what they should expect if they ever engaged Soviet ground troops. It was an important assignment, and few individuals had the background or knowledge to write such documents, but Sam found the job tedious and boring. He had written only a few chapters of his first manual when he came across a peripheral opportunity that offered him much more excitement. He eagerly accepted the chance to make his workday more interesting.

Sam's new opportunity involved facilitating interviews with recent Soviet military defectors. These individuals were selected from a handful of Soviet military non-commissioned and commissioned officers who, for a variety of reasons, ended up on the Allied side of the Iron Curtain. Given the highly secretive nature of Soviet society, current intelligence was difficult to come by and Russians who defected to the West held a treasure trove of useful information. Having fled from the Soviet Union, they were willing to share their knowledge in hopes of helping the American cause in a variety of ways.

Their reasons for leaving Russia were as varied as the men themselves. Some of these officers had gotten in trouble with their superiors. Others had become disenchanted with Soviet military life, and there were those who simply had gotten drunk and carelessly wound up with a call girl on the wrong side of the Iron Curtain. Regardless of the reason, once a man had left the Soviet Union, the mistrustful KGB made a return very unattractive. When Soviet officers exited the Communist domain, therefore, American clandestine services made every effort to gain their cooperation. Defectors who assisted the CIA were assigned serial numbers—Defector Serial #000—and those of special interest would be flown to the United States, usually to Washington, so that military liaisons could record whatever useful information they gleaned. Some of Sam's old CIA friends in Europe had recommended to their superiors at CIA headquarters in Washington that a Detachment R graduate who had been helpful to the agency in the past would be a good candidate to represent the Pentagon's interests in these interviews. When asked whether he was interested, Sam jumped at the opportunity to be the contact point between CIA and Army intelligence for Soviet military defectors.

Sam's bosses in Army intelligence granted him unusual freedom to carry out his role in this endeavor. They approved his selection of a centrally located office in the Pentagon for use as an interview room and turned a blind eye to the scrounging and midnight acquisitions he made to help create an atmosphere conducive to the effective eliciting of sensitive information from former Soviet officers. Sam obtained an imposing walnut desk, a leather chair, and a beautiful Arabian rug to make the place more comfortable. He visited a special storage facility in the Pentagon where he selected colorful and dramatic paintings of European scenery from the extensive cache of art confiscated during World War II. To complete his renovations, he installed a small bar to keep cognac, cheese, crackers, and other drinks and snacks on hand. Sam wanted to make his office attractive so the defectors would feel comfortable and more willing to talk.

Outside the office, Sam went to great lengths to develop trusting relationships with the defectors. He had long ago discovered that Russians responded well to civil and respectful treatment, and he wanted them to feel relaxed when they talked to him, the first step in making them cooperative during interviews with American military representatives. To help make their lives more pleasant, he obtained a supply of Russian books, periodicals, and Russian music records for their enjoyment. If he learned that a defector played a musical instrument, he would acquire it for him and accompany the fellow's music with his guitar. From time to time, Sam took his new Russian friends fishing, and on occasion, he would drink with them, although he generally considered that to be a risky diversion because alcohol made the Russians depressed. He even took a few of his assignees down to the family farm in Rice, Virginia, and toured them around the property while regaling them with tales from his childhood. Sam worked hard to share experiences with the former Soviets because it helped develop a bond with them, and it gave him practice as he continued to perfect his own Russian. As he and his Soviet contacts learned more about each other, he gained valuable insights into the Russian psyche, and the Russian defectors became better acquainted with the customs in the United States. Since most of the defectors eventually resettled in the U.S., Sam's work served a dual purpose. It encouraged a trusting relationship between Sam and the defector, and it provided the defector with opportunities to prepare for a new life. Most of the defectors gratefully accepted Sam's interest in their wellbeing, and the relationships they formed led to informative interviews that were highly beneficial to interested American military personnel.

Sam felt true compassion for all his assignees, but the first defector assigned to him was one that he never forgot. DS441 (not the real serial number) had been a Soviet major. One night after a wildly drunken spree in East Berlin, he wound up in bed with a German girl across the sector border in West Berlin. He had not sobered from his orgy until a full three days after his night of revelry. By that time, the girl had tipped off Western military authorities that he was with her, and it was too late for him to return across the border. He begrudgingly cooperated with the CIA operatives who picked him up in Berlin and sent him to D.C. Sam met DS441 shortly after the Russian defector's arrival in early October, and immediately he began working to construct a bond of trust between the man and himself. After spending some time becoming acquainted with the former Soviet officer and ascertaining his range of knowledge, Sam made sure that relevant offices in the Pentagon knew of the man's presence and interview potential. Part of his responsibility was to act as interpreter during the interviews, so Sam facilitated most of the interactions that DS441 had with Americans.

During their many hours and days together, the two developed a trusting friendship. During the Christmas season of that year, 1951, Sam invited DS441 to his South Arlington apartment to share in his family's holiday festivities and to help trim the Christmas tree. Sam recognized that his buddy had recently been feeling lonesome and, as a result, was drinking too much. Sam and his guest sat in rocking chairs laughing and talking, listening to Christmas music, and drinking beer as if DS441 were a welcome, distant cousin to the household. Sam did what he could to comfort his subdued friend, and although DS441 left Sam's home with pangs of nostalgia, he expressed great appreciation for Sam's interest in his happiness.

Early on, when Sam started drafting Soviet military tactics manuals and began to handle Soviet defectors on the side, memories of his exciting missions and dangerous adventures with Merrill's Marauders motivated him to establish a connection with the U.S. Army's Office of the Chief of Psychological Warfare (OCPW), especially that office's unconventional warfare division. OCPW was in charge of organizing unorthodox adventures like the one that Sam had participated in back in 1943-44 when he entered the jungles of Burma. In an effort to gain their favor, Sam gave representatives from that office priority access to interviews with his former Soviet assignees. The Brigadier General in charge of OCPW, Gen. Robert McClure, formerly President Eisenhower's chief of psychological warfare in Europe during World War II, noticed Sam's consideration and seemed to appreciate Sam's interest in his office. McClure willingly opened the door for Sam to begin developing relationships within OCPW.

The most exciting projects during Sam's time working at the Pentagon offered opportunities to escape tedious paperwork and interact with brilliant military personnel from other countries. One of the internationals whom Sam befriended was a Yugoslav Lieutenant-Colonel General named Dushan Kveder, a recent graduate of the Soviet General Staff Academy in Moscow. Some time earlier, the Department of Defense had agreed to provide military arms and equipment to President Tito's Yugoslavia, which was still

Communist but beginning to slip out of the Soviet orbit. The U.S. desired to assist the process, and as part of this endeavor, began providing military arms and equipment, including tanks, to help the Yugoslavs defend their newly emerging independence. To reciprocate for the American military aid, the Yugoslavs sent Kveder, a rising figure of prominence in their army, to lecture at prominent U.S. military service schools and colleges, and Sam was picked to be Kveder's escort officer, interpreter, and personal assistant during his American tour.

His lecture's topic was Soviet military doctrine and tactics as they were currently being taught at the Soviet military academies, and he gave roughly the same presentation at every college he visited. Kveder used hundreds of slides containing Russian graphs, charts, maps, and other information as the outline for his talks. He could not speak English fluently, so he would give pieces of the presentations to Sam in Russian, their common language, and then pause while Sam translated for the audience. Because Sam had a far better handle on the Russian language than Kveder, he had a significant advantage in grasping the information that Kveder was trying to communicate. Soon after they began their tour, Sam became so familiar with the subject material that Kveder had only to provide his introduction to his particular audience and then allow Sam to recite the lesson.

Classes always found it humorous to hear Sam's lengthy translations of his friend's several words in Russian. Kveder would talk for ten seconds, and then Sam would provide the audience with a half-hour lecture. Occasionally he would present Kveder with one of the session-ending student questions, and Kveder would jokingly respond that Sam already knew the answer to that question and should just answer it himself. Everywhere the pair went, Kveder and Sam were wined and dined by the leaders of major American military institutions, and during this time Sam gained tremendous exposure to important senior military officers.

Back at the Pentagon, Sam continued to work on manuals detailing Soviet military tactics. From time to time, he would become frustrated by the holes in his knowledge concerning specific military questions as they pertained to the Soviet army. Even though he had dedicated half a decade to studying Soviet military culture, he still could not grasp all the nuances of their military habits. It occurred to Sam that the wealth of knowledge of a few native Russian military experts would enhance American understanding of Soviet military policy better than he possibly could. He remembered the Russian area expertise of his old Detachment R professors, and accordingly secured permission from the Chief of U.S. Army Intelligence to establish a team of five senior Soviet military expatriates as The Soviet Consultant Group. In late fall of 1952, he went to Europe to find, recruit, and retrieve capable men for the project.

The first person he thought to invite to the group was Aldan. When approached, Aldan weighed the idea carefully and then agreed to move to Washington. Sam appointed him senior officer and went on to build the rest of the group.

Eventually Sam accumulated an advisory team that represented all major components of the Soviet military, and they proved an invaluable aid to his work, particularly with interpreting and explaining obscure details in Soviet military periodicals. Over the years, subsequent military defectors, judged to be of long-term value, were added to The Soviet Consultant Group. At first, these consultants provided accurate information for Sam's Soviet field manuals, but eventually they worked on much more important projects. The formation and influence of The Soviet Consulting Group became the most valuable work Sam accomplished during his initial two years in Army Intelligence. When he finally left his Washington office to go to the Infantry Officer's Advanced Course at Fort Benning, The Soviet Consultant Group had become so valuable that he was replaced as the group's advisor by a full Colonel who was soon to be promoted to Brigadier General.

After two years of working for Army intelligence in D.C., Sam returned to Fort Benning for the Infantry Officer's Advanced Course. He became a student in the same courses he had taught ten years earlier. He arrived at Benning in the fall of 1953 as a Junior Major, wearing Army fatigues for the first time since his days with Merrill's Marauders nine years before. The courses were hard, for Sam had not thought in any detail about infantry combat for years. Surrounded by precocious young officers who had recently been working in these areas, some of them for years, Sam again felt that he had to work twice as hard as the others to catch up with his fellow students.

At first, Sam lived with his family at the home of his father-in-law, Lemuel Downing, Sr. He fell into the fun-loving and leg-slapping revelry that Pa Lem so enjoyed. It was not many weeks, however, before Sam realized that lugging his maps and manuals home to study in the distracting atmosphere was going to undermine the high level of learning that he required of himself. With full support from his wife, Sam moved to Benning's bachelors' quarters during the work week so that he could concentrate on his studies. This arrangement proved successful, and Sam was soon able to catch up with his contemporaries.

By the end of the course, he was in the top twenty-percent of his class, and he still managed to spend time with his family on the weekends.

In the spring of 1954, with Sam's classes winding down and graduation approaching, Sam and Brenda restlessly awaited his next assignment. She worried that he might be called to serve in a place where she could not join him. Caring for the children as a single parent was very difficult for her, especially since their daughter was showing signs of being handicapped and required special attention. Although Sam's pursuit of professional excellence forced him to spend less time than he would have liked with his children, he made every effort to play a big part in their development. Sam had been providing Brenda with emotional support and doing the best he could to help take care of the children, but he knew as well as she did that his work limited his role in the family.

On one occasion Jackson, their second son, had contracted a horrible case of pneumonia, but Brenda, juggling his care as well as that of the other two children, had to leave Jackson alone in the children's ward at the Fort Benning hospital and hurry home to Sam, Jr. and Susan. That evening, when Sam had torn himself away from work to visit his sick son for a few minutes, Jackson had clung to his father like a spider, desperately frightened and miserably sick. Sam cried when he had to leave his son and wept every step of the walk in that evening's rain back to the barracks and his imperative homework assignment.

Previously, Sam had received assignments that allowed his wife and family to accompany him. In the spring of 1954, however, the standard requirement for Benning's graduates was to immediately begin serving an obligatory overseas tour without family. For Brenda, the thought that she would be left behind to take care of the family for an extended period of time was simply unbearable. Still, as they had expected, a few days before the completion of his Advanced Officers' School, Sam received orders posting him on a one year "unaccompanied" assignment in Korea.

Brenda panicked. She told Sam that he simply could not leave her. Sam agonized over his duties as a husband and a soldier. His allegiance to his family and his country seemed to be pulling him in opposite directions. Traditionally, no one ever questions Army assignments, but for the good of his family, Sam wrote the most difficult letter he had ever written. He addressed the Office of Chief of Infantry of the Army Personnel Directorate in Washington and requested that his unaccompanied assignment to Korea be deferred until his family situation stabilized.

For a full week he worried that the letter might spell the end of his career as a military man. When he received the response, however, he was overwhelmed by the gracious acceptance of his bold request by the personnel department. The officer in charge of his deployment agreed to look for a position where Sam could serve his country and still attend to domestic needs. The next Saturday, while Sam was fishing in his brother-in-law's bass pond, he received a call that offered just such an opportunity. Sam gladly accepted the special assignment as a consultant on Soviet military affairs in the Office of the Secretary of Defense (OSD) in Washington, D.C. Eager to show his gratitude, Sam reported to his new assignment soon after moving his family into a comfortable home in Falls Church, Virginia.

Sam's new assignment in the Pentagon reestablished his connection with The Soviet Consultant group. Aldan, who had been saddened by Sam's departure for Fort Benning, was especially pleased by his friend's return. Work with The Soviet Consultant Group and the continuing strain of adapting to a new cultural environment had been fraying Aldan's nerves for months and he was drinking heavily.

One day, as Sam was working busily at his new office in the Pentagon, his telephone rang. A hushed voice from a worker at The Soviet Consultant group's office whispered a plea for him to get over there immediately, that something involving Aldan had gone terribly wrong. Sam raced from his office and rushed to the offices on Pennsylvania Avenue and Twelfth Street. Leaving his car double-parked illegally on the curb in front of the office, he scrambled upstairs. A surprising scene greeted him as he reached the office. Aldan had crowded the other members of the office onto three desks in the center of the room and was menacingly waving a pair of shears at them. His mind seemed to have snapped and he was looking to kill someone.

Sam knew he had to act fast. He needed to devise a way to distract his friend from seriously injuring one of the staffers, and then he had to take him to a psychiatric hospital for treatment. With some fast talk and strong entreaties, Sam convinced Aldan that they were late for a doctor's appointment that they had scheduled earlier, and that he had arrived with the express purpose of taking him there. Somehow, Aldan agreed and Sam carefully got Aldan to the car. For the entire trip to the psychiatric ward on the grounds of Walter Reed Army Hospital, Aldan babbled nonsensically. He followed Sam meekly through the sliding doors into the waiting room, though Sam remained alert for any hint of aggression. He hurried into the waiting room and tried to relay his situation to the receptionist without triggering a violent response from Aldan. He winked at the lady as he slowly explained to her that he and his friend were here for their weekly appointment. The receptionist remained impervious to Sam's not-so-subtle hints. She replied that she could not find their appointment and that Sam had clearly come to the wrong place.

Aldan's growing agitation at the lady's persistent denial that they had an appointment was quelled only when an enlisted medic passed by and recognized the situation. Somehow, he quietly gathered several other medics in white coats, and together they succeeded in restraining Aldan long enough for them to get him into a padded cell. Cursing and spitting at Sam for betraying him, Aldan resisted the whole way to the cell.

Aldan stayed at Walter Reed for about three weeks and then was moved to a CIA secure facility on Maryland's Eastern Shore. There he could be comfortably isolated near the beach with his books as he regained his health. Sam made an effort to visit him regularly, and their relationship was soon repaired.

Professionally, Sam's work continued to thrive. He was chosen to organize a sensitive project involving the development of all-source profiles of key members of the Soviet military high command for the Office of the Secretary of Defense. Sam's assignment was to study the thousands of intercepted radio and telephone messages in U.S. intelligence files and from that information to build dossiers on senior Soviet commanders. He was to provide info on their individual professional histories, as well as on their personal habits, traits, and idiosyncrasies, and he was to look for any personal weaknesses that might conceivably be used against them. Sam spent weeks assiduously combing through the material. Although he was able to pull together some very useful information, the project was not as fruitful as the OSD had originally anticipated. Sam decided to present the situation to Aldan to see if the ex-Soviet officer could provide any assistance on the subject.

Sam drove to Aldan's isolated Eastern Shore facility with a list of two hundred officials on whom he was being asked to provide in-depth biographies. After discussing his problem with Aldan and brainstorming about how to go about completing the project, Sam allowed the older man to have a look at the list. Aldan took a look the names on the list and exclaimed, "I know these folks!"

He had attended to the Voroshilov General Staff Academy with some of the men in question and figured he could provide an accurate depiction of their personalities. Aldan amazed Sam over the next several weeks by completing one hundred and sixty of the two hundred profiles. Not only could Aldan provide the profiles that were needed, but he wrote with a marvelously clear, clean, and articulate command of the Russian language to produce word pictures that could not be matched. Some years later, during his lengthy Moscow assignment, Sam met and associated with many of the individual officers on the list. Aldan's uncanny depictions deeply impressed Sam with their glowing clarity and accuracy.

During this same period, Sam began to work with a former KGB Captain named Nicolai Khokhlov. Khokhlov was a Soviet KGB officer who had been dispatched earlier from Moscow to Frankfurt with an assignment to kill a well-known Soviet émigré political leader who was working with Americans. In fact, he was to shoot his target in the face with a bullet from a manipulated cigarette case. But Khokhlov changed his mind. He wanted to escape Russia, and he decided to seek sanctuary in the man's house. The CIA quickly provided him with safe lodging and carefully debriefed him on all he knew about KGB operations in the West. In return, Khokhlov's only request was that the Americans help him get his young son and wife out of Moscow. One of the American agents foolishly promised to help reunite his family, but in truth, the promise could never be kept. It presented far too many risks ever to be attempted. When he realized that the promise was false, Khokhlov fell into deep, brooding anger over perceived American perfidy.

Sympathetically, Sam tried to console Khokhlov for his loss. He wanted to help him begin adjusting to American life, and to that end, Sam would fly to Khokhlov's safe house on the Eastern Shore several weekends a month. The two of them enjoyed sculling around the bay in a flatbed boat, raking up oysters and drinking beer. At first, Khokhlov was horrified that Sam was eating the oysters. The Russians had made few advances in refrigeration technology to preserve meat, especially fresh seafood, and all the shellfish that he had seen in Moscow had spoiled by the time it reached his table. When Sam slurped down his first oyster, Khokhlov was genuinely alarmed that it might kill him. It was not until Khokhlov saw for himself that Sam suffered no ill effects that he gave oysters a try. Then Khokhlov found them to be delicious, and he and Sam would down dozens of oysters with cold beer in a single afternoon.

Sam's visits and his safe refuge did not diminish Khokhlov's bitterness that no effort was being made to exfiltrate his wife and small son out of Moscow. He missed them terribly. When he heard that Sam might be traveling to Moscow in the near future, he drew the address and a small map of the alleys around his apartment for Sam to take with him when he visited the Soviet capital. The task reminded Sam of his days taking pictures of old buildings for his Detachment R professors, but it would be several years before he had the chance to take a look at Khokhlov's residence in Moscow. On his first attempt, he discovered that he was being followed. He debated taking a picture of the place, but decided it was risky and would perhaps incriminate Khokhlov's family, who might still be living there. Instead Sam took a clear mental picture so he could describe the area in detail to Khokhlov. Of course, the Russian expatriate was greatly disappointed that no picture could be produced, but he satisfied himself by listening to Sam's description. Like many of the other displaced Russians that Sam came to know, Khokhlov retained a strong emotional tie to the Motherland despite his hatred for the current government.

On 29 May 1955, early on a Sunday afternoon, Sam received a long distance telephone call from a cousin in Rice, Virginia, telling him that his mother had just passed away. Mis' Helen had been ill for months from a series of strokes, so the news did not come as a complete surprise to Sam, but it was still a sad blow. Sam had been living and working at such a fast tempo that he thought about home only during infrequent brief lulls in his high-pressure activities. Somehow, he felt that Mis' Helen would always be there, which was, of course, a foolish thought.

When he returned to the family farm in Southside Virginia for the funeral, Sam experienced a sensation akin to the shock he had felt during his first visits to his wife's comfortable home in Alabama. The contrast between the high-paced, stressful city life he was living in D.C. and the life on the farm, which had not changed much since his childhood, gave him the feeling that he was in a time warp. Sam had no regrets about the career to which he was dedicating his life, but the loss of his mother struck a chord in his heart that from that day forward redoubled the attention he paid to his family.

As a career combat infantry officer, Sam was constantly warned by staff officers in the career infantry personnel branch that he was allowing large voids in his infantry experience to accumulate. They advised that if he wished to keep pace with his fellows, he should pay more careful attention to performing some of the mandatory jobs expected of a military officer. He interpreted their advice as a hint that if he wanted to get promoted, he needed to gain more experience as an infantry officer. Sam knew that one of the most highly valued qualifications in the infantry was to become an airborne (paratroop) officer, and he decided that the quickest thing to do was to take five weeks off, go to Fort Benning, and become airborne qualified. Late one evening after work at the Pentagon, he broached the subject with his immediate boss who agreed with his the plan.

Sam received orders to report to airborne training at Fort Benning in July of 1955. Knowing he had just six weeks to prepare himself for the arduous program, he put himself on a demanding workout schedule. He had not worked out seriously for ten years, since his days with Merrill's Marauders. He began going for runs around the neighborhood early in the morning and late at night, and as if the jog was not challenging enough, he began to encounter neighborhood dogs, who waited for a chance to chase him and nip at his heels. One morning, he had to jump a fence to avoid a pack of aggressive dogs milling around a neighbor's front yard.

By the time Sam reported to the Airborne School at Fort Benning, his training schedule had paid off, and he was in peak condition, prepared for all the physical obstacles the program could offer. Over the five-week course, he completed the five jumps requisite to receiving a certification badge and also the additional special three jumps to earn the jump master status, necessary so that he could direct jumping activities for his platoons in the back of the plane. One obstacle arose during the training that would plague Sam for the rest of his paratrooping career. From the windows of C-47, C-119, C-123, and C-130 planes, and helicopters, Sam confirmed what he had long suspected: he had severe acrophobia. Heights terrified him.

Nothing could assuage the fear that clenched his heart every time he prepared to leap from an airplane, and even though he was carefully harnessed in with a safety cord, he even trembled when he was required to make the routine training jumps from elevated platforms. He dreaded each of the 102 static line jumps of his career. Sam's hands would break into a cold sweat as he desperately cupped the reserve chute on his chest. Sheer will was the only thing that allowed him to work through his fear of heights and complete parachute training.

He felt like a sleepwalker, head spinning in a daze, as he hooked up, scuffled to the exit, hurtled out into the air, plummeted toward the earth, and began his glide back to solid ground. Each time, however, as the roar of the plane died away and he was left in the absolute stillness of the atmosphere, he felt as if he had conquered the universe. But he would not allow himself to enjoy the euphoria of the parachute fall too much. He still had to worry about making a safe landing in the appropriate locations. When, in spite of his fear, he had finished the program and earned his certification as a paratrooper, Sam returned to the Pentagon with a sense of pride that he had achieved his goal despite his acrophobia.

From the spring of 1954 through early fall 1955, Sam worked from two offices. One was in Jackson Place, across the street from the White House, where he worked part-time for the Operations Coordinating Board—or "OCB," later to become the National Security Council—and the other was in the office of the Secretary of Defense in the Pentagon building.

Throughout this period, Sam remained in constant contact with CIA officials at the operational and policy levels. When the CIA officials asked if he would be interested in serving the CIA in Germany on a three-year loan from the Army, he agreed to the proposal, despite the alarm of his career managers. In fact, his Army superiors warned Sam that he was committing career suicide as an infantry officer. But Sam was thrilled that, once again, he could be matching his wits with the Cold War enemy out on the battlefront with intelligence operators. Tackling an assignment with a spice of danger and taking calculated risks in a dramatic atmosphere excited Sam in a way that was akin to the feelings he used to get as a boy hunting on his father's farm.

In preparation for his undercover duties, the CIA enrolled Sam in a course on clandestine tradecraft. Sam relished the training, and his grades were literally "off the chart." He had a natural affinity for living by his wits, and his experiences in Burma and as a courier during his years in Detachment R had allowed him to refine those skills. He was ready to put them to a new test.

In early January 1956, Sam and Brenda again boarded a ship out of Manhattan Harbor, just as they had done almost seven years earlier when Sam attended the language and area school. This time, however, circumstances had changed. The CIA provided first-class amenities. Sam, Brenda, and their children stood at the railing of the *SS United States,* the premier luxury ocean liner in the Atlantic, among passengers who were the epitome of upper crust American society.

From their position on the deck, the family could look down on the rest of the ships in the water, including one old tub of an army transport that wallowed in their wake, much as the *SS General Taylor* had done in the wake of the *SS Queen Elizabeth* on their first voyage to Europe. Their family had grown since those days, with nine-year old Sam, Jr., six-year old Susan, and three-year old Jackson, whom the family called "Hap." As they gazed out at the vanishing New York City skyline, Sam noticed John Wayne standing next to him. "Look, look, Daddy!" exclaimed Sam, Jr., "It's Gary Cooper!" That evening at the ship's bar, Sam told John Wayne about his son's mistake, and the famous actor burst out with laughter. For the entire trip, Sam remained struck by how far he had come since his last journey across the Atlantic.

THE BERLIN BATTLEGROUND

IN JANUARY 1956, the Cold War between Russia and the United States was in full swing. The Soviets were determined to take over the world for Marxist Communism and American was bent on thwarting their every effort. Only a decade removed from the atomic blasts at Hiroshima and Nagasaki, both superpowers possessed the wherewithal to destroy each other and the rest of the world many times over in only a matter of hours. The possibility of nuclear war haunted citizens of both nations like a dreadful shadow. While the free Western countries suffered from fear of looming atomic obliteration, countries of Eastern Europe lived in subjugation behind the Iron Curtain. Moscow successfully isolated these satellites from the free world, and though occasionally a country would try to rise up and throw off the Communist cloak, in each instance it would be sharply restrained by Soviet forces.

The Soviet leadership, headquartered in Moscow, remained shielded from Western influence and hid behind the behemoth that was the huge Soviet military force. Unlike Allied forces, the Red Army had not demobilized after World War II, and by the mid-50s, it was the largest army on earth. It further achieved its intimidating influence with the constantly spreading tentacles of the infamous KGB, an acronym for Soviet Security Forces, which resembled a combination of the American's CIA and FBI, only on a much larger and more pervasive scale. KGB agents probed relentlessly into any soft spot they could find in Western society, especially in the United States. Moscow also possessed a massive propaganda machine. It easily dwarfed that of Hitler's Nazi Germany in the 1940s, and it used all available means to discredit Western democracy. The Soviets kept their eyes peeled for opportunities to exploit any mistakes or weaknesses of their enemies and to foment and spread discontent throughout the world, especially in underdeveloped countries.

Until his CIA assignment in Berlin, and with the exception of his liaison duties with the Soviet military during Detachment R, the Russians with whom Sam had worked previously were refugees and defectors who had left the Soviet Union. These people had fled of their mother country in three waves. The first wave of expatriates left Russia after World War I and the

Bolshevik Revolution. Americans generally termed them "White Russians," because, until their efforts against the Bolsheviks, they had fought with the White loyalists against Communist Reds in the Russian Civil War. These anti-Bolsheviks, who were loyalists to the defeated and executed Czar, numbered about one million, and a large portion of them were wealthy, aristocratic people. When the Bolsheviks took over Moscow, the defeated forces settled in Western Europe as world citizens and quickly immersed themselves in large cities such as Paris, Berlin, and Belgrade. From their new locations, they continued to plot and scheme how to overthrow the Communists and regain their precious homeland.

During the 1920s and 1930s only a trickle of people escaped across the tight Soviet borders to the free West. Consequently, White Russians outside the homeland created a culture divergent from that of their brothers and sisters back in the Soviet Union. With no interaction across the border, the two societies developed in isolation from each other for twenty years. The language and habits of Russians outside Soviet influence began to become almost foreign to those who remained inside Russia. A true cultural and philosophical gap developed between the separate generations of Russians, and it was manifest in the different accents and idioms of the spoken language. Sam was sensitive to these differences and vigilant in his efforts to see the world from the perspective of Soviet citizens in Moscow, not just that of Russian expatriates.

The second wave of Russians who left the Soviet Union came to the West during World War II. When the Nazis invaded and occupied European Russia all the way to the Volga River, they opened what had previously been a completely sealed frontier. To supplement a dwindling native labor force, the Nazis transported to Germany thousands of prisoners from the Russian cities they had conquered. After the war, most of these liberated prisoners chose to remain in the West rather than return to their homes in Russia. The Soviets made an extravagant effort to reclaim their lost citizens, but under Stalin's iron fist, the KGB often would return them to Russia only to imprison and then, far too often, to execute them. The Soviet military and security forces regarded any Russian who had ever lived in the West to be a potential traitor who needed to be carefully watched and controlled, perhaps even eliminated. Needless to say, as news of the brutal Soviet behavior toward their returned people filtered abroad, Russians in growing numbers chose to remain outside their homeland. Thus an estimated five million Russians lived outside the Soviet Union after World War II. Sam's faculty at Detachment R included many displaced Russians from this wave, and later, during an assignment in Berlin, he would work with members of this group again as they helped him handle agents in Soviet-controlled East Berlin.

The third wave of Soviet defectors, if this tiny trickle can be called a "wave," came to the West after World War II, from the late 1940s until the 1980s. Very few people escaped the Soviet Union during these decades, and U.S. intelligence was forced to rely on information they could gain from the ten to fifteen annual defectors who contributed to American military intelligence. These few defectors were of critical interest to the United States, and since Sam had interacted with several members of this group of defectors while he was an interview facilitator in Washington, he had some preparation for dealing with them when they arrived in Berlin fresh from Soviet territory.

Sam was assigned to serve at CIA's Berlin operations base starting in January of 1956. The German capital had been devastated during World War II, first reduced to rubble by British and American bombings. What was left was then then smashed to pieces by the conquering Soviet tank divisions and artillery. The city was just beginning to pick its way out of the ashes and to begin restoration. It was located in the Russian quadrant of occupied Germany, one hundred miles behind the East German border. Just as Germany itself had been divided into four Allied occupation zones, the city was divided into four sectors, with the Soviets controlling roughly half and the Allies controlling the other half. West Berlin, divided among the French, British, and Americans, provided a tiny green island of freedom in a vast red sea of Communism.

The sole reason the Soviets had thus far spared the Allied piece of the city from their looming tanks and troops was that they knew attacking West Berlin would spark World War III. Because of the looming threat of nuclear war, military agents in Berlin could not engage in direct military battle, but Berlin was still a battleground, just one of a different sort. It was a place where clandestine services squared off in a deadly twilight war, hidden from public view. Berlin was a place of conflict in the shadows, and an assignment there became an opportunity for enterprising CIA officers to make names for themselves. CIA's Berlin Operation Base (BOB) was thus a proving ground for aspiring spy handlers and future CIA managers. BOB operated under Chief William K. Harvey and his fast-talking Irish second-in-command, David Murphy, but its ranks teemed with talented men and women. Thrilled at the opportunity to be mentored by the very best American intelligence professionals in this world, Sam joined the BOB.

It was under these conditions that Sam moved his family to Berlin and re-entered the high-stakes fray on a three-year tour with the CIA clandestine services, under the Deputy Director of Plans (DDP), an office that generally oversaw all deeply-secret dark activities by the CIA. For the most part, top management of the DDP consisted of hardened veterans of the Office of Strategic Services (OSS), the American spy and covert paramilitary service during World War II. A surprising number of these men were privileged sons of the Ivy League. Characterized by an almost reckless and debonair mastery of the calculated risk, they were an unusually sophisticated and intelligent subculture. Once again, Sam was among a group of elite men, and amid these brilliant coworkers, he could not help but feel immense pressure to exceed even his own expectations of himself. Theirs was a land of dirty tricks, which proved to be quite possibly the most dramatic, colorful, and romantic world of Sam's entire professional career. He worked in a no-man's land, in the middle of the delicate overlap between two opposing superpowers who daily threatened to annihilate civilization. The assignment was dangerous and difficult, but critically important, and he enjoyed every bit of it.

Sam's first duty at BOB kept him quietly in his office reviewing Soviet propaganda mail. Throughout the Cold War, the Soviets conducted a massive propaganda program in hopes of increasing discontent in the West. They accumulated the names and addresses of hundreds of thousands of their expatriates and regularly sent them mail encouraging them to return home and to bring with them helpful information about the West. Often, displaced Russians who had felt safely immune from notice by Stalin's regime would be terrified to receive what amounted to recruitment letters from the Soviet Union. Many were shocked that the KGB had tracked them down and worried that the Americans might suspect them of collaborating with the Communists. Many of the recipients of the propaganda tended to feel that the quickest way to remove the shadow of suspicion from American intelligence about their involvement with the Soviet Union was to turn in the letters. Part of Sam's new job was to review such letters as a means to garner any useful intelligence they might provide. It was a simple job, a trial assignment from his BOB superiors to make sure Sam was a capable officer.

Soon Sam was given the additional responsibility of assisting in the screening of East German refugees who had escaped to West Germany. Floods of East Germans crossed the sector border in Berlin every day, especially on the weekends. The Berlin sector border was far more porous than the zone border, so most Germans who wished to slip from behind the Iron Curtain focused on the crossover points in the city. As they passed through, any individuals who could conceivably be helpful to military intelligence were sorted from among the refugees and sent to a BOB special facility for questioning. Sam joined a team of CIA agents who interviewed these escapees and tried to glean any bit of information that might help their intelligence efforts against the Soviets. Of the dozens of people whom Sam interviewed daily, he usually could pinpoint four or five who might offer helpful intelligence, and these he would invite to a safe house for further conversations. The assignment offered Sam an opportunity to polish his German, the language in which all interviews were conducted, and also to learn more about conditions in East Germany.

Sam proved his effectiveness and was given the additional responsibility of supporting case officers in their operations. As the agency did elsewhere, the CIA in Berlin practiced the principle of compartmentalization. Sam was told only enough about other operations to be able to play his supporting role proficiently. In this connection, one of Sam's well-remembered support assignments came at the request of a senior case officer, "Agent R," whom Sam vaguely understood to be working with undercover East German agents. One day Agent R stopped by Sam's office and asked if Sam would do him a huge favor by being at a specific intersection at exactly 1300 hours the following afternoon. Agent R stressed the importance of arriving at the corner at *exactly* one o'clock. Sam agreed and spent a few hours that afternoon driving around the neighborhood to get a feel for it. He timed several runs until he felt sure that he could get to the designated alley within a few seconds of the stroke of the hour. The next day, Sam arrived in the vicinity of the intersection a few minutes early. After satisfying himself that he was not under surveillance, he waited until two minutes before the hour and then began the drive, setting off in his black Ford sedan at about twelve miles per hour. At the stroke of one, Sam peered down the alley and saw Agent R, coat flailing, briefcase in hand, running pell-mell toward him. He opened the door and Agent R dove in with a shout, "GUN IT, SAMMY!"

The two men drove around Berlin until they were certain they had lost any tails, and then Sam dropped off Agent R at a safe house. Sam never knew what had transpired before he picked up Agent R. All he knew was that he had successfully done exactly what he had promised, just one part of a covert operation, and Agent R had pulled off his mission and managed to succeed because Sam held up his end of the assignment. As the agent got out of Sam's Ford, he said, "Thanks, Sammy. I knew I could depend on an Army man."

Because of his fluency in Russian and his extensive prior experience in dealing with Soviet defectors, Sam could deal effectively with Russian defectors who crossed the border. Occasionally, the CIA helped Russian officers with higher military status arrange their escapes, and once they had defected, Sam would often be chosen to greet them and get them to a West Berlin safe house. After comfortably settling the defector under the care of an old German housekeeper and a couple of security officers, Sam would arrange a few interviews to see what sort of information he could provide the American military. The whole process was similar to procedures he had practiced at the Pentagon, except that in Berlin, Sam performed the interviews by himself. Sam became adept at these conversations, and he was frequently in demand to debrief important individuals.

When one of the CIA's case officers left Berlin, Sam moved from handling peripheral assignments, which he had been doing for about three months, to assuming responsibility for that agent's operation. This task involved training, equipping, and providing documentation, money, and other forms of support to a small group of adamantly anti-Communist young women. These ladies, who were in their twenties and thirties, all of them exceptionally smart and attractive, were motivated to revenge themselves on the Soviet military in East Germany for injustices and abuse that they and their families had suffered at the hands of the Red Army. In the final weeks of the war, as the Soviets approached Berlin from the east, they cut a wide swathe of violent destruction. Inflamed by the atrocities which the Russians had perpetrated on German soil, these victims were bent on revenge. The Soviets, unfettered by any rules protecting noncombatants and unrestrained by their officers, vented their hatred with a rampage of rape, pillage, and destruction. In its way, the violence left a burning hatred in the minds and hearts of thousands of people, including the women with whom Sam was to work.

They had only one weapon to use against the Soviets, their beauty, but they knew how to use it to the greatest advantage as they endeavored to seduce, entrap, blackmail, and, where possible, destroy various Soviet military representatives. In their bitter, dirty game, they targeted officers, the higher ranking the better. Sometimes they failed and were exposed, which meant certain torture and execution after a long period of interrogation. But sometimes they succeeded, and the results of their successes were at times almost incalculably valuable to American intelligence communities. For Sam, working with this loosely affiliated group of women was the most difficult and demanding assignment that he had to fill in the course of his entire intelligence career.

Sam continued with the operation of this intelligence ring until mid-fall of 1957. Then one day, on the heels of an unusual success involving a female agent bringing an important Soviet official over to the West, Sam was called in to handle a defector of questionable status. There was suspicion among the intelligence community that he might be a phony, a Soviet intelligence agent sent to infiltrate the CIA. Sam worked by himself with this defector for several days, trying to disentangle his convoluted story. On the third day of the interviews, Sam had turned his back to the defector and was reaching to pour himself a cup of tea when he heard a slight sound and saw a movement out of the corner of his eye. He turned just in time to see the alleged defector coming at him with a fistful of razorblades. Sam threw himself lengthwise to one side and rammed his boot full force into the groin of his attacker. Fortuitously, Sam had, that day, put on a pair of heavy hard old paratrooper boots, and his kick to the defector's crotch took out the Soviet.

Sam rarely talked to Brenda about the intrigues and dangers of his job, and he certainly never shared with her the close call he had faced during the Soviet agent's attack. It was only when she and Sam attended a cocktail party several weeks later that she realized how close her husband had come to being maimed or even killed. A CIA man, who was deep in his cups, approached Brenda and, pointing across the room to Sam, congratulated her on being married to the luckiest guy in the world. Startled, Brenda inquired what the man meant. The CIA man proceeded to reveal that Sam's Russian friends had "sent a guy after him."

Brenda quickly made the connection between that event and the late night telephone calls she sometimes received, with heavy breathing on the other end, and the sensation she sometimes felt while standing at the kitchen sink that someone was looking at her. She became hysterical and suffered a nervous breakdown.

Sam keenly felt his obligation to Brenda and his children, and it was impossible for him to continue his activities as a CIA operative in Berlin while Brenda was unwell. He requested a transfer. He had no idea what his next assignment might be or whether there would even be another CIA assignment awaiting him once he returned to Washington. Given the somewhat daredevil stance he had been maintaining over the past few years, with one foot in the CIA and the other in the Army, he knew that it could well be that he had come to the end of his career. The CIA might have nothing further for him, and the Army personnel office, whose representatives had been warning him unceasingly about the dangerously unbalanced professional route he chose, might be right. Perhaps he had finally hit the wall in both careers.

As Brenda's condition worsened and Sam made plans to take his family back to the United States, he received a cable from the CIA office in Washington. They praised his work in Berlin and welcomed him back to Washington. The job they offered at CIA headquarters held even higher rank and greater responsibility than he had enjoyed in Germany. With his children in tow and his wife resting, Sam began the return voyage home across the wintry Atlantic. Once again, they sailed on the *SS United States,* alongside a constellation of America's upper-crust society and international elite—movie stars, millionaires, orchestra leaders, famous authors, ranking government officials, and university presidents. While Sam enjoyed associating with his fellow travelers, he could not help but feel out of place knowing that this was not his position in society and that it might never be. He was, however, satisfied with his current career path and the promise of an intellectually stimulating future. He also cherished his exceedingly loyal and supportive family, and while their spirits were subdued on this return voyage, he remained optimistic about their future together.

THE END OF THE CIA TOUR, FORT BRAGG, AND HOLLYWOOD

THE CROSSING ABOARD the *SS United States* had been brief and relatively uneventful. When the ship docked in New York harbor, Sam hurried ashore to buy a couple of newspapers so he could catch up on any world news that might influence a possible change in his next assignment. Although he discovered nothing of vital international importance, he stopped in his tracks when he saw the headline for the day in the *New York Daily News:* "Big Band Director Tommy Dorsey Chokes to Death." This news hit Sam with a peculiar twist. Shortly before he had enlisted in the Army, his first cousin, a manager of several big band swing orchestras and a promoter of musical talent, had begun to take steps to arrange for Sam to audition for the Tommy Dorsey Orchestra. Although that sequence of events had played out some fifteen years earlier, Sam still nourished faint hopes that he might one day become a big band leader. Sam realized as he read the news report that he had long since made his career choice. There would be no going back.

The family quickly disembarked from the ship, and the old Buick was raised out of the hold, rolled ashore, and serviced. Within minutes they were hurrying their way south to Washington, D.C. Brenda, still suffering from nervous depression, anxiously anticipated her return home to her father. She wanted to drive straight through, from New York to Alabama, without stopping. When they arrived in Washington, however, Sam insisted that they stop overnight in a motel before continuing further. He could not have rationally explained his motive, but an eerie sensation convinced Sam that this might be his last chance to see Aldan, his old friend, with whom he had been in regular correspondence during his time in Berlin. Sam's wishes prevailed, and much to Brenda's heated disappointment, they checked into a motel. As soon as Sam had settled his family in their room, he set out to North Arlington to see his old ex-Soviet friend.

Aldan was living with his doting German wife in a flat on Key Boulevard, a short distance up the hill from the Potomac River in North Arlington. Sam climbed the steps to the flat and paused before knocking on the door.

Through a bay window, he could see Aldan sitting in an old rocking chair, a great grey tabby cat lying in his lap and his elderly wife fussing around him, bringing him food and drink and giving him the attention he so enjoyed. Sam knocked on the door and Aldan's wife approached, but before she could great him properly, Aldan recognized Sam's voice. Aldan sprang to the door to give his friend a welcoming embrace. The men spent the next two hours discussing the state of world affairs, especially the conflicting interests of the United States and the Soviet Union. Aldan considered the Cold War to be a full-scale war in every respect, and he often suggested that the fate of the modern world was considerably at stake. After talking about his boredom with the minutia he had to deal with at work and discussing Sam's future, Aldan looked into his younger friend's eyes rather sternly. "From looking at your face and your eyes," Aldan observed, "I believe that you have been drinking too much. I wish that you would be much more careful about imbibing alcoholic beverages."

This chastising comment struck Sam as somewhat strange, coming from a man who had been an acute alcoholic himself, but he took the advice into consideration and, in later times, did indeed limit his drinking habits. In return, Sam asked Aldan about his health. His response was *"Tak Cebe,"* or "So-So."

Aldan admitted that there were times when he had a sort of tightening in his chest that made breathing difficult. While he was not frightened by death, he had a sense that his time was becoming increasingly limited. He then asked for a favor. Upon his death, Aldan wanted Sam to get some Russian soil— some good, honest dirt from the Motherland—and sprinkle it on his grave. He refused to abandon the subject until he extracted Sam's promise, which Sam had no qualms about readily giving. The friends parted with hopes for many future visits during Sam's upcoming assignment in Washington.

Next morning, the Wilson family continued their drive to Alabama. They decided to spend Christmas with Brenda's father, and Sam, Brenda, and the children settled in to enjoy the holidays. It was a well deserved respite of playing card games, tossing football, walking in the woods, sitting by crackling fires, telling stories, visiting Brenda's cousins, and relaxing with family. After Christmas, they headed north to celebrate the New Year with Cap'n Jack at the Wilson farm in Rice, Virginia. There they again experienced the same warm feeling of family that they had relished in Alabama. On the first Sunday in January, they set out for their new home and Sam's next CIA assignment in Washington, D.C.

It was early morning of his first day at work and he was just about to leave the hotel when the telephone rang. Sam immediately recognized the voice of a senior CIA officer whom he knew very well, and the officer came straight to the point. In a somber tone he told Sam that Aldan had died early that morning. Sam recalled the elderly Russian saying, "When I die, get some good, rich Russian soil from my motherland and sprinkle it on my grave, wherever you bury me." Sam knew that his conscience would not let him rest easy until he had fulfilled his responsibilities to Aldan.

Despite Sam's inclinations, there was not much time to grieve. He reported to headquarters of the Central Intelligence Agency's Soviet Russia Division (known as the "SR division") to learn that he had landed a choice assignment. His new position carried staffing responsibilities for activities of clandestine propaganda and for clandestine paramilitary endeavors the CIA supported against the Soviet Union as well as for other covert political warfare activities in and from western Europe.

Clandestine activities fell generally into three categories and the services were organized accordingly. There was first the undercover collection of intelligence. This service was simply dubbed "FI" for "foreign intelligence." Accordingly, for the subordinate branches and sections within each major office of the CIA, each division had "FI" elements. In the SR division, any engagement in foreign intelligence collection was under the auspices of the SR-FI staff. Secondly, extensive activity focused on countering the intelligence efforts of the Soviets themselves. This activity was referred to as "CI," for "counter intelligence." Those individuals in the SR divisions involved in counter intelligence were thus part of the SR-CI effort. The third significant activity arena of clandestine services was referred to as "PP" for "political and paramilitary." The SR-PP was to be Sam's new arena of activity. He inherited the responsibility for CIA activities in Western Europe of a paramilitary or political warfare character that were directed towards the Soviet Union.

He could not have been more delighted. His assignment tied together perfectly the years that he had spent with Soviet expatriates and, later, with Soviet defectors who were anti-Communists and itching to participate in the fight against Soviet Communism. Indeed, looking at his new assignment, Sam could almost see the recipe of a success story already written for him with ingredients he had gathered throughout his intelligence career.

While he did not want to appear arrogant at his office, Sam recognized how advantageous his varied past experiences could be. Not only was he already Army Major with a distinguished combat record, earned behind Japanese lines in Burma with Merrill's Marauders, but he also possessed briefing, staffing, and writing skills learned during his time with the Army General Staff. He possessed a full understanding of the Russians and their language, acquired during his time at Detachment R and his year of clandestine trade-craft experience in the hottest operational area going, Berlin. In addition, Sam had hosts of useful contacts in the Pentagon, including top levels of Army Intelligence, Army Special Operations, and the Office of Special Operations under the Secretary of Defense. Sam had unfettered access to a number of important decision makers in the U.S. armed services. He was fully qualified for his new position, and he gained respect from his coworkers because of his applicable experience and knowledge.

Although Sam had accumulated an impressive résumé, he still felt somewhat inferior to many of the brilliant individuals who worked around him. The CIA, emerging from the Office of Strategic Services after World War II, had within its ranks some very extraordinary and highly singular Americans. Many of them had joined the OSS in hopes of working in the espionage, clandestine, or political warfare area as a specific choice. They preferred being part of attacks against enemies through the shadowy methods of the CIA rather than the Army's direct attacks on the field of battle. They were often well-educated sons of privilege, imaginative individuals who enjoyed working in an arena where they had latitude to use their creative imaginations. They chose to calculate their own risk rather than be a part of some mighty war. Sam was amazed how many of them came from Ivy League schools, and from within that circle, how many came from Yale. He grew to know many talented operatives in the CIA, and developed a respect for the abilities and talents of each agent. Nearly all of them could have found safer jobs, so they were where they chose to be, in a position where they could pursue adventure as they served their nation. Many of them had ancestors among our nation's original founders, and those individuals had especially strong feelings for the Republic, its Declaration of Independence, its Constitution, and its Bill of Rights. Although they rarely talked about these documents, they were completely conversant with them. In fact, they were very well educated in many subjects, as they were products of classical liberal arts education. They would frequently unload on Sam quotations from ancient Latin or Greek, and they knew the history of Western civilization, the kings and queens of France and England, and the czars of Russia, as well as an American schoolchild knows the Presidents of the United States.

For Sam, it was simply exhilarating to be where he was constantly associating with people who routinely sought to identify creative solutions and who approached the arena of strategic warfare and deception with innovative ideas. Sam never tired of the excitement involved in running undercover operations of a paramilitary and guerilla warfare nature and tackling problems even when significant portions of the situations were unknown. His colleagues stretched Sam's mind daily as he worked hard to be on par with them. Once again, life seemed intellectually challenging and exciting. While the CIA is sometimes viewed as a gang of dirty tricksters who bend the rules, ignore fair play, and stop at nothing, Sam found there a certain gentleman's code. Even while they were involved in questionable activities, agents worked to maintain the moral high ground over their Soviet Communist opponents.

In his new assignment, Sam maintained interaction with Soviet émigré organizations, including several that were very active against the Soviet Union. These groups published their own newspapers in which they explained their political philosophies and endeavored to attract new members and active supporters. They also, by whatever means available, tried to smuggle anti-Communist propaganda into the Soviet Union. Two of these organizations even had their own radio stations beaming regular propaganda broadcasts behind the Iron Curtain. Among the members of these organizations were young men who were more than ready to return to the Soviet Union and work from the inside as part of various undercover endeavors to unseat the Communists from power. United States officers in the clandestine intelligence services found these enthusiastic individuals and organizations were fertile ground for anti-Communist activities. In fact, they clamored to help the American cause so eagerly—and on occasion so naïvely and idealistically—that it became necessary to select only the few best of the many proposals they submitted.

One operation in which Sam participated deserves particular attention. With secret aid provided by the U.S. government, that is, by Sam and the CIA, one organization had begun to dispatch huge helium-filled balloons, three to four stories in height, from areas in northern Bavaria, near the Czech border. Fixed to the sides of these balloons were huge baskets filled with packets of propaganda material, carefully researched and even more carefully written. To facilitate the distribution of the propaganda leaflets, the expatriates, with the CIA's help, attached to the balloons' cargo baskets a crude device, fitted onto a bicycle wheel, armed with a sharp cutter or knife, and further connected to an altimeter. As a balloon floated eastward over the Soviet Union along the prevailing west-east winds, it would reach altitudes anywhere from fifteen to thirty thousand feet. Then its lift would begin to deteriorate, causing it to descend slowly and gradually. Upon reaching a predetermined level of atmospheric density, the altimeter would signal to the wheel armed with the cutter, and a number of bundles of propaganda leaflets would be cut free from their positions outside the baskets. These leaflets would flutter to the earth across hundreds of square miles of Soviet territory. With their loads lightened, the balloons would again ascend to higher altitudes, and the process would be repeated, sometimes across the entire Soviet Union, including eastern Soviet Siberia. Eventually, the balloon ran out of sufficient lift to keep itself in the air, and then it would float gently back down to earth.

This particular propaganda leaflet operation gave rise to one of the strangest events of the Cold War. One day, one of these balloons came down on territory in South Korea, which was occupied at that time by American troops. Only a few propaganda leaflets were still stuck to the basket, but the local U.S. military could not identify the origin or purpose of this strange contraption. When the cable query from the United States' Far Eastern Command hit Washington and a copy came to CIA, it went immediately to the SR division and wound up on Sam's desk. He lost no time in seeking to persuade U.S. forces in Korea that they needn't be alarmed. Indeed, the agency dispatched an officer to fly to Tokyo and Seoul so that staff and officers there could be informed about the leaflet operation. No one wanted a misunderstanding to start an international incident or provoke retaliation by U.S. military elements.

During this period, the Soviet Union sometimes organized tourist-type voyages, which were planned as rewards for Soviet officials and party workers. Their ships traveled around the perimeter of Europe with stops in Istanbul, Copenhagen, Helsinki, and significant ports of call in-between. To Sam and his superiors, these trips represented an unparalleled opportunity for face-to-face encounters between hard-line Communists visiting the West, most of them for the first time, and their erstwhile countrymen who had personal stories of Communist abuse. It appeared to CIA officials that if contact might be established on neutral ground and under favorable circumstances, such meetings could well be the most effective propaganda of them all.

They again employed the assistance of the same anti-Soviet émigré political organizations that Sam and his colleagues had utilized for the balloon project. These contacts helped select, indoctrinate, and train special groups of individuals on conversational propaganda specifically geared to their vacationing countrymen. These carefully prepared men and women were then stationed at various ports of call around the Mediterranean and Western Europe where Soviet ships were likely to dock, and they greeted the parties of Soviets who came ashore to wander the streets of the city with offers to act as guides and answer questions about the town. Since the Russians knew little about the local scene, they would sometimes hire the guides. Under optimal circumstances, these tourists would invite their guides to drink tea or eat a meal with them during the course of the day, and the guides would have a captive audience. Subtly, they revealed what the West was really like and what their experiences had been in the Soviet Union. The project had an effect. Several Soviet tourists wound up jumping ship and joining a persuasive guide.

Sam was completely familiar with the Soviet's post World War II repatriation efforts. He had learned of them firsthand as a liaison officer with the Soviet Repatriation mission in Salzburg in December 1948 and January 1949, and then subsequently in Berlin during 1956 when he monitored the work of the Soviet Homeland Committee. He was also well aware of other continuing efforts on the part of the Soviets to induce their citizens living abroad as expatriates to return to the Soviet Union. From the Soviet standpoint, each former Soviet citizen who refused to return home was a vote against the Soviet Communist system. Consequently, they were very sensitive to the existence of anti-Communist expatriate communities around the world, and they continuously worked against them.

From his work with the CIA in Berlin, Sam was already familiar with Soviet attempts at repatriation through the mass mailing of letters all over the Western World. These entreaties to pack up and come home promised a welcome to returning countrymen as prodigal sons and daughters and promised their restoration to full dignity as vital members of the "highly futuristic Communist society." On occasion, there would be a post script in some of these letters which would say something like, "and if, prior to your coming home you are willing to engage in activities that might be helpful to your Motherland, not only would you be welcomed home, but you would be welcomed home as a hero, and gifts of substantial nature would be awaiting you and your family." It was a direct invitation to spy on behalf of the Soviets.

The CIA saw this program as an opportunity to further infuriate frustrated former Russian citizens and possibly to score a propaganda coup. Working with one émigré organization, and using stationery pilfered from the Soviet Repatriation Committee, Sam and his office composed letters that mimicked the blatant spy-recruitment pitch, except with a sharpened tone. They made it all the more evident that the Soviets were interested in these people mostly because they could be used as agents to advance the cause of Communism.

Unfortunately, CIA officers did not carefully monitor the selection of addressees to which these forged letters were sent. In one instance, their partner émigré organization in Western Europe imprudently mailed a number of the letters to Soviet expatriates in the United States, one of whom promptly mailed his letter to the headquarters of the FBI. One early Monday morning, bleary eyed and sleepy, Sam picked up his morning copy of the *Washington Post* from his doorstep and unfolded it to see a headline in the left-hand corner, "FBI Launches Three-Pronged Investigation." Included in the article was the letter which Sam and his staff had prepared.

If the FBI investigation revealed that the CIA had mailed the letter, the blowback consequences would be devastating. Sam immediately approached his boss, who sent him to his boss, who sent him to his boss. Before Sam knew it, he was sitting before the director of the CIA, Allan Dulles, and trying to explain the miscommunication. Sam had the impression that he was going to be thrown out the window, but all Dulles did was slap his leg and say, "I love it, I love it, I love it. Let's just find a way to keep this contained."

Dulles suggested that to straighten out the matter, Sam should talk to the Chief of Counter-Intelligence, the legendary James Jesus Angleton. Dulles also had his special assistant accompany Sam to Capitol Hill where they met with the staff director of the Senate Committee on Un-American Activities, the old McCarthy committee. While Senator McCarthy, who had cut quite an anti-Communist swath in the 1950s, had passed away by that time, his committee was still in existence and being ruled with an iron hand by its staff director, a Judge Morris. As Sam quickly realized, the Committee on Un-American Activities was already in full bay after this supposedly "blatant instance of a Soviet endeavor to spy on American territory." So, with his hat in his hand and accompanied by Allan Dulles's special assistant, Sam went in to see Judge Morris and told him the whole story. When Sam finished, the judge studied Sam for a few moments, then threw his head back and laughed. "Major," he said, "don't you worry about a thing. I am delighted. We will just investigate, investigate, and investigate, and I will make sure that you will have nothing to worry about."

Throughout this period, the ultimate outcome of the Cold War was still very much in question. That we would emerge victorious some three decades later was by no means assured. Even one decade before President Reagan demanded that Mr. Gorbachev "Tear down this wall," no one knew which superpower would win the struggle. For instance, Sam awoke one morning in 1957 to find that a strange object had been launched into space and was orbiting around the world. Sputnik, the first successful satellite and a precursor of space exploration, had launched. Then, when the Soviets successfully sent a manned capsule around the Earth, the cosmonaut stirred America when he screamed into his radio, "I am an eagle! I am an eagle! I am an eagle!"

That the Soviets were first in space was a real smear on the reputation of America's technology development program. It was even more disturbing that no real evidence existed to prove just how advanced Soviet technology might be. When the Soviets began claims that they had many missiles with nuclear devices in their nose cones, there was no alternative but to assume that they did. The Soviets had always surpassed the United States in using smoke and mirrors to disguise their full capabilities, but with no proof that their claims were false, the U.S. had to believe the claims until it could be disproved.

In early 1957, Sam received orders to report to the Command and General Staff College at Fort Leavenworth, one of the greatest military colleges in the world. Any officer who desires prominent positions in the United States Army has to graduate from that college, and during the 1950s, approximately half of the officers in the Army were offered the opportunity. Generally, officers dropped whatever assignment in which they were currently involved in order to attend Fort Leavenworth. Sam was pleased when he received these orders because it showed the military's confidence in his leadership ability and his potential to continue rising through the ranks. However, when he broached the opportunity with his bosses at CIA, they protested, "Sammy, you can't leave us now. You're involved in too many things of importance. We just can't afford to let you go."

Trying to deflect the negative reaction that was bound to follow, Sam suggested, "If you don't want me to go to Leavenworth, would you please let them know in the Army Personnel Office."

His bosses complied, but the Army's response put the responsibility back on Sam's shoulders. If Sam wanted to decline the opportunity, he would have to let them know personally that he chose to defer the invitation. So Sam wrote the letter and carried it to the Army Personnel Office for certification. That office had long believed Sam Wilson's unorthodox career path would doom his advancement, and his letter reignited their suspicion. They threw up their hands in disgust and bewilderment. "You have just committed career suicide all over again!"

Sam left Army Personnel knowing that they had written him off as a pending career failure. They just could not see why he would pursue what they considered escapades while his counterparts were following standard advancement procedures. But they sent the letter, and Sam's placement at Leavenworth was deferred. To the surprise of his nay-sayers, the next year he again received orders to report to the General Staff College, and in late August 1958, a few weeks prior to his thirty-fifth birthday, he enrolled for the class that graduated in June of 1959.

Before Sam left the Central Intelligence Agency at the end of his three-year loan from the Army, he wrote an after-action report which eventually found its way to the desk of Director Dulles. There were two things that Sam emphasized in the report. He noted that whenever the CIA recruited an agent to spy or perform other secret work, the agency required immediate results. Sam documented that this policy significantly differentiated the CIA and the British Secret Service. The British intelligence service were willing to recruit an agent, position him, and then leave him alone for whatever time he needed to establish himself. They ensured that he was alive, properly supported, and safely accumulating his salary, but they did not insist upon immediate results, contacting agents as little as possible until the time came when they could be of critical service. The British were successful with this approach to agent development. The CIA, on the other hand, tended to push for results. Sam felt that immediate expectations should take a back seat to more substantial results.

Sam also noted that staffing of the CIA's training and teaching positions usually fell to agents who had become physically incapacitated or were growing old and lacked their original levels of energy. Sometimes training responsibilities were handed over to officers who had made serious mistakes of judgment. Sam knew from experience that in the military, the responsibilities for training troops or teaching at military institutions are considered second in importance only to active service. The military strongly emphasized the value of experienced personnel training younger servicemen. In the CIA, the most capable and experienced individuals were not asked to teach, and Sam felt that this short-sighted practice kept upcoming officers from reaching their full potential.

While he never expected his after-action report to produce much impact on the upper echelons of responsibility within the CIA, Sam did think it would be helpful for the people he was leaving behind to at least consider his thoughts. Thus, he wrote his after-action report to summarize his tips for improving the service, and he was grateful to hear later that they were well-received by men of influence within the agency.

As a farewell gift to Sam for his contributions, the CIA prepared and addressed to Sam a flowery letter of thanks, but rather than sending it directly to him, they sent it to the Secretary of the Army. This circuitous route meant that the letter to Sam was read not only by the Secretary, but also the Chief of Staff of the Army, the Secretary of Defense, and the Director of the Office of Special Operations, who all added their written thanks and subsequent endorsements to the letter before it finally reached Sam. A copy of that letter, along with its endorsements, was inserted into Sam's infantry officer file, side by side with his request to be deferred from the Command Officers Staff College. To a degree at least, the thank-you letter offset the "career suicide" of his deferral request. With it, Sam's assignment with the Soviet Russian division of the CIA came to an end.

In the spring of 1958, when Sam returned to the office of the Assistant to the Secretary of Defense after his three-year tour with the CIA, there was a new deputy in office, Air Force Colonel Edward Geary Lansdale. Sam had heard a great deal about Colonel Lansdale, who had been overseas until the fall of '58, and he considered it a privilege to spend three months with this gentleman.

While he was still with the CIA, one of Sam's staff officers had described to Sam that he had spent part of a morning and his lunch time listening to the most fantastic individual he had ever heard in his life—a certain "Landslide Lansdale"—the same Colonel Edward Geary Lansdale who helped defeat the Communist guerillas in the Philippines and went on to assist in the election of a new Filipino president. Then Landslide Lansdale began the same kind of campaign in Vietnam. The young staff officer chattered with genuine excitement as he told Sam the details about the man he had heard speak during the morning symposium.

After such a glowing introduction, Sam eagerly anticipated his opportunity to work with Colonel Lansdale, and he was not disappointed. Over the next three months after Sam joined the office of the Assistant to the Secretary of Defense, prior to Command and General Staff College, he and Lansdale formed a close friendship. The duties of his office required that Lansdale travel around America, and often he would invite Sam to accompany him on these trips. He and Sam spent their free time enjoying themselves in different cities. Whenever they were near the ocean, they would walk the beach late at night, drinking beer and having memorable discussions about their lives. Sam found that the rave notices from that CIA lad about Lansdale were true, and the Colonel became one of the most influential people in Sam's life—easily at the same level as the Russian defector Aldan or with Colonel Charles Hunter of Merrill's Marauders.

Lansdale was both a political warrior and a kind of political psychiatrist. A master of subterfuge, a king-maker, and a real wheeler-dealer, he was extraordinarily adept at personal promotion, which he always accomplished in subtle ways without detracting from his overall aura. A Californian, he had attended the University of California, Los Angeles, before the war and then went into advertising and became a successful salesman. During World War II, he entered the Office of Strategic Services, where he worked mostly as a singleton. He moved on his own, devising some of the more significant ideas pertaining to psychological warfare that the United States employed in World War II. In the immediate post-World War II period, Lansdale was in the Philippines as a public relations officer with the 14th Air Force Division at Clark Air Force Base when he became deeply immersed in internal Filipino matters. An astute and insightful observer and a brilliant writer, his reports eventually found their way to the desks of such high ranking officials as the Director of the CIA, Allen Dulles, the Secretary of State, John Foster Dulles, and the Vice President, Richard Nixon. These three powerful men became some of Lansdale's biggest supporters.

While at Clark Air Force Base, Lansdale became personal friends with an obscure Filipino congressman named Ramon Magsaysay—so much so that they referred to each other as "brother," and spent a great deal of time together. Lansdale had maintained some of his OSS connections, which were by this time mostly in high-level positions in the CIA, so there were many hidden political manipulation levers to which he had access. He was able to use his ties in the CIA to help facilitate the appointment of Magsaysay as the Secretary of National Defense for the newly formed Republic of the Philippines, but Lansdale soon recognized that he was working with an individual who had the capacity for far greater things, even the Presidency of the country. He obtained clandestine funding from the CIA, and worked successfully behind the scenes to help gain the election of Magsaysay as the President of Philippines in 1953.

At Magsaysay's request, Lansdale moved into the Presidential Palace in Manila. He occupied a suite that connected to one wing of a huge conference room while the President stayed in quarters adjoining the other side of the conference room. Magsaysay was an insomniac, and on the nights when he could not fall asleep, the Filipino President would walk to Lansdale's room, shake Lansdale awake, and say, "Brother Ed, I can't sleep. Play me something on your harmonica."

Lansdale could play the harmonica quite well, and he always kept one close at hand for that purpose. He would go out to the conference room, slouch down in a corner, and start playing some well-known Filipino ballads. Magsaysay would put his head down on the table and usually fall asleep while Lansdale was still playing, sometimes accompanying his friend's harmonica with contented snores.

Many legends grew about Lansdale. Countless books and articles had been written about Landsdale by the time Sam ran into him in the Office of the Secretary of Defense. Two, in particular, were notable, both in book form and as movies. In 1958, *The Ugly American,* a book by William J. Lederer and Eugene Burdic, which was later made into a movie starring Marlon Brando, featured a main character named "Hillendale," the "ragtime kid." It was a thin guise as a play on the name Lansdale. Hillendale even played the harmonica. Several years later, Graham Green's *The Quiet American* also portrayed a main character who was obviously based on Lansdale. When *The Quiet American* was made into a successful movie, Lansdale's legend was embellished and perpetuated.

Sam was particularly impressed by Lansdale's ideas on political warfare. Simply put, the man was a secular missionary of the American political system. His convictions, or message, stemmed from the Declaration of Independence, the Constitution, and the Bill of Rights. He believed that, through trial and error and a whole lot of luck, our forefathers had bequeathed to us a system of government that was better than any the world had ever known. He believed that, with proper instruction, education, and understanding, the system could work for any culture. Lansdale found that there were people in other cultures who would respond to our basic political ideas. He was fond of noting that when the first Office of Strategic Services detachment parachuted into Ho Chi Minh's jungle headquarters in Vietnam, the first thing the Vietnamese leader wanted from the Americans was a copy of the Declaration of Independence. Lansdale truly believed that the American system could save the world. He was walking propaganda for Americanism.

Secondly, Sam was impressed by Lansdale's observation that in many impoverished developing nations in the world, poverty, illiteracy, and disease are so great that the only viable institution is the army. The army can play a role in either oppressing people or making the soldiers their brothers by taking positive actions—uplifting, helping, teaching, healing, and harvesting crops. Lansdale argued for the optimization of all the potentially positive kinetic energy that an army can represent if thus employed for the good of the people. Sam was deeply impressed by his observations on the army as a catalyst for good.

During the three months Sam was with him, Lansdale identified a number of chores for Sam to complete. In his duties, Sam had no specific assignment because of his temporary status, and thus he was free to help Lansdale with the numerous odd tasks that presented themselves daily to the Assistant to the Secretary of Defense. Lansdale requested that Sam share with the other members of the office some of the stories and lessons he had learned through his experiences in the CIA. During these carefully selected narratives, Sam's audience was usually so captivated by the adventures that he would have to remind them that they were a couple of hours overdue for their return to work. Even with the self-censorship that Sam felt inclined to apply to his talks, Lansdale and his department seemed fascinated by his activities within the CIA. In return, Sam was glad to share with good people who were interested in what he had been doing, and the talks gave Sam a chance to identify with them more completely. During his three months in the Office of the Secretary of Defense, Sam became involved in several very interesting and highly sensitive issues of a strategic nature, where the prestige of the United States was very much on the line. While the stories remain too sensitive for General Sam to feel comfortable including in this book, his activities were important enough for him to earn several citations for service.

While he was working on various tasks for Lansdale, Sam went back and forth to the Army Office of the Chief of Special Operations in the Pentagon. Sam had already established contacts in that office during his first tour with the Pentagon, so he took advantage of the freedom he had with his Defense assignment to re-open and continue those relationships. Sam also convinced Lansdale to put him on "jump status." With that status, Sam had permission to go south to Fort Bragg, visiting folks there and jumping out of airplanes with them. During these jaunts, he successfully renewed connections with the tactical elements of special operations.

In August of 1958, after three months with Lansdale in the Office of the Secretary of State, Sam and his family departed Washington for Fort Leavenworth, Kansas, where Sam enrolled in the Army's Command and General Staff College class of 1959. Although he lagged behind his military contemporaries, and the subjects of study rarely appeared familiar to him, Sam relished the experience at the prestigious school. He worked as hard as he had ever worked to keep abreast of his classmates, but the demands on his time were daunting. In order to accomplish all that was necessary, he scheduled every five minutes of his day.

While Sam toiled and studied at his desk nearly every night of that year, his family encouraged and supported him. Their routine was that, at seven o'clock each evening after eating supper together and doing dishes, Sam would enter his study room and begin preparing for the next day's classes. While he worked in his office, Brenda and the children quietly tip-toed around and spoke in whispers so that he had no interruptions. Sam realized the sacrifice required by his wife and children, and that support spoke volumes to him about the familial love they shared.

Support from his family became especially important to Sam when his father, Cap'n Jack, died on February 7, 1958. He left the college for a few days to fly home for the funeral, and while Sam was in Virginia, he experienced the same sensations he always felt when he returned home. It was like coming back to a stage where he had been in a play and the stage setting had not changed at all. The same people were still there, though maybe a little older, conversations were the same, and familiar objects were still in place. It was the closest thing to turning back the clock that he could possibly imagine. In Rice, he could luxuriate with less stress, less tension, and less haste.

Sam graduated from the Command and General Staff College in May of 1959, and thanks to his dedication, he ranked 102nd in the class of 689 officers. He left the college satisfied with his work, especially in light of the many years he had been away from the military arena. On graduation day, he proudly accepted a promotion to Lieutenant Colonel.

Early in 1959, orders came that assigned Sam to an unaccompanied one-year tour to Korea. By this time, his ten-year-old daughter, Susan, had been diagnosed with mental retardation and further handicapped with petit-mal epilepsy. Attending to Susan's needs as well as other everyday family responsibilities severely sapped Brenda's energy. When she learned that Sam was to be gone for a year with only postal contact between them while he would be thousands of miles away in the Pacific, it was more than she could bear.

"I'm sorry," she said, "I have to ask you to request that the Army defer you again to a situation where you can still help me. I can't do it on my own."

There was no way Sam could refuse such an urgent request from his loving wife. All he could do was sigh, turn, and face the wall. One more time he wrote a letter to the Infantry Branch Office of Military Personnel in Washington. He explained his situation and asked for compassion, but he knew that this could well spell the end of his career. Within two weeks of sending his deferral request, he received a letter from the Personnel Office gently explaining that they understood his situation and that he was being re-assigned to the center for special warfare, Fort Bragg North Carolina, where he would either be assigned to the 77th Special Forces Group, or possibly to the Special Warfare School.

It was fortuitous for Sam that the commander of the Special Warfare Center, who was simultaneously the commandant of the Special Warfare School, wanted Sam to be his Director of Instruction. By the grace of God and the Military Personnel Office, Sam walked out of Fort Leavenworth into one of the best jobs he would ever have: Director of Instruction, United States Army Special Warfare School. The Wilsons traded in their old Buick, bought a green Chevrolet station wagon, and drove from Fort Leavenworth, Kansas, through Arkansas, Tennessee, Mississippi, Alabama (where they stopped briefly at Brenda's home), Georgia, and on to North Carolina. They were assigned quarters the day they arrived, and Sam quickly reported to his new job. Though he did not know it at the time, a door was opening that would lead him into unparalleled opportunities.

The Special Warfare School maintained under its auspices a Special Forces training regimen and two principal academic departments, one of which was the Special Forces Department, the other devoted to psychological warfare. While several other elements were also operating, those two focuses commanded the primary resources of the college. The commandant was a legendary paratrooper named Colonel George M. Jones. Colonel Jones boasted a distinguished record from World War II, and Sam quickly found him to be a man of innate leadership competence who was willing to take calculated risks and who displayed keen imagination and creativity. He also possessed willingness to delegate responsibility and couple it with authority. He became an important and influencing figure in Sam's military career.

Soon after Sam joined the college staff, Colonel Jones carefully described Sam's new task. He observed that the United States had blocked the Communists fairly well along the Iron Curtain, both in Europe and in Asia. But the Soviets were pulling end runs on the U.S. by fomenting revolutions in Third World countries—trying to take them over from within. Colonel Jones believed that "it took a thief to catch a thief," and that the U.S. Special Forces needed to adhere more closely to their founding doctrine, which conceived the U.S. Special Forces as revolutionaries and masters of resistance movements and insurrections. Consequently, Jones felt that on his campus, right there on Smoke Bomb Hill, they should find some of the solutions for blocking Communist take-over attempts in impoverished nations. Jones ordered Sam to see what strategies he could devise and what he needed to implement them.

The Special Warfare School housed a number of very bright and somewhat unorthodox officers. Sam organized and began meeting with a group of them in the evenings to discuss Colonel Jones's idea. Eventually, they decided to initiate a new program of instruction (POI). Not surprisingly, it was full of the knowledge that Sam had gained from Lansdale, Soviet expatriates, and the fake movements the Soviet Union had used to fool the U.S. during his time serving in the field with the CIA. All his experiences were coalescing once again, and Sam could not help but feel that an unseen hand must be guiding him from task to task.

The group soon developed the POI. They briefed it to Colonel Jones, and after making minor suggestions, he gave it his approval. Over subsequent months, they continued to refine and improve the concepts, and the new course became one of Colonel Jones's favorite programs at the base.

A few months into the project, a group from CIA, all of whom were reserve officers, came to Fort Bragg to take their two weeks of annual active duty training. As a trial, Sam and his team boiled the new course down to a two-week program. The CIA officers were impressed and, soon afterwards, the Special Warfare School received a visit from the Department of State's "Senior Seminar" of about thirty mid-level Foreign Service officers, every one of them with potential to become an ambassador. The Senior Seminar wanted to learn what the U.S. Army's Special Warfare School had developed to counter Communist-inspired insurgent movements. They were impressed by the program and by Sam's understanding and development of Lansdale's concepts. Even more importantly, they were excited by the potential the course offered in fighting Communist insurrections. Following the visit by the Department of State officers, Assistant Secretary of Defense for International Security Affairs (ASD/ISA) John M. Irwin III arrived with a special group of staff officers to be briefed on the new program. Secretary Irwin also was encouraged by the potential of the project and felt strongly that it was something the government needed to support.

Late one night, Sam and the team were working in their offices on Smoke Bomb Hill as they struggled to assign a name to the thematic aegis under which the entire project would be placed. They couldn't call it "Counter-Resistance operations," because from the United States' exprience in World War II, "resistance" had a positive connotation, while "Counter-Guerilla operations" failed because it was too narrow. They were combating more than just enemy guerillas. "Counter-Revolutionary" could not be used because it was the Soviet's derogatory term for dissenters. At about 2:30 a.m. that morning Sam stood up at the board and wrote "Counter-Insurgency," a term that fit precisely and one that has been used for the program since that night. For a number of years, the term became a buzzword in Washington, especially during the Kennedy administration.

As the program continued to develop and interest in it grew among Washington insiders, the Department of State, the CIA, and the Agency for International Development each offered to send liaison officers to Fort Bragg to advise and assist with the program. Fort Bragg scheduled the first major course, which would last twelve weeks, to begin in January of 1961.

To Sam's surprise, the Army decided that the program was too political in nature, and they refused to help fund it or to send any students to attend the course. Secretary of Defense Irwin, however, who believed in the program's merits, agreed to provide funding for the first course offering. He also suggested that they canvas allied and friendly foreign countries, especially in the under-developed world, to determine which would like to send students to the program. The first course included a future president of the Republic of South Vietnam, two future ministers of the Republic of South Vietnam, and military officers who rose to positions of great political importance in South and Central America.

During the time that Sam and the team worked on their Counter-Insurgency program, Sam flew to Hollywood, where Warner Brothers had purchased the rights to *The Marauders,* a book published in April 1959 and written by Sam's good friend, Charleton Ogburn, Jr. The main character of the movie was based largely on Sam's adventures in Burma during 1943. Sam had heard that Warner Brothers had bought the movie rights to the book and that Colonel Hunter had been invited to spend some time with them during the filming. Sam's good friend and fellow I and R platoon leader, Logan Weston, had visited the set as well. But people in Hollywood wanted to talk further with Sam. In early December 1960, Warner Brothers requested that he be assigned temporary duty for full time services as technical advisor to the feature motion picture production.

Colonel Jones realized the movie would be good for Sam personally and good publicity for Fort Bragg, but he felt that the handling of the Counter-Insurgency course would be more beneficial for the country as a whole. Unless Sam could find someone to cover the course for him for the six months he would be on set in the Philippines, Sam would have to turn down Warner Brothers' offer. Sam immediately phoned his buddy, Logan Weston, who at that time was holding a staff job in the Army Personnel Office. Weston hesitated to accept Sam's proposal for fear that he lacked the qualifications to run the project that Sam had been creating for a year, so Sam flew to Washington and spent an evening with Weston talking about the parameters of the Counter-Insurgency course. When Weston agreed to assume Sam's duties, Sam was free to pursue the offer from Hollywood.

As a technical advisor on the movie set, Sam earned one hundred dollars a day to cover sundry expenses, while the production company provided meals, lodging, and transportation. With his per-diem allowance, Sam saved enough money for a new washer and dryer and deep-freezer for his family, who were waiting for him back at Fort Bragg. That contribution made Sam feel as if he had provided some compensation for his prolonged absence.

Sam and Brenda Wilson in 1962, before the première
of the "Merrill's Marauders" movie in Farmville.

IN THE OFFICE OF THE SECRETARY OF DEFENSE AND THE CUBAN MISSILE CRISIS

WHILE THIRTY-EIGHT-YEAR-OLD Sam Wilson was consulting Warner Brothers on the feature production of *Merrill's Marauders,* forty-three-year-old John F. Kennedy was sworn into office as the President of the United States. Kennedy brought a new generation of young Democrats with him to power in Washington, including the new Secretary of Defense, forty-four-year-old Robert S. McNamara, who had already had a successful career as president of Ford Motor Company. The brilliant and youthful crowd that Kennedy brought to Washington was soon dubbed the "whiz kids," and although Sam did not know it at the time, he would wind up working alongside many of these new additions to the Executive Branch.

Kennedy entered office and immediately faced a rapidly developing foreign policy problem in Vietnam. The President and those around him in Washington saw the conflict developing in that country as a key attempt by Moscow to promote and establish Communist dominion in Southeast Asia, much like the North Korean invasion of South Korea in 1950. On January 6, 1961, Soviet Premier Nikita Khrushchev delivered a major policy speech before a gathering of world Communists in Moscow. It did nothing to alleviate Washington's fears. In his speech, Khrushchev stressed the importance of international Communist support for wars of national liberation in underdeveloped countries. The essence of his speech blatantly exposed what Colonel Jones had already suggested to Sam at Fort Bragg—the new Soviet strategy was to support guerilla/insurgent movements as a means for Communism to dominate countries from the inside. Kennedy immediately seized upon the importance of understanding the Soviet Premier's speech. He had it translated into English, sent copies to each of his cabinet members and their staffs, and insisted that they all become acquainted with the content of Khrushchev's message.

In the wake of Washington's heightened sensitivity to subversive warfare, Kennedy sought the expertise of Colonel Ed Lansdale and decided to find an appointment for Lansdale that would put him in the middle of the action to counter the Soviet's advances. He initially offered Lansdale the ambassadorship to Vietnam, primarily because of the close personal relationship between Lansdale and the president of Vietnam, but the new Secretary of State, Dean Rusk, objected vehemently and warned Kennedy that he would resign if Lansdale were appointed Ambassador to Vietnam. Kennedy deferred to Rusk's demands, but he saw to it that Lansdale was promoted to the position of Assistant to the Secretary of Defense for Special Operations so that this knowledgeable veteran could actively shape American policy for countering Soviet activity.

Sam was just finishing his work on *Merrill's Marauders* in June of 1961, when he learned that Lansdale had been promoted to the new position. Because of their past relationship, he was not surprised when Lansdale cabled him from the Philippines to offer the position of Deputy Assistant to the Secretary of Defense for Special Operations. Sam readily agreed to the assignment, and after reuniting with his family at Fort Bragg, he moved with them to Washington for another tour of duty with the man he respected more than anyone else alive at the time, newly promoted Brigadier General Edward G. Lansdale.

His assignment as Deputy Assistant to the Secretary of Defense for Special Operations represented the apex of Sam's Special Operations experience during his life in uniform. His career had already been uncommonly varied. He had been a First Lieutenant in Burma with the Marauders as Merrill's chief reconnaissance officer, had been involved in some Special Operations while working for the CIA in the clandestine arena, and at Fort Bragg had focused on developing doctrine and creating workable responses for Special Operations. But this was Sam's first position at the policy level of Special Operations, with a seat at the table with other significant leaders in the area. An added incentive to accept the post as a policy maker came when Sam realized that, though his military rank at the time was Lieutenant Colonel, the civilian rank that went with the new job was equivalent to that of a two-star (Major) General.

As he moved into his new role, Sam continued developing contacts and friendly relationships with key people who would be in Washington for a long time and with whom Sam would work again. He carefully cultivated relationships with individuals in the Department of State, members of the National Security Council staff, and his old friends in the CIA. Sam had learned over the years how valuable these connections could be.

Sam's office complex was comprised of twelve to fifteen people, with representation from each of the military services, including officers with various Special Operations capabilities and a senior liaison officer from the CIA. Shortly after Sam arrived in the Washington office, Lansdale departed for a trip to Vietnam for several weeks, and in his absence Sam was left in charge. During this period, Sam had opportunities to develop relationships with both Secretary of Defense McNamara as well as his deputy, Roswell Gilpatric, a prominent lawyer from New York. Because of the tremendous span of control the Secretary of Defense had over the multi-billion dollar empire of the Department of Defense, it had long ago become necessary to delegate much of the responsibility to the Deputy Secretary. The outcome of this arrangement made Gilpatric's position as Deputy Secretary of Defense by far the most powerful sub-cabinet position in the Executive Branch. Over the weeks when Lansdale was in Vietnam, Sam crossed paths with Gilpatric often, and the two men developed a congenial friendship.

In response to the heightened concern over Communist subversive warfare, the Kennedy administration created a highly sensitive, top-level policy group called "the Special Group/Counter Insurgency" (SG/CI). Members of this group included Attorney General Robert Kennedy; the military representative of the President General Maxwell D. Taylor; Deputy Secretary of Defense Roswell Gilpatric; Director of the CIA Allen Dulles, who was often represented by his deputy; Chairman of the Joint Chiefs of Staff Lyman Lemnitzer; and Deputy Undersecretary of State U. Alexis Johnson. Other senior governmental officials were called in from time to time on an as-needed basis to augment group discussion. SG/CI was a very busy group thrust right where the current action was in the international arena, and Sam's responsibilities as Lansdale's assistant often put him in the midst of the powerful group.

One of Sam's primary duties was to provide staffing support for SG/CI through Lansdale's boss, Roswell Gilpatric. Gilpatric frequently took Sam to SG/CI meetings, and occasionally he requested that Sam provide briefings before the group on the overall subject of Special Operations. Initially, Sam thought it was unusual for Lansdale to delegate these sensitive tasks to him, but later he realized that because of the volume of the work the SG/CI required, his boss was keeping himself free to concentrate on other priorities.

During his tenure with the Department of Defense, Sam was an active participant in the most threatening and dramatic international event of Kennedy's administration: the Cuban Missile Crisis. The Cuban Missile Crisis tested the resolve and nerve of everyone in Washington and Sam's sometimes brash and unorthodox but always productive actions during the crisis distinguished him among his peers and gained him the respect of his superiors.

One of Kennedy's political platforms before the 1960 Presidential election was the dominance of the Soviets in missile capabilities. He asserted that the U.S. was very much outgunned by the Soviets in term of nuclear-tipped intercontinental missiles and that Eisenhower had fallen asleep at the switch, allowing the Soviets to establish almost insurmountable strategic superiority in weapons. In actuality, Eisenhower knew that this was not the case. Reliable intelligence showed that the Soviets were bluffing about their capabilities to the extent that nuclear-warhead count estimated about five thousand for the U.S. and three hundred for the Soviets. In the early 1960s, the Soviets could not rocket a warhead beyond Europe while the U.S. could reach every part of the Soviet Union. But this information had been obtained through such secret and highly sensitive methods that Eisenhower could not reveal Kennedy's error. In part, Kennedy won the election by basing his campaign on unsubstantiated statistics and, two years later, the Soviet's actual missile deficiency persuaded Khrushchev that it was necessary to put medium and intermediate range missiles within range of American soil.

In early winter of 1962, Khrushchev and the Soviets began preparing to ship nuclear-capable medium and intermediate range missiles to Cuba with plans to aim them towards American cities and other strategic U.S. targets. The United States began to learn about the planned installation of these Soviet missiles in Cuba beginning in late August of that year. On Monday, 15 October 1962, President Kennedy and his cabinet received pictures photographed by a U-2 high altitude reconnaissance aircraft. They showed the SS-4 medium-range nuclear missiles being shipped by a Soviet convoy to Havana, and accompanying intelligence reports detailed the planned installation of these Soviet missiles in Cuba beginning in late August. Kennedy knew he had to respond. He could not allow those SS-4s to be installed so close to American soil. The countdown to Armageddon began. The crisis, later detailed by Robert F. Kennedy, Jr., in his book, *Thirteen Days: The Cuban Missile Crisis,* played out with a situation that was palpably tense, not just for Washingtonians but also for ordinary U.S. citizens. A great deal of behind-the-scenes secret communication transpired as the United States attempted to dissuade the Soviets from their intentions. Finally, on October 28, just before additional missiles reached the pivotal quarantine line in the Atlantic, Soviet transport ships carrying the missiles slowly turned around and headed back to Moscow, and Americans heaved a collective sigh of relief. Khrushchev's subsequent speech revealed that he had backed down, but the crisis brought us closer to a nuclear exchange with the Soviets than at any other time during the four decades of the Cold War.

The handling of the Cuban Missile crisis was a fast-paced operation, the highest intensity that Sam had witnessed since active combat. The urgency of the situation forced Sam to take action in the name of the Secretary of Defense, in some instances without clearing the action in advance before making decisions above his rank. He had to exploit his "authority by association." "The Secretary of Defense wants . . . " or "Mr. McNamara would like to have . . . " became phrases that Sam occasionally employed to get otherwise impossible work accomplished. Despite Sam's efforts to keep his superior abreast of his activities, he soon learned that, as a young officer close to the seat of power, he was playing a very dangerous game.

During the period when all evidence suggested that Khrushchev was intractable in his resolve to establish missile bases in the western hemisphere, the U.S. began preparing to invade Cuba. The Kennedy administration realized that it would be advantageous for Special Forces teams to infiltrate Cuba ahead of an invasion to establish contacts and support with anti-Castro elements in that country. In an effort to identify potential anti-Castro groups within Cuba, they called on recent Cuban refugees. Preparations were fast-paced, as all planning, training, and positioning had to be accomplished before the missiles were in place. In reality, the operation could only be accomplished if a tremendous amount of red tape were ignored.

Working with Sam on this project was a young staffer named Joseph Califano, one of the junior "whiz kids" in the Office of the Secretary of Defense and a man who later became the Secretary of Health, Education, and Welfare in the Jimmy Carter administration. At the time, however, Califano was simply a bright, civilian staff officer working alongside Sam. The two worked all day and all night for seventy-two hours to set up the process for young Cuban refugees to be identified, recruited, indoctrinated, trained, and then inserted as members of Special Forces' teams prepared to infiltrate Cuba. When Sam and Califano hit bureaucratic log jams, they would drop the name of superiors to make things happen, thus circumventing a bureaucratic system that otherwise would not respond quickly, even in a crisis. They had to bluff, cajole, and fake to make the necessary arrangements within their extremely truncated timeframe.

One of Sam's projects involved communicating the Americans' intentions to the Cuban people. Since Castro controlled all the public communication outlets in the country with an iron grip, it was difficult to access the mass news media in Cuba. Sam needed to help solve this dilemma, and he needed to solve it quickly. With others, he came up with a solution, but he knew he would never succeed, at least not in time to be of value, if he followed all of the procurement procedures prescribed by law. Sam circumvented the lengthy legal channels and found people who could do what he wanted, told them to do it, and billed the government for their services. Much like his efforts to assist the training of the Cuban Special Forces teams, he occasionally had to overstep his ranking.

Sam's solution was to work with the U. S. Air Force to equip two EC-121 aircraft with a television station suite and independent transmission abilities and position each plane in international airspace just off the coast of Cuba. There, the planes could loiter and transmit American communication to Cuba with sufficient power to blot out Castro's local stations. The airplanes also broadcasted by radio from the same aerial platforms. The operation was dubbed "Caronet Solo," and although it was expensive, this technique became so important to the U.S. military that it was retained from that point on as a part of the American Armed Forces capability. Eventually, for daily operational control, it was placed under the Pennsylvania Air National Guard, where it still remains.

To augment television and radio broadcasts from aerial platforms, Sam realized the benefit of having a stronger land-to-land radio signal to Cuba. Using the name and the authority of the Secretary of Defense, he commandeered an army radio station that was being shipped to Laos. Sam ordered it taken off the docks in San Francisco, had the pieces put in trucks and vans and organized for shipment to the southeastern coast where it could be used during the crisis. The radio station was assembled on Dog Island in the Gulf of Mexico, where it had a clean transmission to Cuba, and though it was expensive, stepped on some toes, and stretched a few laws, Sam believed the radio project was necessary.

One of the most exciting moments of Sam's life occurred while he was preparing for the potential conflict with Cuba and the Soviets. Late one night, sometime between midnight and two in the morning, Sam sat in the Oval Office of the White House with President Kennedy, the acting head of the U.S. Information Agency (USIA), and a successful businessman from Detroit surnamed Wilson, though of no relation to Sam. This Wilson and that Wilson assisted President Kennedy as he personally composed a propaganda leaflet that pictured a Soviet nuclear missile field and launchers, with a caption describing their purposes and why it was necessary for America to force their removal.

The President himself chose the words to express the dangers the missiles posed to the United Sates and to appeal for understanding of the U.S. position from the Cuban people. When the draft was finished, Sam put the leaflet in an envelope and gave it to a courier officer who piggybacked on a U.S. Air Force F80 jet from Andrews Air Force Base in Washington to Pope Air Force Base at Fort Bragg, where he delivered it to the Commander of the Army's Special Warfare Center, Brigadier General William P. Yarborough. At Fort Bragg the leaflet was edited, translated into Spanish, and then printed. In short order Yarborough's Psychological Operations Group had four million copies ready to scatter over Cuba in preparation for a United States invasion. The pamphlets remained at Fort Brag for two years, until Sam received a message from Fort Bragg while he was on assignment in Vietnam, "Colonel Wilson, what are we supposed to do with these four million Cuban leaflets that we are holding here in the warehouse?"

As tensions increased between the rival superpowers, the very real possibility of the Soviets releasing their nuclear missiles against targets in the United States loomed heavily over the Western hemisphere. The U.S. was at the brink of war, and people knew it, although the public did not realize as well as Sam and Washington insiders how precarious the situation had become. As one of those insiders, Sam recognized the true extent of the threat, and he called his brother, who lived in rural Virginia, some three hours south of D.C., to arrange emergency sanctuary for his family and the families of other members of his office. It was a controversial step to take. Not everyone in Washington could be included in his planning, but Sam felt it important to do what he could to assure the safety of his colleagues and of his family. When he finalized the project, he called his entire staff into his office and gave them each a sealed envelope with emergency instructions. When the moment came, and Sam believed *when* was more likely than *if,* he would pass the word to open the envelopes, and they would execute as quickly as possible the enclosed instructions to safeguard themselves and their families.

Several months after the Cuban Missile Crisis had passed without dire consequences, two gentlemen with dark suits and black briefcases walked into Sam's office to speak to him about a very confidential matter. The purpose of their visit, they explained, was to ask Sam where the government was to find the ninety million dollars required to fund the projects that Sam had initiated in the name of the Secretary of Defense during the Cuban Missile Crisis. Sam had assumed that those expenditures had already been covered, and he had to admit to the two agents that he did not know the answer. Sam realized that he might be indicted for his fast and loose use of government money during the crisis. He worried his way through anxious days until nearly a week later, when the Secretary of Defense issued instructions to approve the expenditures from funds available to him.

Sam resolved that, from them on, if he ever found himself in the midst of another crisis, he would have someone with budgeting experience sit beside him to keep track of any money he was spending on behalf of the government. He needed to know the sources for funds and necessary expenditure approvals so that he was protected after the crisis had passed. Fortunately, in this case, Sam's actions brought him positive recognition. In fact, he received high applause from both McNamara and Gilpatric. Some months later, when he was already a student at the Air War College at Maxwell Air Force base in Montgomery, Alabama, Sam was called out of class to receive a long-distance phone call from the Deputy Secretary of Defense. Secretary Gilpatric informed Sam that he had been moved to the top of the promotion list for becoming a full Colonel. The honor was a reward for his performance when he was working for McNamara and Gilpatric, especially during the Cuban Missile Crisis.

Gaining recognition for his initiative and action during the tense days of the crisis was gratifying, but as Sam considered his role in the Defense Department, he realized the danger of power by association. He resolved that he would always act in well thought out and balanced ways, even in the peak of a crisis, so that he could avoid any abuse of power, even when his superiors allowed or even encouraged it. He further resolved never to forget that he was dealing with deadly serious situations that required good judgment and careful wielding of power.

With the Cuban Missile Crisis behind them, the Office of the Secretary of Defense redirected attention to problems in Vietnam. During an earlier period of duty in that country, Lansdale had established an extraordinarily close relationship with the President of South Vietnam, Ngo Dinh Diem. By 1963, Ngo Dinh Diem was mired in the crisis of a Communist-inspired and supported insurgency from Communist North Vietnam. For several years, Diem asked Washington to send Lansdale back to Saigon to work with him, but Washington had refused his requests. Lansdale's unorthodox methods had earned him considerable hostility from within the bureaucracy. There were a number of people who believed that returning Lansdale to South Vietnam was too risky.

During the months of December 1962 and January 1963, Diem's calls for Lansdale began to come to Washington more frequently and in increased volume. McNamara was opposed to Lansdale returning, even on a visit, so Lansdale asked Sam if he would go on the trip in his stead. For the public, they would describe the assignment as a staff orientation visit, but Lansdale would arrange for Sam to meet with President Diem while he was there. In late January 1963, Sam flew to Vietnam with an armful of Lansdale's handwritten letters to important figures in both the Philippines and Vietnam, including President Diem. Sam remained in South Vietnam for about ten days, during which he attended to numerous tasks for the Defense Department, joined South Vietnamese military paratroopers in a jungle operation, and visited U.S. Special Forces camps along the mountainous western Vietnamese border.

Sam left Lansdale's letter with President Diem's executive assistant on the very first day he arrived in Saigon, but he heard nothing from the President until the evening before his departure. Late that night, he received a message from the President's office that Diem wished to see him early the following morning.

Sam reported to the waiting room of the President's office promptly the next morning and was quickly ushered into his personal office. Through an interpreter, Diem spent the next several hours in a monologue of complaints about the war, his many problems, and his need for Lansdale to return. Meanwhile, Sam was checking his watch. He was all too aware that his Pan-American Airways flight for the United States was scheduled to depart Saigon at 10:30 that morning. Finally, as his departure time approached, he cautiously interrupted the President to say that he was scheduled to be on a commercial flight out of Saigon some thirty minutes hence and needed to leave their meeting. Diem turned to his interpreter. "Tell them to hold the plane," he ordered.

Then he resumed his one-way conversation with Sam until noon. When Sam could finally disengage himself and hurry to the Tan Son Nhut Airport, he arrived to find that the plane was still sitting at the gate with the engines idling and its passengers sweltering in the Saigon heat. On his return to Washington, Sam reported the essence of Diem's message to Lansdale, and Lansdale reported Diem's pleas to his superiors. Once again, no action was taken, and the position of South Vietnam and its President remained precarious.

AIR WAR COLLEGE AND VIETNAM

WHILE SAM WAS SERVING in the Secretary of Defense's Office, he faced a familiar situation of conflicting demands. Early in 1962, at the age of thirty-nine, he again received an appointment to the National War College, but both Robert McNamara and Ed Lansdale counseled Sam that his work at his current post was essential, and they could not afford to let him go. They promised, however, that if he would defer the appointment for just one year, they would ensure that he could attend the war college of his choice at that time. Sam agreed to stay in the Secretary of Defense's Office and, once again, the people in Army Personnel threw up their hands and said, "Wilson is as crazy as ever. He's committing career suicide again."

The next summer, when the time for his enrollment came, Sam selected the Air War College, a decision he based on his favorable experience in 1943-1944, when the Air Force did so much to help him behind Japanese lines in Burma. The Marauders had depended on planes for food, water, weapons, evacuations, and support for their ground operations, and Sam had not forgotten how the relationship between the ground and air troops had enabled Merrill's Marauders to survive and operate effectively. He wanted to learn more about air power and about how air power and ground power could best collaborate.

Sam accepted his appointment to the Air War College for the school year beginning in the fall of 1963. In August of that year, the Wilson family emptied their Washington home and once again moved south, this time to the outskirts of Montgomery, Alabama. Brenda was back in her beloved home state and only an hour-and-a-half drive from her father's home. The whole family reveled in the new appointment that promised a less demanding schedule than Sam had ever enjoyed. Indeed, the Air War College proved to be a gentleman's course, relaxing and non-taxing, giving students enough time to read, fish, hunt, and be with their families.

Sam particularly enjoyed the guest speaker program at the Air War College. About three times a week, various prominent American public figures would give guest presentations to the class. Their speeches fascinated

Sam because they were so relevant to his career and to the fate of his country. Much of the rest of his class time was spent in directed seminars led by highly-select officers. At the end of the year, Sam was honored to be named the distinguished graduate of the United States Air War College, class of 1964. From his point of view, the year there had been so enjoyable that it was more like a sabbatical than an official appointment.

In the spring of his session with the Air War College, Sam learned that the Air War College had requested of the Army Personnel Office that he be given a three-year assignment as a member of their faculty. Although it was not an appointment that would lead him to positions of higher responsibility, it would be a comfortable and enjoyable one. When he shared the news with Brenda, she was ecstatic. She and Sam both agreed that though a faculty position might not further his career, it would be beneficial for the entire family. Sam could spend time with them, more time than had been possible with any other assignment. Just as he was preparing to settle into Montgomery family life, however, Sam got a phone call from Ed Lansdale asking that he report to Washington to be interviewed for a key job in Vietnam.

One of the most successful programs run by the United States in Vietnam was a grass roots economic project under the auspices of the United States Operations Mission (USOM) in Saigon, a program that was being handled by the Assistant Director of USOM's Office of Rural Affairs. The incumbent director of that office, Rufus Philips II, a brilliant officer, was relinquishing his position and had returned to Washington. Consequently, one of the most promising operations in Vietnam was left without a leader. Washington was casting about intensely, trying to find a suitable replacement for the director, and Lansdale offered Sam's name as a promising candidate. Thus Sam was offered this position and assigned to the U.S. Foreign Service on a temporary basis under the provisions of a rather obscure piece of legislation called the Participating Agency Service Agreement (PASA). PASA allowed the Foreign Service to bestow upon its appointees whatever rank and pay level was appropriate for their duties, and under the auspices of PASA, Sam was placed on temporary duty with the Foreign Service to work with the Agency for International Development (AID) as a reserve Foreign Service Officer at a rank equivalent to an Army Major General, quite a promotion for a Lieutenant Colonel. Sam relished the new duties and the opportunity to join another challenging and creative field of responsibility.

A disappointed Brenda agreed to remain for the first year of this new assignment in their existing quarters in Montgomery, where she would have the support of her family nearby. Since it was Sam Jr's first year at the University of Alabama, she would be close enough to offer support during his acclimation to college life. Then, if Sam's tour of duty were extended beyond one year, she would have the option of moving to the Philippines or to Thailand to live with other American military families. In Asia, she would be close enough that Sam could visit for long weekends. The next summer when, not surprisingly to either of them, Sam's tenure in Vietnam was extended, Brenda relocated to the summer capital of the Philippines, Baguio, a beautiful mountain city about one hundred miles north of Manila. Once his family was living just a plane ride away, Sam was able to visit Brenda and the two younger children with some regularity.

The conflict in South Vietnam represented a classic case of a Communist-supported insurgent political organization endeavoring to subvert an existing government from within. The Communist underground organization in South Vietnam called itself the "National Liberation Front," and their paramilitary arm referred to themselves as the Viet Cong. The Viet Cong had developed an extensive underground network of spies, informers, and couriers, and they had a well-organized guerilla force, many of whom were Vietnamese farmers working in rice paddies during the day and at night becoming black-pajama-wearing warriors carrying AK-47s and attacking South Vietnamese targets.

The Office of Rural Affairs, of which Sam had been appointed director, worked to help local governments be more effective and responsive to the needs and wants of the indigenous people. South Vietnam consisted of forty-four provinces, and a USOM representative with a small staff was located in each province. Their charge was to assist in improving the local economy, and their efforts included agricultural assistance, road building, especially farm-to-market roads, construction of irrigation systems, and rudimentary public health services. Beyond their economic concerns, one of USOM's major focuses was to improve the local education system. They also studied the country's widespread saltwater intrusion problem and found that digging deep wells of fresh pure water was one of the most helpful things they could do for the local peasantry. Because of the constant struggle between the republican government's forces and the Viet Cong, there was a steady and growing stream of refugees from areas in which the fighting was most intense, and the USOM took part in establishing refugee camps to meet the needs of displaced people until they could be resettled.

The old Office of Rural Affairs, which under Sam's direction became known as the Office of Field Operations of the Aid Mission, attracted a number of very interesting people from various walks of life. Among the USOM personnel in the South Vietnamese provinces were fifteen young Foreign Service Officers. Although it was the first Foreign Service tour for most of them, nine of the young officers would eventually go on to become ambassadors. In addition to the young Foreign Service Officers, there were several retired military men, unconventional and unorthodox singletons who loved the outdoors. There was also a deputy sheriff from Orange County, California, a former champion prizefighter, several former actors, and teachers. Basically, the people Sam worked with loved to attempt things that were dangerous and exciting but had a chance of great success. They relished helping people to secure themselves, grow better rice, enjoy better health, form strong government institutions, and they were gratified when, through their efforts, they won locals over to the side of the government in Saigon. The heterogeneous group members were volunteer salesmen for democracy.

Sam worked at this task almost eighteen hours a day, seven days a week, for about twenty months. He traveled daily throughout the countryside to monitor his subordinates in the field and to ensure that various forms of support (building materials, wheat, rice seed, or live poultry) were getting to their desired destinations. He worked with Special Forces detachments that operated in concert with the rebel anti-Communist forces along the mountainous Cambodian and Laotian borders. He also worked with CIA operatives stationed in the South Vietnamese countryside, helping where he could to establish intelligence nets and providing support as the men developed and trained the natives to fight against the Viet Cong.

Often at the end of a long day, as he prepared to leave some remote village and return to his office in Saigon, Sam would turn to local provincial officials and pose a somewhat rhetorical question in his broken Vietnamese: "Tell me, my friends, what have the Viet Cong done for you today?"

They would avert their eyes and scuff their sandals in the dirt, avoiding a direct answer to his smart-alecky question. Point made, Sam would then climb aboard his helicopter and flutter back to the capital city, quite pleased with himself and even more pleased with the accomplishments of his volunteers.

One day, while going about his regular check-up routine in the Mekong Delta, Sam was caught in the middle of a very bloody firefight. Fortunately, this was one of the rare occasions when the Army of South Vietnam emerged victorious over the Viet Cong. Indeed, they found the Viet Cong battalion commander sprawled beside the trail with half his leg missing and a gaping wound in his left shoulder. Sam bent down over the man and gave him a cigarette while somebody else gave him a shot of morphine and brought him some tea. They were waiting for a helicopter to evacuate the VC commander for further treatment and interrogation when Sam decided to see what he could learn from the man. He gave Sam no tactical intelligence whatsoever, but as Sam pursued questions that reached more distantly into the man's past, he found he was willing to talk about his own life. At twelve years of age, the man had been recruited as a courier to fight against the French in the first Indo-Chinese War. He had been sent south carrying two rounds of mortar ammunition. After marching hundreds of miles, he delivered his package to a gunner, who promptly discharged the rounds towards the enemy and told the young boy to return home for another load.

The Vietnamese boy had no intention of walking hundreds of miles just to bring another inconsequential load for someone to shoot aimlessly into the dark, so he stayed with the rebels from that point on and fought as a guerilla. He had been wounded five times, nearly died from fevers, and could show several scars from fights he survived as a Viet Cong guerilla. As he talked, there emerged a picture of dismal human deprivation. The man's whole life was a gripping story of human suffering.

When the wounded man paused for breath, Sam offered him another cigarette and saw to it that he was given another injection of morphine. Then, with the sound of a helicopter approaching in the distance, Sam asked him, in the best Vietnamese he could muster, "Tell me, my friend, what did the Viet Cong ever do for you?" In response, the man rose up on his one good arm, glared balefully at Sam through morphine-glazed eyes, and spat at him. "They gave me the chance to sacrifice."

The comment worried Sam. There were few natives who carried equivalent dedication to capitalism.

Sam soon learned that he had to be aware of the cultural difference between an American working in a foreign area and the indigenous people. Vietnamese did not think or act like Americans, and when U.S. troops attempted to elicit American-like reactions from them, they failed. One example of the difference between the two cultures was evident after Sam endeavored to improve the breeding stock of some hogs that were being raised in one of the Vietnamese provinces along the coast of the South China Sea.

When Sam first visited that province, he was taken to some of the hog farms. He was struck by the small size and overall appearance of the hogs. They were hardly larger than small dogs: thin, razor-backed, and hairy. While they were strong and their meat was delicious, the pigs were too lean to produce much grease. Sam figured that by helping them breed larger hogs, he could show these farmers how to achieve better results from the tremendous effort they were expending on the small razor-backs. Representatives from AID in Washington went to the Midwest to locate a big boar hog.

The hog they secured for Sam weighed about 300 pounds and had a pedigree as long as an arm. It was a regal animal, with a Latin name, something like "Gustavus Adolphus Maximilian VII." Sam approved the pig for the mission, so the U.S. military flew Gus in solitary splendor across the Pacific Ocean in the belly of a C130. He landed on a dirt airstrip near the town of Binh Dinh, where Sam organized a welcoming celebration and ribbon cutting for his arrival. Gus was loaded into a big crate on the back of a truck, and he was taken out to one of the hog farms. There, they turned him loose in the big hog lot with a bunch of small sows. Sam worried a bit when he realized that Gus was huge in comparison to the small females, but he figured that love would find a way, and he left the issue for others to monitor.

About six months later, Sam returned to check on Gus. He was met by the Province Chief and the Assistant Province Chief of Agriculture. When he asked them how the pig was doing, they said that he was the most wonderful thing they had ever seen. Sam drove with them to the hog farm, and there, standing proudly like a small elephant, was a mountain of a hog, easily two hundred pounds heavier than when Sam had left him. Sam could hardly see the pig's eyes because his cheeks were so fat. He was shocked by the hog's altered appearance. The Assistant to the Chief for Agriculture filled him in on

Sam Wilson with Vietnamese village children.

the South Vietnamese's incredible pig-growing secret: "Yes, it's amazing how they grow when you castrate them." Sam had to shake his head and move on.

A highly time-consuming aspect of Sam's work involved hosting visits by important people—mostly American congressmen, senators, well-known correspondents, governors, and figures from the American entertainment world. For example, Sam spent a week with the president of Columbia Broadcasting System, traveled around the countryside with the Deputy Secretary of State, briefed and escorted a delegation headed by Senator Edward Kennedy, and spent ten days acquainting former Vice-President Richard Nixon with the dynamics of the war in Vietnam.

Richard Nixon came to Vietnam twice during Sam's tenure there—once in 1965, when Sam gave him a tour of the countryside, and again in the late summer of 1966, when Sam hosted Nixon at his house. There were aspects of Nixon that impressed Sam. First, he was a very quick study. On one flight across the country, Sam advised Nixon, "Mr. Vice President, the war in Vietnam is a forty-four-province war, with a different conflict being fought in each province, so we can't take a cookie-cutter approach. We have to adapt to the local situation. The war in Vietnam is a political struggle with violent military overtones. It's a struggle that has to be won by the Vietnamese themselves, with our intelligence support and its systems. But we cannot win it for them. The most important American in this struggle is the official down below the province level—the American district advisor. The most important Vietnamese in this war is the district chief. It is at that level that we will win."

When the plane landed, newsmen greeted them on the airstrip. "Mr. Vice President, how are you enjoying your visit? What things have you learned about the War here in Vietnam?"

To the flurry of inquiries, Nixon calmly replied, "I've always said that the war in Vietnam is a forty-four-province war, and it has to be fought according to the specifications of each province. This is a political struggle that has to be fought on the district level . . . " He repeated almost word for word what Sam had just been telling him. Sam shook his head in amazement. The man had a mind like a tape recorder.

During Nixon's last visit, while Sam was serving as the U.S. Mission Coordinator and working directly for Ambassador Henry Cabot Lodge, they were having drinks together in Sam's quarters on a Saturday evening before they were scheduled to helicopter to a Southern province the following Sunday morning. Sam began telling Nixon about how he was providing information about the war in Vietnam back to Farmville to his brother John at WFLO in Farmville, Virginia. John would send him a list of questions, and Sam would take his portable tape recorder and find himself a spot where there was an interesting background of war-related sound, such as planes landing and taking off or the sound of a hot firefight, just to provide a little atmosphere. There, Sam would carefully read his brother's question into the recorder and give his response to the question. Then he would read the next question and give his response to it. When the tape arrived back at WFLO in the mail, his brother would sit down with his taping equipment and dub his voice over Sam's where the question was being asked. The effect was to produce an interview that sounded like a real-time conversation taking place between two brothers, one asking questions and the other providing answers, with the sounds in the background emphasizing that something of interest was going on in Vietnam.

Nixon laughed and said it was a great idea. Then Sam asked Nixon if he would be willing to join him in his next production during the trip they were to take the next morning, with the helicopter blade whopping in the background. Nixon and Sam orchestrated the recording so that John would be able to make it sound like a three-way conversation. In order to add even more reality, Sam held up a 3x5 card, saying, "John Wilson speaking," to indicate that Nixon should direct his response to Sam's brother. Nixon then began his responses with phrases like, "Well, John, Sam and I were talking about that just last night..." They did everything they could to make it sound like a folksy three-way discussion. Not surprisingly, the tape was a huge hit for WFLO radio in Farmville.

When Nixon flew through Manila en route to the States, he called Sam's wife to let her know how much he appreciated the support she provided Sam. He called her in the middle of a typhoon, so the connection was fuzzy, and at first Brenda was a little confused, not knowing to whom she was talking or what he was trying to say. Eventually, however, she pieced together the situation. When she hung up the phone, she rushed to tell the children who had just called her and what he had said. The future President of the United States also wrote thoughtful letters to Sam's son at the University of Alabama, to his daughter at the Evergreen Presbyterian Vocational School in Louisiana, and to his brother, John Wilson, at WFLO Farmville, telling them that he had worked with Sam and enjoyed their time together. Sam never forgot Nixon's thoughtfulness.

One of Sam's projects in Saigon was to work with young Vietnamese students at the University of Saigon in an effort to encourage their interest in the economic assistance work he was doing in the countryside. As Sam was initiating the project, then-U.S. Ambassador Maxwell Taylor asked Sam to come to the Embassy and read a cable that had just arrived from Washington. The cable informed him that twenty college and graduate-level students from across the United States had been selected to visit Vietnam for a firsthand look at the war. It was 1965, when student anti-war protests were just getting underway, so Ambassador Taylor was inclined to reject these students. Sam did not agree. He suggested that Taylor turn the students over to him so that he could put them to useful work.

The students soon arrived from prestigious schools like The University of California-Berkeley, Tufts University, and The University of Michigan. Sam assigned each one to a separate provincial representative in one of the forty-four provinces of the country. He told his representatives to allow the students to participate in real projects and to let them work hard for the summer. For his part, he checked on them frequently, and he found that, for the most part, they were excited about what they were doing. In fact, they saw the war in a light that was different from what they had envisioned in the United States. When fall 1965 approached and it was time for them to leave Vietnam and return to their schools, Sam suggested to Ambassador Taylor that they have a special presentation for the U.S. and foreign media as part of the standard daily press briefing that was given by the Joint U.S. Public Affairs Office (JUSPAO).

Each day at 5 p.m., JUSPAO provided a news briefing on the events of the day from its headquarters in Saigon. These briefings, in which successes were liberally exaggerated, soon became known as the "five o'clock follies." The ambassador initially was a little hesitant to have American college students report their observations on the war, but once Sam took responsibility for any potential negative backlash, Taylor finally gave the go-ahead. Had he written them himself, Sam could not have scripted the students' presentations better. Each individual had his own story to tell, and every single one of them was positive. The students were full of zeal about improvements in the local provinces that they had seen growing in the areas of local security, economy, and government.

Of the original twenty students, eighteen were present. One had dropped out early and returned home, and another was recovering from wounds sustained during a Viet Cong attack on the small building in which he had been sleeping.

On the night he had been injured, the student heard something moving against the wall next to him. He had been barely able to duck under his bed before the charge went off and blew in the wall. Sam visited the young man about thirty-six hours later, just after the arrival of his father, who had chartered a private plane to visit Vietnam. The father fumed angrily at Sam until his son interrupted, "Hey Dad, that's my boss. It's not his fault. He's the greatest guy I've ever worked for. I didn't use my head. I was sleeping in the wrong place." At one time or another, most of the students had been shot at, but even the student who was injured reported a positive overall experience.

One of the journalists who attended the JUSPAO briefing was a young New Yorker by the name of Jimmy Breslin, a witty Irishman who had become iconic for his writing ability. On the night of the student presentation for the press, Breslin and Sam met for drinks and later joined Vietnamese students and the American college students at a party. By the end of the evening, Sam allowed his tongue to slip to Breslin, a mistake that quickly made its way to print. Sam learned an important lesson—if he were not careful he could dig his own grave with his mouth.

When Sam was approaching the end of his second year of duty in the Foreign Service, President Johnson relieved Ambassador Taylor of his post in South Vietnam and assigned Ambassador Henry Cabot Lodge for a second tenure in the country. During Lodge's orientation, Sam briefed the ambassador and drove him around the countryside so that he could see first-hand some of the things that the U.S. was endeavoring to do to assist the Vietnamese. Sam's department was responsible for winning back the loyalty of the Vietnamese peasantry from the blandishments of the Viet Cong, and he was proud that they were performing well. During the bleak years of the Vietnam War, the program of reform that Sam was running shone as one of the few bright spots for the United States.

A few hours after the two men had completed their tour, Lodge called Sam and asked him to come to the Embassy. Sam suspected what Lodge wanted, so he was not shocked when Lodge asked him to join the embassy staff and work with him directly, in the capacity of the United States Mission Coordinator. Sam would be able to continue to build upon and broaden the scope of the programs that he already was carrying out with the U.S.'s economic mission. Sam told Lodge that he would let him know the following day. He returned to his office and immediately made a long-distance call to Brenda in Baguio to tell her what he had been offered, and to ask if she would support him if he accepted Ambassador Lodge's invitation. It was difficult for her to know what the new offer entailed, but she knew it represented a significant promotion. As usual, Brenda gave her full support for Sam to pursue the offer. Sam accepted the appointment and began what developed into an extended position in Vietnam.

Lodge promised Sam that if he accepted the job, he would see to it that President Johnson appointed him to the personal rank of Minister, which would make him senior to all of the three-star military officers in Vietnam and would provide him with additional protocol clout. Sam held the title of Minister for ten months, a designation that allowed him to work on the same sorts of things that he had been doing in his earlier assignment, but with greater authority and control over more funds and material to support useful projects.

Several months into his work in South Vietnam, it had become evident to Sam that there was a basic flaw in the way that the United States organized its activities there. Operations in Vietnam were too divided to be effective. Each agency and department operating in Vietnam reported back to Washington without any meaningful collaborative obligations. This created a bureaucratic morass, in which people were frequently working at cross-purposes, a situation that proved very frustrating for Sam as he tried to initiate economic programs requiring teamwork in each province.

To discern a possible solution to the problem, Sam asked permission of Ambassador Lodge and General Westmoreland, the Senior U.S. Military Commander, to be assigned to a province in the Delta and assume total control over all American activity in that province. He wanted to prove the principal of success found in unity of command and purpose, and he also wanted to shift the focus of the American soldiers in that region. Sam knew that, in past wars, certainly in World War II, the main objective of ground combat action was to impose one's will upon the enemy by winning battles and conquering hills. The war in Vietnam was different, and the objective was no longer a hill. It was the hearts of a people.

Sam proposed that he be given six months in Long An, which at that time was considered a province which could go either to the Americans or to the Communists. At the end of the six months, he intended to produce measurable gains in the province's security and economic and political situation. If the experiment worked, he would suggest that the United States adopt the same system for each of the forty-four provinces. Essentially, Sam believed that one senior U.S. representative should be completely in charge of all American activities in each province. Lodge and Westmoreland agreed to Sam's proposal, and in mid-November 1965, Sam took control of all

American activity in Long An.

It was not an easy task, but Sam was given the necessary authority to establish the chain of command he needed. He carried the rank of Minister, which made him senior to all U.S. military in the area and gave him control over the Agency for International Development, the U.S. Information Agency, and the CIA, all three of which were already operating in Long An.

The experiment proved sufficiently successful that when President Johnson was briefed about Sam's achievements in Long An during a Vietnam War Conference, held on the island of Guam on March 15, 1967, he interrupted the briefing before it was finished. "I don't need to hear any more," the President said. "This is the way I want it done throughout the country."

The Office of Civil Operations and Revolutionary Development Support (CORDS) was born at that meeting. Under CORDS, each province in which Sam's proposal was implemented showed positive progress. The first director of CORDS was U.S. Ambassador Robert Komer, who served for the first year and a half. He was followed by William Colby, a future director of the Central Intelligence Agency.

In May of 1967, Sam was asked by the newly appointed U.S. Ambassador to Vietnam, Ellsworth Bunker, to extend his duties in the country for another year. Sam was enjoying the work he was doing in Vietnam, but he decided it would be best to discuss the matter with his family before he accepted Ambassador Bunker's offer. Sam flew to Baguio in the Philippines to consult with Brenda. Brenda had already spent two years in Baguio and she was ready to take the family home. For Sam, the decision was more complex.

In his last year in Vietnam, Sam had received a great deal of positive publicity for the success of the CORDS experiment. He had participated in television interviews, and a number of magazines had run articles about his adventures in the provinces. In July 1965, *Reader's Digest* published an article about his position as one of "The Quiet Heroes of Vietnam." In February 1967, *Newsweek* did a special article about him, and in June of that year, the editor of *Time* magazine, Hedley Donovan, had traveled to Vietnam and had written an article for *Life* magazine, which included comments about Sam and his work. As far as the war was concerned, Sam had fared quite well. He had survived thus far intact, with his family still together and supporting him. In the process, his efforts had attracted a lot of attention from his higher-ups. Staying in Vietnam would likely lead to similar opportunities for the future. As further enticement, there was an offer for a permanent top-level Foreign Service officer's rank. Sam had every professional reason to accept the appointment, but after some serious thought and conversations with his wife, it became clear to him that he needed to return his family to something approaching normalcy. He needed to return to the Army.

After a few days of deliberation and to the delight of this family, he decided to return to the United States. He moved down three levels in protocol rank and was reassigned to Fort Bragg, North Carolina, to command a Special Forces group. The Wilson family sailed from Manila in early June 1967, on the luxurious *SS President Cleveland*. They thoroughly enjoyed the vacation-like trip back to San Francisco, the port from which Sam had sailed almost twenty-five years earlier during World War II when he was on his way to Burma and what would become Merrill's Marauders.

FORT BRAGG

SAM'S SECOND ASSIGNMENT to Fort Bragg proved to be the longest time he spent in one place during his entire military career, from July 1967 through February 1971, and during that period he spent more time with his family than ever before. In February of 1968, he had saved enough money to purchase 150 acres near his family's farm in Rice, Virginia, and that rural get-away proved to be a relaxing haven for Brenda and him when they needed to escape the pressures of military life. Over the years after the initial purchase, Sam expanded his holdings, built a house, and made improvements to the farm.

Among military circles, Fort Bragg is known as the home of the Airborne, America's first guardians of freedom, and forces from Fort Bragg are the first troops deployed to defend the nation in emergency situations. As the home of the Airborne, Fort Bragg's activities center around flight and aircraft.

Sam's first assignment at Fort Bragg was as the Commanding Officer (CO) of the 6th Special Forces Group (Airborne), oriented on the Middle East. Sam's talented Lieutenant Colonels boasted an average of twenty years of experience in the Special Forces, and each knew Special Forces operations like the back of their hands. Sam had to work to gain the respect of these Lieutenant Colonels and the respect of the cadre of elite non-commissioned officers in the group, men who came from colorful and exciting backgrounds, many with years of experience working with Special Forces in the bush. They were gunfighters and knife-throwers, black-belt karate and judo experts—the type of quiet heroes about whom books are written and movies are made. The men knew that Sam had spent some time with the CIA and in the Foreign Service, but they were waiting to find out exactly what sort of man their new CO was.

Sam's initial approach was simply to walk around the compound, to watch carefully, to ask questions, and to listen attentively. He had long ago learned the importance of being a good listener. He also tried to appear at unexpected places at odd hours. He wanted to make sure his men were excelling on every level at all times. As he conversed with the men around Fort Bragg, he would selectively tell stories from his past to give them a taste of the sorts of activities he had experienced, but he was very careful not to be an arrogant braggart. He would drop a story here and there, and then let the men pick it up, pass it around among themselves, and add their own embellishments.

As he began his tenure as CO of the Special Forces Group, Sam took time to carefully organize his staff meetings. He worked to ensure that everyone had an opportunity to contribute his views. Sam placed great emphasis on keeping his group's communication channels open from all directions. Especially during the initial period, he avoided emphatic pronouncements on any subject and endeavored to be factual, rational, and wise. He made a point of showing sincere personal interest in all his troops, remembering an old adage that said, "Take care of your troops and the troops will take care of you."

From the very outset, Sam worked to craft a comprehensive mission statement for the group, and once he had written the statement, he made sure that everyone knew what it was. While retaining final authority, Sam concentrated on delegating responsibility whenever feasible, a technique he had picked up from Lansdale and Hunter. Sam always tried to explain upcoming tasks with great care, and then he backed away to give subordinates space to do their jobs. Sam also realized the importance of liberally crediting the good work of others. He often remembered the saying, "If you don't care who gets the credit, you can do anything."

At a time of great personnel turbulence, with troops coming and going from Vietnam on a weekly basis, Sam looked for every possible chance to provide useful training for his troops. He devised a program in which a handful of men were dropped into the swamps and forests of the military reservation to survive for a few days with nothing more than a pocket knife, some stout string, a compass, and a few matches. The maneuver showed the troops that, by using creativity and diligence, a resourceful individual can find ways to stay alive under dire circumstances. While it was not necessarily a pleasant experience, it was realistic and useful survival training for what they might face in the future.

Sam also set up a corral and borrowed five or six mules from surrounding farms. He had members of his Special Forces teams practice handling the animals. One day, the Corps Commander of the 18th Airborne Corps happened to see Sam's troops working with the mules. He turned with some irritation and asked, "Sam, what in the hell are you doing here?"

Sam replied that the operational areas for which his group was training were places where mules, camels, and other beasts of burden had to be used to carry the munitions of war. From his experience behind the Japanese lines in Burma during World War II, he had learned that an entire division can be blessed if they have a couple of good muleskinners on hand to help load and transport needed weapons, equipment, and supplies. The Corps Commander, a three-star General, scoffed, saying, "Good God, Sam, a helicopter can go any place a mule can go and some places that the mule can't."

The General was angry, but Sam had learned from experience that a mule can carry a lot more food and supplies than a man can carry by himself, especially when the platoon is being supplied by air drops in areas where the enemy has air superiority. Sam was to remember that General's remarks in the 1980s, when a call went out from the CIA for mules to help support the *Mujahedeen,* who were fighting against their Soviet occupiers in Afghanistan.

Special Forces troops are generally not of the spit and polish variety. As a rule, they do not especially care for inspections or parades. But Sam felt that an occasional parade to the music of a marching band added to the unit's *esprit de corps.* He insisted that the troops at Fort Bragg should spend some time learning how to march in formation and should hold regular parades. On these occasions, wives and children of the troops would be invited to attend, and without fail, the kids always enjoyed the marching bands, colors, salutes, and the playing of "The Star Spangled Banner." It was not too long before the grizzled Special Forces veterans began to agree that the additional formal training was worth it. Maneuvers polished the men, made them shine their shoes, shave, and begin to take pride in themselves and their unit.

Not too long after Sam took over the 6th Special Forces Group (Airborne), he was invited to Washington to deliver the same briefing on the war in Vietnam that he had already delivered to President Johnson and General Westmoreland, but this time he was requested to brief Secretary McNamara, the three service secretaries, the Chairman of the Joint Chiefs of Staff, and the Chief of Staff of the Army. The assembly was particularly interested in Sam's Long An unification experiment and the conclusions that Sam drew from that operation. At that presentation, Sam reiterated his suggestion that the U.S. must increase its focus on local South Vietnamese commanders through American advisors. Sam drew most of his thoughts from nuggets he had gleaned with Lansdale's nation-developing philosophy. The briefing proved to be the first of many presentations that he was asked to make about his Vietnam tour and his experiences with the Soviet military.

One of the most exciting projects that Sam undertook as CO of the Special

Forces group at Fort Bragg was a summer field exercise that he code-named "Orbit Wings." During Orbit Wings, Sam and the other leaders developed an elaborate scenario that created a mythical country, extending from Montana to Arizona. As they worked on the maneuver, Sam drew on his combat experience against the Viet Cong in Vietnam and on his knowledge of the Soviet wars of national liberation in third-world countries. In the exercise's scenario, a mythical country had been infiltrated by an insurgent army (which Sam arranged to be played by police), while the insurgents' "advisors" to local law enforcement elements were played by the National Guard. On the other hand, Sam's real Special Forces troops were deployed to provide counter-insurgent aid to the people of this nation. The objectives for Orbit Wings were two-fold. First, the men received valuable experience in developing and running guerilla warfare operations. At the same time, the troops learned how to defeat guerilla attacks being conducted by Communist revolutionaries.

The exercises lasted several weeks, and, in some areas, especially in Utah, parts of New Mexico, the southeastern end of Arizona, and the area around El Paso, Texas, the local population became considerably involved. Local radio stations and newspapers described the mythical revolution taking place in their midst. Sam developed separate, small scenarios throughout the exercise. For instance, he often ordered a platoon to exfiltrate a local revolutionary leader from a town where the insurgents were beginning to close in on him. While they were carrying out these orders, one platoon actually placed the individual they were seeking to rescue in a coffin and drove him in a hearse out of town and 100 miles through "enemy" police road blocks until they got him to safety.

Orbit Wings was very productive. The troops learned a great deal, and the local public enjoyed the experience. It gave them a good taste of what was going on in the Special Forces community. After drafting their proposal for the first summer's exercise, Sam invited U.S. Air Force special operations units to participate as well. The two services pooled their training money so that they could each afford the exercises. The first had been such a success that by the second summer, they were attracting enough attention that some in higher headquarters became aware of Orbit Wings. Military authorities began insisting on controlling the exercise to ensure that no offense to the public was perpetrated. After their investigation of the mythical counter-insurgent operations, authorities instigated such stringent regulations that Sam could no longer do all the interesting activities he wanted. Consequently, after the second summer, they were not scheduled again. But the two Orbit Wings operations that did occur were creative, effective exercises that are still discussed in military courses as examples of innovative training techniques.

In the summer of 1968, Sam arranged for his Special Forces to fly to Farmville, Virginia, for a ceremony celebrating the opening of the regional airport. They dazzled spectators with an extensive skydiving exhibition in which the aerial troops jumped from airplanes in various formations, passing batons and carrying flags as they fell from 20,000 feet. Even Virginia Senator Harry F. Byrd, a political icon in his day, came from Washington, D.C. for the occasion. Byrd wrote Sam a highly commendatory letter for arranging such a show for the Southside Virginia public.

In August 1968, Sam organized his men outside Farmville again, this time to replay the Battle of High Bridge, a Civil War skirmish fought in April 1865 between the forces of General Robert E. Lee and General Ulysses S. Grant. In the original battle, the two armies struggled for control of the major railway bridge spanning the Appomattox River four miles east of Farmville. In the reenactment, Sam's troops played the part of infiltrating Union troops while Sam's cousin, Lieutenant Colonel Julian Bradshaw, led local National Guard troops as part of Lee's defending army.

Sam assigned the mission to one of his crack "A" teams of twelve men and created a small command unit to be designated the "B" team. The troops were isolated in a tented area of maximum secrecy and charged to develop a plan to destroy the major railway trestle, named High Bridge, on the Norfolk and Western Railway over the Appomattox River. To make the exercise more demanding, Sam told them they must destroy the bridge at precisely midnight on Saturday, and he emphasized that the bridge was to be destroyed at exactly that time. To ensure that they took the exercise seriously, he warned his men that, if this mission failed, they need not bother returning to Fort Bragg.

On a Friday evening in late August of 1968, the 6th Special Forces Group (Airborne) conducted an administrative airborne operation or "air drop" on Farmville Municipal Airport. Just before sunset, hundreds of local people were on hand to watch the demonstration. The operation was impressive. Soldiers landed on the airstrip and silently melted into the surrounding forests. At that moment, the tactical part of the exercise began.

It was the task of the 2nd battalion of the 116th Infantry of the Virginia National Guard's 29th division to defend High Bridge against the possibility of guerilla attacks. The 116th Infantry had been Sam's first outfit as an enlisted man, and under the command of Julian Bradshaw, who was connected with the National Guard and with whom Sam had grown up in Rice, the battalion provided staunch opposition to Sam's teams. The public's interest in this exercise was whetted by extensive local radio coverage and articles in *The Farmville Herald* newspaper that reported on the contest between two old schoolmates and fellow soldiers. As had been the case during the "Orbit Wings" exercises, public affiliation was equally divided between the two sides. Some supported the local National Guard and the Sheriff's Department (Lt. Col. Bradshaw's counter-insurgent forces). Others supported Sam and his guerilla warriors by providing food and safe havens or by lending pickup trucks.

From Fort Bragg, Sam kept in close radio contact with his Special Forces' guerilla warriors, and they provided him with regular intelligence reports on the local situation. He had them provide sketches of High Bridge and requested that they use specific types and amounts of "explosives," although, of course, the destruction was only simulated. The Special Forces air support dropped "explosives" to designated pastures and fields in the general area around High Bridge in Prince Edward and Cumberland Counties.

On D-Day and H-Hour, the National Guard units were deployed in an extended circle around High Bridge where they aimed to block all efforts from Sam's troops to infiltrate the bridge. Despite the best efforts of the local militia, at precisely midnight there was a series of explosions from Dago Bombs, Roman Candles, large fire crackers, sizzlers, and sparklers which lit up the bridge like a belated Fourth of July celebration. It was obvious that the Special Forces had succeeded in infiltrating to the bridge and destroying it. What Bradshaw and his men did not know was that Special Forces troops had been infiltrating for several days, climbing up into the superstructure one by one and hiding there.

Lt. Col. Bradshaw knew that the bridge was to be blown at midnight, so he had focused his attention on stopping all infiltration to the area on the night of the danger. By that time, however, the infiltrators were already inside the bridge and were preparing their explosive charges. When the whistle blew to conclude the exercise, the troops from both sides met at a large bonfire. There, the Special Forces briefed the National Guardsmen on the techniques they had used. They adjourned to the local National Guard armory for a big breakfast in the wee hours of the morning. The exercise proved to be good publicity for both the local National Guard and the Special Forces, and both sides enjoyed the war games. At about seven the next morning, Sam's telephone rang in his quarters at Fort Bragg. He recognized his cousin's voice on the other end of the line. "General Grant, this is General Lee. Request you let my men keep their horses, Sir, for the spring plowing."

During Sam's stint as commanding officer, the 6th Special Forces Group (Airborne) came to be recognized for its high morale and *esprit de corps*. It was described as the best disciplined, best trained, and most combat-ready of the three Special Forces groups stationed at Fort Bragg at the time. For Sam, it seemed all too soon when his experience with them had to be concluded. In December 1968, Sam was given the assignment of helping to establish a new school for training American military advisors and raising the professional profile of effective officers.

Once again, Sam found himself back with the Institute for Military Assistance, the old Special Warfare School. His first assignment, which continued for eighteen months, was as the Director of the new Military Assistance school. Then, in December 1969, he received a promotion to serve as the Assistant Commandant of the John F. Kennedy United States Army Institute for Military Assistance (USAIMA). The Commanding General asked Sam to create a course which taught the concepts of military advisorship he had practiced in Long An. To develop the curriculum for this enterprise, Sam expanded on the class that he had already formulated to educate young soldiers on counter-insurgency techniques, and he tailored it into a more detailed program for soldiers in advisory roles. His team eventually organized a sixteen-week Command and Staff course which they titled the Military Assistance Officer's Command and Staff Course (MAOCSC).

Long before Sam was developing what became MAOCSC, the United States had already established military assistance advisory groups (MAAGs) in a number of countries around the world. In the 1940s, the United States had found that providing military assistance to allies and friends was of vital importance. After the successful conclusion of World War II, the U.S. began to provide military equipment, supplies, and advice to allies who stood strong against the Soviet Communists. For better or worse, the U.S. was in the military advising and training business, and Sam's work in educating military advisors further was a vital step forward in assuring that they understood the philosophic concepts behind effective military advisory doctrine around the world.

The first course was sufficiently successful that the Army continued to develop a follow-up program called the Military Assistance Officer Program (MAOP). Experienced officers who attended courses such as the MAOCSC immediately became candidates for MAOP. This new program particularly focused on understanding the people and culture of the countries with whom the U.S. worked.

When the formal MAOP was officially announced as a government-sanctioned program, Sam was offered the ceremonial first membership in the program. A few weeks after his election to MAOP, however, he received a memorandum rescinding his membership to the program because he was already a member of the intelligence-oriented Foreign Area Specialist Training Program (FAST), and it was felt that officers should not be members of both programs. While Sam had no real attachment to that card, he was furious that the military bureaucracy saw membership in the intelligence-oriented FAST program as precluding membership in the advisory-oriented MAOP.

He immediately contacted his old friend, General William C. Westmoreland, who was by then the Chief of Staff of the U.S. Army, and explained the situation to him. Westmoreland responded immediately by combining the two programs into a new Foreign Area Officer Program (FAOP). Officers belonging to the new program were to be known as FAOs. The ultimate outcome was quite satisfactory to Sam, although he never experienced the pleasure of a ceremonial first membership.

In early summer 1969, Sam was asked by his commanding officer if he would accept the post of Assistant Commandant of the John F. Kennedy Army Institute for Military Assistance, the new designation of the U.S. Army Special Warfare Center. The assignment would give him responsibility for running the Institute for Military Assistance of which his MAOP course was a part. Sam would have been delighted, except for one glitch. The Army places great store in seniority, and there were three officers already at the Institute who were significantly senior to Sam and would be the expected candidates for the position. If Sam were to accept the position, he would put these officers in the awkward position of working for a colonel who was junior to them.

The Commander assured Sam that he would speak with each of the senior colonels, and Sam considered it one of greatest compliments that he ever received when each of the three officers agreed without hesitation to Sam's appointment. Their votes of confidence motivated Sam to redouble his efforts and justify their support. For the rest of the year, he worked diligently, especially in areas that streamlined the institute and improved programs.

Early in the spring of the following year, 1970, Sam was selected for promotion to Brigadier General and assigned to a much-coveted job, Assistant Division Commander for Operations of the 82nd Airborne Division. With this promotion, he enjoyed significant influence in what was nicknamed

"America's Ready Force." Even the infantry career-management personnel who had warmed Sam that his job choices would sabotage his future finally recognized that his career was, in fact, very much on track. The assignment presented formidable challenges, but Sam loved being back with troops.

Since the 82nd Airborne Division was stationed at Fort Bragg, the Wilsons remained in their house on the parade ground, though enhancements were made to it in an effort to make it appear more like a General's quarters. Sam enjoyed a few of the luxuries that marked his high rank, like the private driver assigned to him. He still worked long hours to provide training of the highest quality for the division and personally played an active role in their training. To that end, he assigned himself the task of leading the whole division on five-mile runs every morning, which initially was an exhausting exercise for Sam but which soon became so routine that he could run the route backwards, facing and leading the troops in song.

Sam also organized significant training exercises to keep his troops prepared for battle. These exercises were frequently visited by a grizzled corps commander who had not initially supported Sam's promotion. He considered Sam to be a maverick and an adventurer who was not grounded in tradition, but after many visits to Sam's new training exercises, where he observed the troops' superb performances, he became a strong supporter of Sam's efforts. In Sam's annual evaluation report, the commander went so far as to recommend that Sam be given a division to command by himself.

Early that fall, the 82nd Airborne Division was placed on alert when roughly five hundred American citizens living in Amman, Jordan, were rounded up and held in the International Hotel by the People's Liberation Organization (PLO), a Palestinian terrorist group. The PLO intended to hold them hostage while they worked to overthrow King Hussein and then to assume control of Jordan. The 82nd Airborne stood ready to depart for Insirlik, Turkey, from which they could fly to nearby Jordan and parachute into Amman.

The plan was to air drop the soldiers and then land several airplanes at the Amman airport. The dropped soldiers would secure the hostages and take them to the airport where they could be flown out of the country. It was a very delicate and risky proposal. Sam prepared to board a C140 jet at Pope Air Force base from which he would fly to Turkey, when King Hussein's military attacked the Palestinian insurgents and utterly vanquished them in what has become known as the "Night of the Long Knives." The U.S. no longer needed to become actively involved.

In the fall, Sam was given responsibility for conducting a two-day demonstration with the 18th Airborne Corps, to which the 82nd Airborne Division belonged, for a large Congressional delegation that visited Fort Bragg each year to assess the readiness of America's premier strike force. A few days before the demonstration, Sam's immediate superior, the Division Commander, remarked in passing to Sam that he had been called in by the Corps Commander and asked, "Are you confident that Wilson can pull this thing off?"

The Division Commander told Sam that he had responded, "If Wilson can't do it, I'll fire him and get someone else."

Sam cheerfully replied, "Thanks for the vote of confidence," and, more determined than ever to do a first class job, he returned to his preparation.

At one point in the day's agenda, about half of the 82nd Airborne's troops were to parachute all at once before the visiting VIPs, who would be watching from bleachers. Elements of the Special Warfare Center and several of their Special Forces groups would also play a part in the demonstration. The winds aloft were quite brisk on the appointed day, well above parachuting's generally accepted limit of seventeen miles per hour. As Sam took his command position in a tower to the rear of the stands, he saw that there were hundreds of people preparing to watch the spectacle. The Special Forces troops were scheduled to drop first, and Sam saw that as the aircraft carrying the Special Forces troops approached the drop zone, the needle of the wind indicator hovered between nineteen and twenty miles per hour. At the last minute, Sam's old commander, a Major General who was in the command tower with him, aborted the drop. There was an audible groan from the watching crowd when this decision was announced over the loudspeaker.

After the first Special Forces planes flew over without dropping their troops, they were followed by Sam's armada of C130s. As the planes turned on the final leg of their approach pattern, Sam checked the wind speed indicator; it was stuck at nineteen miles per hour. Remembering the groan from the crowd when the last drop had been cancelled, he simply said, "The hell with it," and gave the order for the drop to proceed. Sam was confident that his men were skilled enough to do the job, and he had no desire to disappoint the VIPs. As his decision was announced, a cheer rose from the stands.

Mercifully, there was a lull in the wind just as the first trooper jumped from the cargo doors. Much to Sam's relief, the drop went off without a single injury. The success of the 82nd Airborne's drop made Sam's old boss and friend (half) jokingly vent at Sam, "You crazy SOB, I guess I should have done the same thing."

Upon reflection over the scenario that night, Sam decided that he would rather be lucky than smart anytime.

In November 1970, Sam received a long distance telephone call from Paris from Nguyen Cao Ky, Vietnam's former Prime Minister and South Vietnam's current Vice President. Ky informed Sam that he had been involved in talks with a North Vietnamese delegation in Paris and had decided to return to Vietnam via the United States the following weekend. While he was in the United States, he hoped that he and his staff could visit Sam at his farm in Virginia. Sam immediately agreed. As soon as he hung up, Sam immediately called Brenda to tell her the news and ask that she begin preparing to host a retinue of foreign dignitaries, headed by Ky, Vietnamese ambassador to Washington, the Chief of Staff of the Vietnamese Air Force, and a number of other South Vietnamese staffers and support personnel. Sam and Brenda needed to accommodate forty people at their farm.

With some help from his old office in the Institute for Military Assistance, from his old Special Forces group and from the 82nd Airborne, Sam and Brenda planned every detail of the visit. They designated an escort for each principal visitor, worked up the right kinds of menus, set up tents, had outdoor latrines dug, and provided basic piping so that their guests could have fountains of potable water. After extensive preparation, Sam and Brenda were able to meet, greet, feed, and entertain the South Vietnamese retinue for a delightful three-day weekend. The visitors shot skeet, rode horseback, fished, and hunted quail during the day. At night, they played cards and listened to Vietnamese music by a crackling open fire.

One of the most memorable events during the visit occurred when Sam brought Ky to Hampden-Sydney College to attend a football game against Randolph-Macon College. A bevy of Secret Servicemen drove from D.C. to ensure Ky's security on the trip, adding to the forces provided by State Police and members of the Sheriff's Department who were already posted at the farm to safeguard Sam's important guests. It was quite a convoy that set out behind State Police cars, with their blue lights flashing and sirens wailing, and descended upon Hundley Stadium and Fulton Field that November Saturday afternoon. The game was underway when they arrived, with Randolph-Macon leading by a touchdown. When they departed towards the end of the fourth quarter, Hampden-Sydney was comfortably ahead and well on the way to a win. Ky took credit for the victory, saying that his visit brought Hampden-Sydney good luck.

Toward the end of Sam's tour with the 82nd Airborne Division, General Westmoreland arrived for an inspection visit. Although he was excited at the chance to see his good friend again, Sam was a bit concerned that Westmoreland's favorable personal attention to him might be resented by his Corps Commander and immediate boss, but Sam's worries were unfounded. The visit did, however, initiate widespread rumors speculating that Sam might eventually be promoted to Major General and given command of a division.

But then, Russia beckoned.

In early December 1970, Sam received a phone call from Brigadier General Daniel Graham, a long-time contemporary of Sam's in intelligence matters. "Greetings, Sam," said Danny, "the American Ambassador in Moscow awaits your early arrival."

Without saying a word, Sam slammed the phone on the receiver. He sat in his chair, wondering if the call had actually occurred. Then the phone rang again. This time the voice said, "It's me, Sam. It's Danny. Don't hang up. I'm serious. We have established a new position: Defense Attaché in Moscow. We want you to fill it."

At that time, all American military attaché officers in embassies around the world had separate Army, Navy, and Air Force office components, with each component reporting directly back to Washington, but with no one locally in charge. Sam knew full well from a number of experiences that one way to ensure things will go wrong is to have no one in charge. The United States government had seen that difficulty and sought to correct the problem. Sam was glad to hear of this development, but he was shocked that he had been selected to lead the implementation of a new command structure in the backyard of his country's most dangerous enemy, Moscow.

Sam faced a dilemma. In a sense, his current position represented a comfortable home-like situation for him. He found it deeply satisfying to be back with troops, particularly with the elite paratroopers of the storied 82nd Airborne Division. He had been fully accepted by the non-commissioned officer cadre of the 82nd, which was no mean feat in itself. Also, the holders of his personnel file in the General Officer Management Office in Washington seemed finally to be placated. They assumed that Sam had recovered from the dangerous malady of itching foot and his addiction to wandering off his career path. Sam was beginning to listen to those rumors that he was in line to take over the 82nd Airborne Division, which could mean eventually a straight shot through the XVIII Airborne Corps to four-star General status.

And here he paused. Moscow was calling him. The U.S. was very much in the grips of the dangerous Cold War, and the war could shift to active, even nuclear, at any time. Such a development would gravely threaten the existence and freedom of American people. "Moscow calling" rang in his ears. All his language and area education and training, and all his prowling the alleyways and dark byways of East Europe as he recruited agents, debriefed defectors, and devised innovative ways to thwart Soviet expansionist plans or to defuse Communist wars of national liberation—the myriad aspects of his diverse training—would come together in this assignment. Sam once again would be dealing with the enemy, this time face-to-face in his very lair. Sam could sense the spice of danger. There risks would be far greater than anything he faced when jumping out of airplanes at Fort Bragg. And there was so much more at stake. The 82nd Airborne Division would only be involved if the U.S. went to war and, given the abundance of nuclear weapons on both sides, everyone realized that war should be avoided at almost all costs.

On the other hand, Sam's family was living comfortably in a nice home on the edge of the parade ground where they were safe and secure. There was time for backyard cookouts, horseshoe pitching, football games, and attending church together. Moscow would require a separation that would end all that. It was a huge crossroad for Sam. He took the left fork . . . Moscow.

MOSCOW

BRENDA AND THE CHILDREN were less than eager to uproot and move to Moscow. They loved the stability of Fort Bragg and the opportunity to see their oft-absent father and husband on a regular basis. These were not easy conditions to relinquish. Eventually, the family compromised, and it was decided that Brenda would go to the farm in Rice with David and Susan while Sam took Hap with him to Moscow. Hap had been struggling during his freshman year at the University of North Carolina, and both parents felt it would be beneficial for him to join Sam for exposure to the language, music, and culture of Russia.

In early February 1971, Brenda moved north from Fort Bragg to the farm in Virginia. Sam subsequently moved into the VIP guest house at the base, where he spent several weeks transferring his responsibilities at Fort Bragg. In early March, Sam reported to the Director of the Defense Intelligence Agency as the new Defense Attaché for Moscow. His first few weeks were dedicated to orientation on attaché matters, administrative procedures, diplomatic dos-and-don'ts, and intelligence requirements for the new position. While in the nation's capital, Sam paid courtesy calls to the Director of the Central Intelligence Agency, the Director of the National Security Administration, and the Army, Navy, and Air Force Intelligence Chiefs. To each of them he pledged assurances that he would be aware of their needs and would try to be helpful to them from his new post in Moscow. Sam also visited selected embassies of the U.S.'s European allies in Washington, and finally, he paid a lengthy visit to the Soviet Embassy.

Over the phone, Sam had arranged to arrive at the Russians' Washington Consulate at precisely ten o'clock on Tuesday morning. Always a stickler for promptness, Sam pulled into the neighborhood of the consulate a quarter of an hour early. To kill the time, he paced the sidewalk for a few minutes and smoked a cigarette. He then walked up to the front door of the consulate, knocked on the door, and was warmly greeted by his old friends from Moscow. He spent several hours socializing and assuring the Soviet representative that he would be working on behalf of both countries to maintain peace during his tenure as Defense Attaché in Moscow. The Soviets, as was their custom, attempted to induce Sam to drink vodka with them, and Sam found himself slightly out of practice in keeping up with their consumption habits. When he stumbled out to his car in the early afternoon, he had just enough presence of mind to drive himself back to his office.

Not two hours after he returned from his visit with the Soviets, the Director of Army Intelligence phoned. The man suspiciously inquired what Sam had been doing that morning. It seemed that FBI surveillance of the Russian consulate had taken footage of Sam nervously pacing up and down the sidewalk shortly before ten o'clock. The surveillance operatives suggested that he appeared hesitant about going into the consulate, but finally made up his mind, threw down the cigarette, and disappeared through the doors.

As a result, The Army Intelligence Chief asked Sam to clarify why he had gone there. Sam assured the Chief that he was still as patriotic as ever and had no intention whatsoever of betraying his nation. He carefully explained exactly why he had visited the Soviet embassy and assured him that there was no reason for anyone to be suspicious of his actions. Although he apologized for failing to coordinate his visit with the proper authorities, he sensed, as he had on several prior occasions, that some of his counterparts tended to be suspicious of his close relationships with the Russians. Sam's almost native fluency in their language and the ease with which he seemed to establish rapport with our most bitter enemies sometimes caused other American observers to suggest that he overstepped the boundaries of cautious diplomacy.

With the controversy over his Soviet consulate visit resolved, Sam and Hap left for Moscow. Father and son were very close, and Hap was excited about the prospect of visiting the country his father had studied for so long. They stopped in Frankfurt, and detoured briefly to visit the headquarters of the Commander in Chief of the U.S. Army in Europe. Sam took the opportunity to talk to the Commander's Intelligence Chief and members of the staff concerning Moscow and about how Sam's work might be useful to European headquarters.

Sam soon became frustrated by the selfishness of the leadership of that office. It became clear to him that the major general serving as the Director of Intelligence of the U.S. Army in Europe thought that Sam would be working for him, and he lost no time in telling Sam what he should and should not be doing on his new assignment. In a slightly tense conversation, Sam informed the general that he would be as helpful to the European office as possible, but his command line ran independent of that office. It was not the European

Director of Intelligence who would write Sam's evaluation report. Rather, Sam worked directly for the Director of the DIA, who in turn worked for the Secretary of Defense and the Chairman of The Joint Chiefs of Staff. His command line was quite clear. The only person for him to report to in Europe was the American ambassador in Moscow. After an icy silence, the Army major general said, "Thank you. That concludes this interview."

Sam was reminded of other times when he had been working for the U.S. government and constantly had to be aware of the zones and areas of authority and the responsibilities and boundaries that separate them. There are differences between solid lines of command, dashed lines of administration, and dotted lines of coordination, and while a man can be helpful to many administrators or coordinators, he can only serve one master.

Nearly as soon as Sam arrived in Moscow, he learned that the Air Force attaché, a very senior colonel, had been expecting to be promoted to Sam's newly designed position and had been shocked and dismayed when he learned that the promotion was going to an officer from the 82nd Airborne. This Air Force colonel considered that he was the expert in intelligence, and that he knew the Soviet Union better than anyone else in America. He was quite resentful that they tapped someone from the operational field, someone whom he presumed knew nothing about the area. He resented Sam even before they met.

Initially, he was surly and disrespectful. Sam knew that he had two choices. One was to punish the disrespect. The other option was to win the man's confidence, and Sam chose to try to the latter. It soon became obvious that the colonel's command of the Russian language was weaker than Sam's, and that although the colonel knew certain areas of intelligence, his background in operational intelligence was meager compared to that of the newly appointed Defense Attaché. It was no easy task, but eventually Sam won the loyalty and later the friendship of both this officer and his very intelligent and talented wife.

Sam's first visit to Moscow had been in the winter of 1948, and during the dark, grim days of Stalin, when people scurried around the city locked in the vise of an absolute police state. Sam had returned on a number of subsequent occasions and observed that conditions had progressively improved, but it was still far from the free and easy life that existed in Western Europe and the United States. Hap and Sam arrived in Moscow in May 1971, just as the flowers were beginning to bloom and the air to brighten. The first suggestions of a sort of détente between the two superpowers wafted in the air. In Washington, American officials, including Secretary of State Kissinger, began sensing the possibilities of an uneasy peace with Moscow. Over the next several years, this fleeting promise of cooperation between the two nations gave Sam and the other forty-four members of his office more access to representatives of the Soviet military's high command than had been enjoyed by Americans in Russia for decades. Sam was determined to take maximum advantage of the improved access.

Still, suspicion and distrust colored the relationship between the two superpowers. Americans never left the U.S. Embassy in Moscow without having at least one, if not several, Russian surveillance tracking their every move. U.S. officers continued to assume, with justification, that their living quarters and offices in the Embassy were bugged. On occasion they would find microphones hidden in their bookshelves or underneath their desks. They also knew that the cooks, maids, washerwomen, the local barber, and all serving personnel who were provided to Embassy officials were in the employment of Soviet intelligence. Nothing of any sensitivity or possible intelligence interest could be left unattended, even within the sanctity of the Embassy. Only the confines of a few secure offices were safe.

If Sam ever neglected to remember how closely he was being watched, the Russians quickly reminded him. At one time, Sam brought a 16mm film reel to Russia with him, a film given to him by British Independent Television. It depicted the details of his experiment in Long An and also included recordings of a series of his presentations. He kept it with him as a useful memento of his activity in that period. One day, however, he made the mistake of taking it to his quarters in the Embassy, rather than locking it away securely in his office. He put it on the desk in his study before he went to bed, and the next morning, it was gone. The old saying, "Big brother is watching you," applied to Sam and all Westerners in Moscow.

Sam had been in Moscow for only a few weeks before he was presented to the Chief of Staff of the Soviet Armed Forces, a four-star General, Viktor Kulikov, during a reception commemorating the national day of Poland, one of the Soviet's satellite countries. Sam was presented to General Kulikov by a Red Army colonel, whom Sam knew was also a member of the Soviet KGB. As he presented Sam to General Kulikov, the Colonel introduced him by saying, "This is Brigadier General Wilson, who has come to us from the American 82nd Airborne Division. General Wilson is the first American General to serve in Moscow since World War II."

While the statement was not entirely accurate, Sam did not endeavor to correct the exaggeration. The colonel continued, "And we are certain that General Wilson has come to us on a special mission. Is that not correct, Comrade General?"

Sam responded to the entrapping question quickly, "Of course, I have a special mission. Do you want to know what it is?"

For the first time, he had Kulikov's full attention. The general turned around and said, "Yes, I would like that."

Sam continued, "My mission is to study the Soviet Armed Forces from stem to stern in consummate detail and to learn your strengths and your weaknesses, your capabilities and your limitations, and to pay particular attention to your intentions."

Kulikov's face split with a broad grin, and he said to an aide, "Sklar, bring the vodka. I'd like to have a drink with this fellow."

From that point, thanks to his boldness in their initial encounter, Sam was able to build a healthy relationship of respect with the Chief of Staff of the Soviet Armed Forces General Staff.

Sam found that American intelligence officers in Moscow were playing what he considered to be a silly game of cops and robbers with their Russian surveillance counterparts. The Americans would wander around Russian military installations with their cameras and try to snap photographs of Soviet weapons. Occasionally, they would wind up in shouting incidents with the Russians. Police would be called, the cameras confiscated, and the attachés would be detained for questioning. After some posturing and intimidation by the Russians, they would release the Americans with threats that those types of activities could result in expulsion from the country.

In Sam's view, the value of the intelligence that officers were able to gain with their cameras in open Soviet cities like Moscow and Leningrad was minimal. With the diplomatic access to Soviet military representatives improving, he decided to place a greater emphasis on face-to-face dialogue with Soviets rather than such secretive maneuvers. He believed he could gain far more valuable information by asking specific questions of key Soviet personnel. With this theory in mind and in light of Washington's continued insistence on photographic work, Sam divided his staff into two groups. The larger group consisted of "white hats," those who concentrated on correct diplomatic behavior by working to develop relationships with key Soviet figures and creating opportunities to discuss useful subjects that the Soviets were willing to discuss. The second, smaller group was the "black hats," and Sam made sure that these people were assigned only when they had a few

months remaining in their Moscow tours. He decided that if an attaché were
to be kicked out of Russia because of flagrant disregard for the country's rules,
it would be someone whose tenure was already drawing to an end. Sam's
approach resulted in significant improvements in intelligence yield for the
Moscow office.

The Defense Attaché's office contained a file room where strategic
intelligence collection requirements (SICR's) were stored. Shortly after Sam's
arrival, he sat in this room and began to examine the intelligence collection
requirements. It did not take long for him to realize that they were so
intricately detailed that he could probably spend three years just trying to read
them all. Since SICR's were constantly being revised, he would then have to
start reading them again to catch up on the revisions. To Sam, the inordinate
number of requirements signified a case of bureaucratic practice run amok to
the point of uselessness.

Sam decided to address this matter with his boss, the Director of Defense
Intelligence Agency, General Don Bennett, on the first opportunity that
arose. The time came soon enough, when Sam returned to Washington about
three months after his initial arrival in Moscow. Sam approached the Director
of the DIA and said, "In my new post, I am having difficulty ascertaining
what your intelligence priorities are for me. What I really need from you is a
simple listing of the key intelligence questions that you want us to work on.
Could we sit down and develop the list of your intelligence priorities?"

With the aid of some of the key members of the Director's staff, the two
met and devised eleven specific areas on which Sam would gather intelligence
while in Moscow. The entire list was composed of real-world questions that
made sense, like the first one which read, "Can you learn anything about the
status of American POWs from Vietnam who have been taken to the Soviet
Union?"

General Bennett then proposed that they have the Chairman of the Joint
Chiefs of Staff critique the list. The Chairman added two questions of his
own and then suggested that they check the list with the Secretary of Defense.
The Secretary of Defense added one more question, making a list of fourteen
intelligence collection priorities. The list of specific questions gave Sam useful,
directed objectives for his assignment in Moscow.

When Sam returned to Moscow, he requested that the list be sent to him
so that he could begin his collection work. To his surprise, the embassy in
Moscow was considered too insecure to house such a sensitive list. Sam had
no choice but to wait two weeks for a trip to London, where he received the

list in the American embassy. For security, he memorized the priorities and destroyed the print version. When he returned to Moscow, he assembled his key subordinates in the acoustically secure conference room, the ACR.

The ACR, or Bubble, as the Americans called it, was really a room within a room, with the inner chamber suspended two feet from the ceiling, two feet off the floor, and two feet from the walls. The walls themselves were layered and rushing air swirled between the layers. When one entered the suspended conference room and closed the door, it felt like a vacuum. Only in that specially constructed "safe" room could Americans talk freely without fear of being overheard by Soviet spies.

When Sam's attachés gathered with him in the ACR, they also memorized the priorities as he quoted them. With everyone in sync on their missions, their efforts took on an efficient and directed character. It was these questions that drove intelligence collection of the Moscow operation thereafter, and its success was soon recognized in Washington.

Sam found that being idiomatically fluent in Russian gave him a great advantage at his post. He was conversant in a number of subjects that might have been closed to him otherwise. For example, while he was at Detachment R, he had majored in Russian and Soviet military history with a particular focus on the Soviet-German Front during World War II. His knowledge on that topic made him extremely popular among Soviet officers. It was not uncommon that he would find himself discussing battles from the Soviet-German front with someone who had been there. The Russians would, of course, know more than Sam about their piece of the battle, about what had been seen, felt, heard, and experienced, but often Sam knew more about the overall dynamics of the battle.

At one cocktail reception Sam was talking with a Soviet major general who had been a participant in the battle of Stalingrad in the winter of 1942-43. As the major general talked about the battle, he said, "Commander Zhukov came from Moscow to take command in October 1943."

Sam interrupted, "Excuse me, Sir, but I believe he came down earlier and, at Stalin's direction, primarily to inspect the front and oversee preparation for your counter-attack."

The man blinked, paused thoughtfully, and said, "Yes, I believe you're right."

He continued his story, "Then, when we brought our main forces across the Volga south of the city and began our counter-offensive against the Germans . . . "

Sam held up his finger again, "Excuse me, Sir, but I think you attacked initially against the Romanian Third Army, north of the city on November nineteenth, and the next day, November twentieth, you moved against the Romanian IV Corps south of the city . . . I have been told that Zhukov thought the Romanians there on both flanks would not fight as strongly as the Germans, so he went after them first."

After a number of these instances, the major general turned to Sam and said, "Who in the hell are you?"

He was shocked that Sam knew so much about the history of his country. Sam tried very hard not to be offensive or overbearing when sharing his knowledge of Russian military history, but he used it often enough to gain respect from the Soviets, and in turn, they were more willing to talk to him.

During the occasion of President Richard Nixon's visit to Moscow, in May 1972, for the Strategic Arms Limitation Talks known as SALT, the Soviet Politburo held a banquet in honor of the American President. Individuals occupying key positions in the American embassy were invited as guests, and Sam was expected to be there. Greeting the guests at the reception was a receiving line made up of the thirteen members of the Soviet Politburo, the ruling circle at the heart of the Communist party and the Soviet Government. As he proceeded through the reception line in his military dress uniform, Sam noted that immediately behind each member of the Politburo was a personal aide who whispered information about the individuals coming through the line. As Sam approached President Brezhnev, he could hear the aide telling the Soviet leader in a low voice, "This is General Wilson. He is a paratrooper, and he speaks Russian fluently." Brezhnev, very surprised by this flattering description of his American guest, turned, looked at his man, and exclaimed, "What do you mean?"

Sam approached, clicked his heels, and extended his hand.

"Say something in Russian," ordered Brezhnev.

"Of course, Comrade, Genius-like Secretary," replied Sam.

His response was a play on words, as the Russian words for "genius-like secretary" and "General Secretary" (of the Communist party of the Bolsheviks) differed by only a slight intonation variance. Sam began to complete his sentence, but Brezhnev looked at his name tag and said, "Wilson, Anglo-Saxon? That's impossible, a man who speaks Russian the way you're speaking it can only do so if he's learned it with his mother's milk. How do you explain that?"

Sam answered, "Well, Comrade President, you see, America is still the great melting pot. We have Americans of Russian ancestry, German ancestry, Spanish Ancestry, and Indian Ancestry. And I . . . I am a Russian of American ancestry." At that point President Brezhnev threw back his head and said, "I love this guy."

He grabbed Sam in a big bear hug. Sam had passed his language fluency test.

He did not realize it at first, but Sam eventually learned that it was a great advantage to him that he had come to Moscow from the 82nd Airborne Division. In a police state, and during this time period the Soviet Union was indeed a police state, the word "intelligence" is an ominous word. Sam came to Moscow to represent the American Armed Forces to the Soviet Military establishment, not simply because he was an intelligence officer. He was also a combat arms officer who had fought in battles and jumped from planes. Sam found that the Russians received him differently than they did Americans from intelligence backgrounds. Sam could pretend to be a brother-at-arms with the Russian military leaders, and the intelligence officers could not.

The primary opportunity to have interesting conversations discussing military history, military theory, strategy, doctrine, operational art, and even tactics with the Soviet leaders usually occurred at diplomatic receptions where military representatives of various nations gathered socially. On these occasions, Sam would often single out a Soviet commander and endeavor to engage him in conversations about pertinent topics, anything from the current state of the world to military aircraft. Sam found these conversations to be invaluable to his intelligence collection mission, and he made certain that he trained his subordinate officers to employ similar strategies.

One of the subjects which Sam eagerly explored was the Soviet concept of airborne operations. He wanted to learn how the Soviets intended to use their parachute divisions in a conflict with America. Several days before a reception honoring the Romanian National Day, Sam pulled together all the documentation he could find on Soviet airborne operations. He carefully prepared himself for an encounter with a man he knew would be at the reception, a Soviet lieutenant general who was the Chief of Operations and Plans for the Soviet Armed Forces General Staff.

The night of the reception, Sam found the general, and they clicked wine glasses. They had always shared a reasonably affable acquaintance, so talk came naturally. The General's opening gambit to Sam was, "How's the spy business going these days?"

Sam's calculated response was, "I'm no spy, I'm a combat arms commander.

Furthermore, I am a paratrooper."

He said, "We know that. You came to us from the *et dus* (the 82nd Airborne)."

Sam answered, "Yes Sir, in fact, that's exactly what I want to talk to you about. I have a question."

"Let's hear it," replied the General.

"The 82nd division, when it stands to force, can have as many as twenty to twenty-two thousand soldiers and personnel ready to deploy. You, on the other hand, have seven separate airborne divisions."

"How do you know that?" The General was taken aback with the extent of Sam's familiarity with the Soviet military.

"Come on, everyone knows that," chided Sam. "In fact, you have an 8th division, but it is just a training division. The point is, each of your divisions is roughly seven thousand troops, which means that the 82nd is three times the size of each of your airborne divisions. We are heavy, you are light. The question is, who is right?"

The General paused to think carefully. "Tell me, Paratrooper. Who is your worst enemy?"

Sam pointed to the tank emblem on the General's lapel.

"Go to the head of the class," applauded the General. "Tell me, how deep are you willing to drop the *et dus* in the rear of my armored formation?"

Sam protested the incomplete question. "For me to answer that, you've got to give me some facts about the existing situation. We have to have a scenario. Where are we? On the central plains of Europe or darkest Africa? Who is attacking whom? What is the force ratio? Who has air superiority? How long have we been fighting? Are we up to strength? All these variables have a bearing on my answer."

"OK," agreed the General. "We fix you a scenario."

The pair finally agreed that their situation put Sam's division in Europe, where the Soviet War Pact Forces had broken through NATO Forces onto the plains of Europe. Their advance had stalled, and the Allies were getting ready to try a counter offensive, involving the 82nd Airborne as part of the attack. They also decided that the general was the commanding general of the Soviet First Guards' tank army.

Sam thought to himself about how far behind his opponent's lines he might drop his troops. "Thirty-five kilometers, maybe fifty. Push me, I'll go sixty-five," he told himself. But he exaggerated his response, "Sixty kilometers, maybe even eighty kilometers. Push me and I'll go ninety."

The Soviet general was amazed and called over his buddies as he further exaggerated Sam's already exaggerated response. "This Son-of-a-Gun is going to drop his *et dus* one hundred kilometers in the rear of my First-Guards tank army."

They began to bang their glasses, stomp their feet, and yell in excitement. When the ruckus died down, the general asked Sam to prolong the scenario. "How long can you stay there and hole up with your troops until the main NATO force somehow breaks through our lines to relieve the pressure that I'm going to put on you?"

"Haven't I taught you anything?" Sam inquired with feigned incredulity. The general turned red in the face at Sam's response. "We have to further explain the scenario. When I dropped, did I drop on a single large airhead or do I now hold multiple isolated airheads? What were my losses when I dropped the *et dus*? What is my state of supply? Most importantly, what is the weather, and who has air superiority?"

By this time, Sam had seven or eight Soviet officers working out the scenario for him. They finally provided the details and then demanded to know what he would do. Sam ventured, "Ok, three, maybe five days. Push me, and I'll stay ten."

His exaggerated response excited the Soviet officers. From that initial repartee, Sam verbally war-gamed the 82nd against the Soviet general's tank army at social gatherings for eighteen months. After every encounter, Sam wrote up his opposite's reactions. After a few submissions to Washington, he learned that his war-game scenario had accumulated quite an audience in American military circles. People were avidly awaiting his next report.

Months later, when Sam returned to Washington after his Moscow assignment and was promoted to Deputy to the Director of Central Intelligence, he called the Chief of the Strategic Research Division for the CIA and said, "Hank, I've got an idea for a little study. The Pentagon probably won't like it, but I think that you can do it and it will be valuable to us."

Sam described how useful it would be for the CIA to prepare an analysis of how the Soviet military viewed American military forces, with chapters addressing Soviet views on American amphibious warfare, armored warfare, and air-assault operations. The helicopter became the "horse" for the U.S. military in Vietnam. What did they think of that? He also was interested in Soviet views on the U.S. doctrine for use of air-ground support, and on the use of air power in general. Especially having in mind the 82nd Airborne Division, Sam concluded by suggesting that it would be useful to have a chapter on how the Soviets viewed American airborne warfare concepts.

Forty days later, Hank dropped a draft of the project on Sam's desk. Sam thumbed through most of it casually because he really just wanted to read about the 82nd Airborne Division. He was delighted when he found a passage that read, "For some reason which we cannot fully explicate or understand, the Soviets have an extraordinarily exaggerated view of the capabilities of the 82nd Airborne Division." Just as he had hoped, Sam's conversations with the Soviet generals must have reverberated through the Soviet military system.

In the spring of 1972, Sam's son Hap returned to the U.S. and the University of North Carolina to continue his studies. Shortly thereafter, in May 1972, Brenda, Susan, David, and an American nanny joined Sam in Moscow. Sam wanted his family to be comfortably situated, but the summer of 1972 was the hottest summer in the recorded history of the city. The temperature was constantly in the nineties, sometimes climbing to 100 degrees Fahrenheit. The heat continued day after day.

Moscow's buildings were poorly air-conditioned, on the occasion when they were air-conditioned at all, so there was no escape from the heat. Russian gasoline was inferior to that in the U.S., and their automobile engines poorly engineered, so Sam could look down the wide boulevards of Moscow, some ten or fourteen lanes wide, and see disabled vehicles parked with their hoods up and Russian drivers beating on carburetors with hammers. Conditions grew even more unpleasant when two Soviet fighter pilots ignited peat moss in a swamp outside of Moscow. The moss burned underground for weeks and then eventually began to emerge in forest fires throughout the region.

The Soviets sent tanks to help extinguish the fires, but nothing could stop their burning. The sky over Moscow grew gray and cloudy from the fire's smoke. Sam could smell it constantly. It stung his eyes, burned his nose, and added to the intense heat, all of which made conditions miserable.

It was especially hard for Sam's family. Moscow's sweltering environment proved extremely difficult for Brenda, and it proved impossible for Susan. Brenda longed for the peace and comfort of the Virginia countryside, and Susan needed careful attention. In August, they returned to the States though, even in Virginia, the health of both Susan and Brenda continued to deteriorate. Eventually, Sam had to request relief from his Moscow assignment.

Finally, in the middle of August, rain came to the Moscow area. The storm lasted for two days, washing the sky clean and putting out the forest fires. The air began to smell sweet again. Just at that time, Sam was scheduled to return to Washington to prepare for a regular conference. He normally paid a visit to his friend, General Kulikov, before he returned to the U.S., so he was driven to Ministry of Defense in the gentle falling rain. Kulikov was standing at the window looking out at the rain when Sam arrived. He turned to Sam and commented, "Praise the Lord. As the peasants say, rain is coming down like it is being poured out of a bucket."

Then he shifted his tone abruptly and said, "You know what, Wilson? If we have this problem that we're having with a forest fire on three sides of Moscow, what would we do if we had to deal with a nuclear attack? This just reminds us how serious it would be. The living would envy the dead. You know, despite our differences in view, we really must work very hard to ensure that such a day never comes."

Kulikov requested that Sam tell his bosses in the United States just what he had said, and Sam willingly obliged.

Throughout his tenure in Moscow, Sam made regular return trips to Washington during which he would report to the Joint Chiefs of Staff about conversations he had been having with their counterparts in Russia. The chiefs seemed to find these sessions valuable, so much so that they insisted they be continued, despite the long travel time required for Sam.

In November of 1972, Sam began to experience what his doctor called laryngial spasms, spasms of the larynx. He had also developed a serious problem with the acronym GERDS–Gastro-Esophageal Reflux Disease. As early as 1964, before he went to Vietnam, Sam had been diagnosed with a hiatal hernia, a bulge in his esophagus, and that hernia had exacerbated the gastro-intestinal problem while he was in Moscow. His GERDS condition further deteriorated because Sam was not controlling his diet as he should have with a carefully planned regimen and no alcohol. In Moscow, however, Sam ate the meals the Russians provided for him at his house, and at embassy functions he feasted on whatever culinary specialty was served—rich dishes, spicy tidbits, and decadent deserts. With the demands of his attaché circuit, it was not unusual for him to drink and smoke heavily and often.

One day, Sam was sitting at his desk when, all of a sudden, his throat closed, and he simply could not breathe. He stood up and gasped, unable to get breath into his lungs. He instinctively raised his arms, and in doing so sucked in a little air, but he quickly felt faint. Thankfully, as he grew faint, the muscles in his throat relaxed. He began to breathe a little easier and slowly recovered from the scare. From that point on, however, similar spasms would periodically hit Sam without warning. They felt as though someone had choked his windpipe, and they were always frightening.

His condition forced him to be evacuated to the military hospital at Wiesbaden Air Force Base in Frankfurt. From there, he was transferred to Walter Reed Army Medical Center in Washington.

Since August, when Brenda, Susan, and David had returned to the States from Moscow, Sam had been keeping in touch with them through post cards, letters, and regular phone calls. He realized that his wife and daughter still were not well, especially Susan. He cautioned his sons to be very gentle as they informed their mother of his illness. He wanted to downplay his condition until the doctors determined exactly what was wrong. Despite his sons' efforts to calm Brenda's fears, she was at his side when Sam woke the morning of his second day at Walter Reed. She and Susan had driven up from the farm to be with him. The family was together again, but this time Sam was not on his feet and his daughter was quite ill. It was not the homecoming from Moscow that Sam had planned.

Sam eventually recovered, at least in part, and soon Susan also improved and was placed in the psychiatric ward at Walter Reed. For Thanksgiving, the military District Director of Washington flew Sam from Walter Reed to his farm in a helicopter. Already there before his dad, David threw a smoke grenade so that the pilots could judge the wind direction as they landed in the field across the lake from the farm house. David met the helicopter with a tractor and trailer, ready to haul his father to the house. For the next ten days, Sam stayed there and improved his health. By early December, he had recovered sufficiently thathe could head back to complete his duties in Moscow, but his heart was heavy with the knowledge that Brenda's health was failing.

By February, Sam decided that his family's growing health problems demanded his attention. The time had come to return to the U.S. The family was suffering. Both Susan and Brenda were experiencing health problems. Sam, Jr. had broken his leg in a night parachuting-operation exercise at Fort Bragg. Hap, who had returned to the University of North Carolina, was beginning to require psychiatric treatment. Sam's family needed him. He explained his situation to the Director of the DIA and to the Chief of Staff of the Army, and although he figured that he would be forced to retire, there was no other option but to go home and care for his family.

His military superiors in Washington saw things differently. They discussed what possibilities were open to help Sam. They wanted to station him so that he could still contribute his experience and talents to the U.S. military while simultaneously keeping an eye on his family. All agreed that it was too early for Sam to retire as a Brigadier General.

The Chief of Staff of the Army at that time was a former tank warrior named Abe Abrams. He had been in Patton's Third Army during World War II and had built a reputation as a genuine American hero. He recognized that they had to help Sam, but he also wanted to retain Sam in the American military. As a solution, Sam was given a less-stressful assignment in Washington as the Director of Estimates for the Defense Intelligence Agency. There, he would be close enough to be with his family but he also could remain active in American military policy development.

WASHINGTON FINALE

WHEN SAM RETURNED to Washington from Moscow, he had no way of knowing what the future would hold for him, and it is unlikely that he would have guessed that for the next four and a half years he would remain in the nation's capital. During that period he held five different jobs in what became a very turbulent cycle in which he would assume a position, learn it thoroughly, and begin doing worthwhile things in it, only to be promoted shortly thereafter. He spent such a short time at each assignment that an outsider might have assumed that his superiors did not value him.

In early March 1973, at the age of fifty, Sam began serving as the Director of Estimates for the DIA. Brenda and Susan had decided to stay at the farm in Rice, and Sam considered his future too unclear to warrant the purchase of a house in Washington. Fortunately, Brenda had an elderly cousin named Helen Newton who lived in D.C. and who doted on Sam. She offered him rooms in her home, which was very conveniently located on the edge of Rock Creek Park and across the street from the Chinese Embassy. She had plenty of space and gave Sam his own suite in her apartment. The most fortunate thing about the apartment was that Sam had only a ten-minute commute across the Roosevelt Bridge to his new job. His workload was so heavy that he woke at four every morning and rarely got home before ten in the evening, but Sam often could escape to the farm for Saturday afternoons and typically remained there until Sunday evening.

At the Directorate for Estimates, Sam worked with a group of military intellectuals, about half of whom were high-ranking civilian professionals. Their job was "estimative intelligence," especially determining long-range threats to U.S. foreign policy and national security interests for fifteen to twenty years down the road, the approximate length of time necessary to develop and deploy major new weapons platforms, such as capital items like aircraft carriers, submarines, and bombers. The Directorate for Estimates projects the political, economic, sociological, and military situations of other countries for coming decades, and from their estimates, the U.S. government plans programs and forecasts budgetary requirements necessary for the defense of our interests against future threats. The Directorate for Estimates also works with our closest allies, the British, Canadians, Australians, and New Zealanders, to develop international intelligence estimates for potential threats of mutual interest. It is a complex, demanding, intellectually challenging, and strategically vital undertaking. Before or since, Sam never faced more daunting intellectual challenges.

From time to time, it was necessary for Sam to give briefings on these estimates to the Chairman of the Joint Chiefs of Staff as well as to the Secretary of Defense. Sam well recalls his first briefing to Defense Secretary James Schlesinger, who had a reputation for chewing up and spitting out people who dared tell him something he had not anticipated. Sam happened to open his briefing with a statement concerning the value of working with our close allies on estimates and how much we gained from their insights. He was just proceeding to the meat of his briefing when Schlesinger raised his hand and cocked his head with irritation.

Sam said, "Mr. Secretary, if you'll give me four minutes, I'll provide you the basis for my assertion. If you're not satisfied by that point, I'll be happy to save you some time by departing."

Schlesinger removed his pipe and told Sam to proceed. When Sam finished the basis for his presentation, he asked the Defense Secretary if he could continue.

Schlesinger encouraged him, "Go on. This is becoming interesting."

Sam's friendship with Secretary Schlesinger, which developed into a strong one, began at that moment.

In October 1973, everyone was surprised when war suddenly broke out in the Middle East between the Israelis and the Arabs. In Sam's world, surprises of that nature meant that the American intelligence net had failed. It was an extremely tense period, because the United States was backing Israel and the Soviet Union was backing the Arabs. The United States brought forces to defense-ready positions (Def Con II), just one level short of deploying the forces for war. They saw the Soviets making similar moves, especially with their airborne divisions. For several days, the Israeli situation remained desperate. Then gradually, the tide began to turn and eventually the Israelis commanded a stronger position than they had before the conflict began.

Sam was directed to fly to Moscow and talk to some of his old acquaintances in the Soviet military high command to ensure that a foolish move did not cause an already tense situation to worsen. In Moscow, Sam managed to see his old friend, General Kulikov, at a reception, but as Sam greeted him, Kulikov gruffly complained, "Don't you remember the things I said before? Are your chiefs crazy? The situation in the Middle East has become very dangerous!"

Sam said, "Comrade Chief of Staff, we saw your airborne divisions being alerted and prepared for immediate operations. What else would you expect but for us to go to a similar alert level?"

The General paused, and then said, "Well, all right. We've just got to be very careful."

Fortunately, by this time, the war was beginning to wind down and the two superpowers remained on the sidelines.

On his return to America, Sam flew from Moscow to London, where he transferred to another airline and for the flight across the Atlantic found himself seated next to an American surgeon from Boston. In the course of their conversation, Sam discovered that the surgeon was a lieutenant colonel in the Israeli Army Reserve. He was an American citizen, and American citizens are not supposed to hold positions in someone else's foreign army. But he was called to active duty as the war broke out, and his medical talents were badly needed. He was able to describe the war in some detail from the vantage point of an Israeli field hospital facility, and his remarks formed the basis for part of Sam's report to his superiors upon his return to Washington.

Sam was promoted to Major General in June of 1973. On the heels of this happy event, Sam received a telephone call from the command sergeant major of the 82nd Airborne Division who said, "A little bird tells me that you may soon be coming our way to take over the division. Is this so?"

Sam had to tell him that he had heard nothing about it, but that it would be good news if indeed it were true. It would mean that Sam would be back at Fort Bragg and his family could live with him on post, and he would enjoy being back with the troops. In late fall 1973, however, Sam was asked to transfer from his position as Deputy for Estimates in the DIA to the Office of Deputy for Attachés and Training. Sam moved into his new office in January 1974 and rumors about the potential post at Fort Bragg slowly subsided.

As Deputy Director for Attachés and Training, Sam was responsible for the preparation of attachés for their upcoming assignments around the world. He supervised and coordinated their activities while they were on station, and he was responsible for ensuring that they were appropriately debriefed and cared for when they completed their assignments. At the time, the United States had military attachés in about one hundred countries around the world. In some of the smaller embassies, there might be only one attaché, but in larger countries, there could be up to fifteen supporting personnel. In

Moscow, the Defense Attaché's office consisted of forty-four employees. In total, Sam had about four hundred attachés preparing for their upcoming assignments, about four hundred more already stationed in embassies, and about four hundred in the post-assignment process.

Although it lasted only about nine months, this was one of Sam's favorite jobs of his entire military career. He compared it to his time as one of Merrill's chief reconnaissance officers during the North Burma campaign of '43 and '44, when he would set up a patrol base deep in enemy territory and then send out separate patrols to determine what was happening in the surrounding area. In Washington, he was at a patrol base sending attachés to a hundred different countries to gather intelligence and to represent the United States.

With attaché officers scattered around the world, this assignment required Sam to grab his diplomatic passport and make trips to areas he had not yet visited, not even in his diplomatic courier days where he visited countries "peripheral to the Soviet Union." In addition to being able to help resolve problems in the local offices, these travels allowed Sam to add to the number of countries around the world that he had visited. At one time, he had visited just about all of the countries that appeared on the world map.

In the United States military services, an attaché has three major functions. First, he is the military advisor to the American ambassador in whose embassy he serves. Second, he represents his military service to the host country's military service. Finally, he is responsible, in professionally unobtrusive and non-flamboyant ways, for gathering intelligence about the host country's military. Attachés are intelligence collectors, but they avoid the spy business. The attaché's ability to produce relevant information generally depends upon the relationships he forms while at the station. Only in rare instances will an attaché with an appropriate background be called upon to become involved in any espionage.

This assignment enabled Sam to apply everything he had ever learned about leadership to ensure that the United States had properly qualified people on the job. One problem that quickly became apparent to Sam was that attachés had no suitable space at the DIA complex to work or address necessary personal business when they returned to the United States. To help accommodate these valuable officers, Sam was able to establish an area at his office with bulletin boards, telephones, safes, street maps, and even a coffee maker and a television so that the attachés had a comfortable environment to sit when they came back to visit. He also provided them with a secretary to take dictation, run errands, and answer questions. Returning attachés appreciated these support services, and morale immediately improved.

In July 1974, Sam received a telephone call from the office of the Director of Central Intelligence, William E. Colby, asking whether he was interested in taking a job as Colby's Deputy Director. Sam replied that he would be interested, and, several days later, he received a call from Colby's special assistant asking if he could talk with the Director. Sam agreed. He had very high professional regard for Bill Colby, especially for the work that he had done over the years in Southeast Asia. When Sam entered Colby's office, the two men shook hands. Colby quickly began the conversation with "Now, Sam, the first thing I want you to do when you get here is . . . " Sam caught his breath. Colby had not even asked Sam if he wanted the job, or if he were interested in the job, but he treated him as though he already had accepted the offer. Despite Colby's somewhat rash assumption, he was completely correct. Sam took on the position as Deputy Director of Central Intelligence, a three-star position, with enthusiasm.

Some three weeks later, Sam left his old post at the DIA and moved his office to CIA headquarters in Langley. Sam also moved from his Washington residence to on-post quarters at Fort Belvoir in Northern Virginia, and he brought Brenda and Susan from the farm to be with him. Once again, they had commodious quarters. They also had two enlisted aides to attend to the family's needs. Sam was even assigned a car with a driver. He quickly settled into the new routine.

During that time, Director of Central Intelligence Colby had two major responsibilities. The first assignment was to direct the Central Intelligence Agency. But beyond that, he also had overall policy supervisory responsibility, including ultimate budgetary authority, over the other major offices and elements of the US intelligence community. Sam had been brought on as deputy to help carry out this second responsibility. He had his work cut out for him. His first obstacle was that he had important supervisory responsibilities but not the appropriate authority to accomplish them. The job was also made difficult because lines of responsibility and authority were poorly defined. The confusion often created misunderstandings and developed frequent tensions among the higher command of American intelligence. For example, the Director of the DIA was responsible for looking to the Director of Central Intelligence for policy guidance in intelligence matters, in putting together budgets and programs, and for coordinating operations involving more than one agency. At the same time, the Director of the DIA worked directly for the Secretary of Defense and the Chairman of the Joint Chiefs of Staff. This situation produced a dilemma because it was unclear who had the ultimate authority.

Several years later, when Sam became the Director of DIA himself, he met with President Jimmy Carter and was briefing the President and assembled heads of the intelligence community's offices and agencies. When Sam referred to the Director of the CIA as the "titular head" of the intelligence community, President Carter interrupted him and said, "Stop right there, General. The Director of Central Intelligence is THE head of the intelligence community. He is your boss, and don't you ever forget it. Do you understand me, General?"

Though he held his tongue, Sam wanted to say, "Mr. President, will you please pass this clarification on to the Secretary of Defense and the Chairman of the Joint Chiefs Staff, who at the present time both suffer from the delusion that they are my boss and that I report exclusively to them."

As the Deputy to the Director of Central Intelligence, Sam was once again rising to go to work each morning at four o'clock and rarely returning to his quarters before ten at night. With Sam so engaged in work, Brenda began spending most of her time back at the farm in Rice, and while Sam was saddened by her absence, he understood it was best for her happiness and well-being. At the same time, Sam could not help but enjoy his work at a level where consequential policy decisions were being made. He was at Langley with CIA professionals, many of whom he had come to know well over the years, and he often worked with key members of the White House staff. Professionally, it was a dream job.

In the middle of December 1974, an article appeared in the *New York Times* by a correspondent, Seymour Hersch, exposing a number of times when the U.S. intelligence community had broken the law and trampled on civil rights in the quest for information. This article and its follow-up initiated a tumultuous period which Sam's counterparts dubbed "the intelligence inquisition." American public media watchdogs were in full bay looking for intelligence misdeeds on the part of the CIA and other agencies. Congress assumed a mission of finding the guilty parties and cleaning up the "mess," as they saw it. One Senator, Idahoan Senator Frank Church, referred to the CIA as a "rogue elephant run amok." Two separate committees were established: the House Select Committee on Intelligence, led by Democrat New York Congressmen Otis C. Pike, and the Senate Committee on Intelligence, led by Senator Church. On several occasions, Sam was called to appear before both committees to defend the intelligence community. One of his speeches in particular was sufficiently well-received to be read into the *Congressional Record*.

By the time Sam's was serving his final tenure in Washington, a number of his friends in the CIA had risen to top executive positions in the clandestine services. Sam spent time with these old buddies and became conversant with some of the key, on-going operations of that time. He was able to further his bond with his colleagues during the daily morning meetings that Director Colby held with the CIA staff. Sam always enjoyed working with the clandestine services, and even though he was a military man and wore his uniform most of the time, he found that they treated him with warmth, consideration, and trust.

As another part of his service for the intelligence community, Sam returned to Moscow several times and maintained his ties with acquaintances in the Soviet military. All of his work in intelligence combined with his official duties to make his life extremely busy, but during those months Sam gained an overall appreciation of the scope and substance of the CIA's undertakings.

One of Sam's fondest memories as the Deputy to the Director of Central Intelligence was times that he engaged in war scenarios with other, senior, U.S. policy-makers at a secret underground facility in Maryland. On one occasion, they were war-gaming a Soviet invasion of Iran from the north with the U.S. team endeavoring to respond with available forces coming up from the south and west. The U.S. side was headed by the Secretary of Defense, James Schlesinger, and Sam had been selected to command the Soviet forces arrayed against him. At the end of three days, Sam had the Red Soviet Russian forces driving the U.S. into the Persian Gulf. Sam hoped that in the process of the war games, Schlesinger and his fellow invaders had learned a few lessons about how to handle troops when or if they ever attempted such an invasion.

Sam had assumed the post of Deputy to the Director of Central Intelligence in September 1974, and he continued in that capacity until Colby was replaced by newly-elected President Ford in 1976. Colby's successor, appointed by President Ford, was George H. W. Bush, who had been serving as the American ambassador to the People's Republic of China. Sam continued his responsibilities as Deputy under George H. W. Bush for several months, and his first task was to brief the new Director on the intelligence community as an institution. During their sessions together, the two men came to know each other quite well and ultimately became good friends.

After several months as Bush's Deputy, Sam was offered the job of Director of the Defense Intelligence Agency by newly appointed Secretary of

Defense, Donald Rumsfeld. Sam left his office in CIA headquarters in early January 1976 and was temporarily appointed Deputy Assistant Secretary of Intelligence in the Pentagon while he awaited official appointment as the Director of the DIA, an appointment that became official in May 1976.

Sam assumed the directorship of the Defense Intelligence Agency at a time when the entire U.S. government was in a budget crunch, and an extensive planning and review effort was underway to completely reorganize defense intelligence. Because of severe resource constraints, one of the options being considered was the dissolution of the DIA. Sam was convinced that this would be a very serious mistake, and he worked to prevent such action.

The DIA had initially been established in 1961 as part of an effort to coordinate the intelligence operations of the Army, Navy, and Air Force. Defense Secretary McNamara established the DIA as the intelligence advisor to the Chairman of the Joint Chiefs of Staff and to coordinate the separate activities of military intelligence services. Even then, there was a great deal of resistance to this attempt to unify the varied elements of military intelligence, and progress proved slow and painful. Still, progress had been made, and the benefits of coordinating intelligence efforts were obvious. Sam believed that all that progress would be undone if the DIA were eliminated. Bureaucratic battles can be acrimonious and bitter, but cooler heads prevailed and the threat to the DIA's existence eventually dissipated.

During the Cold War period, the number one intelligence priority involved documenting Soviet capabilities, limitations, and intentions. The core intelligence question for the United States and its allies was whether the Soviets believed they could fight a war against the United States and its allies at nuclear levels and emerge victorious. The answer to this crucial question had overwhelming potential for United States strategy in the Cold War, and for strategic purposes, it was critical to the U.S. that the Soviets believe they were too weak to emerge victorious from a nuclear conflict. The full history of this highly dangerous and complex Cold War stand-off is yet to be written in fine detail, but suffice it to say that Sam and the DIA played a valuable role in informing the President of the United States and his key advisors on this basic question.

Sam was close to the situation and evaluated relevant information on a daily basis. He had no delusions about the importance of the Soviet's perception of U.S. strengths, and he often recalled the remark by the Soviet Armed Forces Chief of Staff, Marshal Kulikov, on that rainy day in August 1972: "A nuclear war would be mankind's worst nightmare. The living would envy the dead.

We must do all within our power on both sides to ensure that it never takes place."

Sam headed the DIA at a time when the U.S. remained nose-to-nose with its Soviet enemy. Nuclear missiles on both sides were pointed at each other. It would not have taken much for missiles to fly. If the U.S. detected a salvo of incoming ballistic missiles, the response would be immediate and would involve nuclear missile counter-attacks. Sam understood that his work with the DIA provided intelligence that involved the ultimate fate of the United States.

He was again rising at dawn in his quarters at Fort Belvoir, arriving in his office by six and rarely going home before ten at night. He worked nearly every Saturday for at least ten hours, leaving only Sunday to catch his breath, take care of personal matters, and share a little time with his family. Sometimes, when things were "hot," even Sundays became just another workday.

During this time the United States' strategic and conventional forces and the Soviets were essentially at a face-to-face standoff. To gain an advantage, the Soviets endeavored to move around the U.S. flanks to underdeveloped nations of the Third World. They hoped through revolutionary means to subvert from within vulnerable countries in Africa, Latin America, and Southeast Asia. Sam found the entire intelligence community, including his DIA, strangely uninterested in countering what the Soviets had dubbed "Wars of National Liberation." Combining multiple elements of his past, this time by connecting his Special Operations and low-intensity conflict interests with his intelligence experience, Sam worked to raise the visibility of this indirect threat and to repel the effects of Soviet wars of "national liberation."

As Director of the DIA, Sam enjoyed the return visits to Moscow that he was required to make every four or five months. Russians greet November seventh, the anniversary of the Bolshevik Revolution in Russia, with great celebration and festivity each year. Sam realized that the various social occasions associated with this holiday would afford him maximum access to senior Soviet military leaders and staff officers, so he made a particular point of returning to Moscow over that holiday in 1976. He was especially interested in attending the Soviet Armed Forces parade across Red Square.

At the parade, Sam sat in the visitors' stands in a reserved VIP position. As it was concluding, he saw his old friend, General Kulikov, descend from the top of Lenin's mausoleum where he and the Politburo had been viewing the demonstration of Soviet military might as it crossed the square. Sam was aware that on such occasions Kulikov greeted all the foreign military attachés, so he made his way to the spot where the general was standing and was first in line. Kulikov was pleasant and cordial. They chatted, and then Sam hurried over to the edge of the square where the Commander of the Moscow Military District, a three-star colonel general, and the overall Parade Marshal, a two-star lieutenant-colonel general, were standing. Sam was in his three-star military uniform when he approached them, and he saluted them with pleasantries about the celebratory occasion.

Turning to the senior of the two generals, he said, "Well, what's new?" The colonel general responded with the Russian peasants' saying, "Nothing is new. Everything is as it was."

At this point, Sam objected, saying, "That's not possible, Comrade General. That offends the Marxian dialectic."

The general turned and looked pointedly at Sam as he said, "Well, Samuel Son-of-Jasper, according to Marx, everything is in motion and everything is in the process of change. In reality, here in Moscow everything is in motion, but nothing ever changes."

While only a sophisticate in Marxian dialectics would understand the underlying meaning of those words, Sam realized that the general had just spoken words of high treason about the Soviet Communist system. Sam marveled that the general trusted him enough to criticize the Communist system in front of him. The general was admitting that, even in the Communist capital of the world, the system was frozen in time. If a Communist Party Commissar had heard that statement, the three-star general would have been arrested for speaking blasphemy, yet he knew he could speak to Sam with impunity.

Sam's position as Director of the DIA required that he travel extensively in the Middle East, North Africa, the Far East, South America, and all over Europe. In the spring of 1977, he flew to Teheran, Iran, with orders to brief the Shah of Iran on the military capabilities of Iraq. This briefing required special permission from the Office of the President because it included sensitive information about Iraq's technological and military capabilities. The briefing lasted over three hours and involved more than two hundred illustrated slides. Moscow had, by that time, provided Iraq with an overwhelming and frightening amount of war material. While Sam was describing the build-up of arms, he watched the Shah grow pale and increasingly subdued. When Sam finished his briefing, he asked the Shah if he had any questions. The Shah paused and said, "I would like for you to give this briefing to my senior commanders and the Iranian Imperial Staff. Can you do it?"

This was quite a demand, especially since President Ford had only given Sam permission to present the information to the Shah. Sam glanced at Ambassador Richard Helms, a former Director of the CIA, who sat in on the presentation. He caught an almost imperceptible nod from Helms. "Of course, Your Majesty," Sam responded. "When and where would you like for me to give it?"

That afternoon, Sam repeated his presentation for the senior members of the Iranian military. There was a palpable hush hanging over the auditorium when he finished. That evening, he was honored at a reception and a banquet that was one of the most lavish affairs Sam had ever attended. Though the atmosphere was greatly subdued, it was a memorable evening. It wasn't many months later that Sam studied photographs portraying the last vestiges of the deposed Iranian Shah's regime. Rows of bodies lay dead before a wall. The Shah's loyalists, including many of the men to whom Sam had given his presentation, had been machine gunned by Iranian revolutionaries under the leadership of Ayatollah Khomeini.

On another of his many trips, Sam was boarding a flight from Italy to North Africa when he heard the raucous laugh of Sam Fuller, the writer and director of the *Merrill's Marauders* movie. Fuller came sauntering onto the plane with an unlit cigar in his mouth. He spotted Sam and stopped in his tracks. The cigar fell out of his mouth and landed on the floor. He bent over to pick it up, looked up at Sam, and said, "I'll be damned! And wearing three stars, no less!"

Sam moved his assistant to a seat next to Fuller's assistant and sat beside his old friend on the flight to Tunis. It was, as always, a joy to sit next to the electric and effervescent Sammy Fuller, who bubbled with acrid humor. During the flight Fuller endeavored to get Sam to forget about his diplomatic mission and join him on his search for suitable locations to reenact the activities of the United States First Infantry Division in the North African Campaign of World War II. To his great chagrin, Sam had to walk away from Fuller's blandishments and stick to the official schedule while Fuller went off on a picnic to Kasserine Pass, the scene of one of World War II's most overwhelming American defeats. The echoes of the funny little man's raucous laughter played in Sam's memory for a long time after their chance meeting and replayed again whenever he saw the film that Fuller produced in Tunisia, *The Big Red One.*

By the summer of 1977, the strain of working long hours was being felt by Sam and his family. Brenda's health had deteriorated to such an extent that the doctor at Fort Belvoir called Sam in one day to talk. As Sam sat there, he heard a dire report, "Your wife has a number of serious maladies. For one thing, her liver is failing. She probably is not going to live more than another couple of years."

Sam believed he had only one option. Brenda had been the tail of his kite as he floated around the world most of the years of their marriage. It was her turn to direct their movements. Sam submitted his retirement papers to effect his relief from active military service, effective 31 August 1977.

On that day, a Tuesday, fifty-three-year-old Sam stood on a reviewing stand at the Fort Bragg parade ground, not far from the house in which he and Brenda had spent four wonderful years. He watched an aerial flyby and a skydiving demonstration in which the Green Berets from his old command passed a baton while they hurtled from twenty thousand feet. Upon landing, they presented the baton to Sam. A procession passed before him with troops from Special Forces units, psychological operations units, a special detachment from the 75th Army Rangers bearing the colors of Merrill's Marauders, and troops of the 82nd Airborne Division. During the retirement ceremony, Sam heard telegrams from the Secretary of Defense, the Chairman of the Joint Chiefs of Staff, the Secretary of the Army, and the Chief of Staff of the Army, all of whom sent their best wishes for Sam's retirement. After the procession, the speeches, and the singing of "Auld Lang Syne," a reception with cold drinks and cake on the parade ground gave Sam a chance to meet with old friends and commanders who had gathered to celebrate his career.

Late in the evening of his retirement day, Sam flew from Fort Bragg to Farmville, where his brother met him at the airport. John drove Sam to his house, where Sam got out of his military uniform, thinking it would be for the last time. He changed into walking clothes, boots, a cowboy hat, and a white brush jacket. Then, just before sunset, his brother drove Sam to downtown Farmville and parked in front of the courthouse. Sam walked from the car to a granite marker that had been erected on the green grass in front of the courthouse. On that marker was a large brass plaque containing the names of fifty local men who went off to World War II but never returned. A number of them had been in the National Guard's Company G with Sam.

Sam hung his retirement medal on the granite maker, gave his fallen comrades his snappiest salute, and turned to walk across the street to the site of the old armory where he had first signed up for the National Guard. Sam knocked on the double doors, but of course no one answered. It was already after six o'clock and the insurance agency that had been housed there for years was closed for the day. Sam hitched up his trousers and walked in reverse the same route that he had traveled at a dog-trot to enlist in the National Guard on that rainy night in June 1940.

He was not endeavoring to be theatric or to engage in a dramatic gesture. Walking the route backwards simply felt like the right thing to do. It was already fully dark when Sam arrived at the old farmhouse. Brenda was waiting in the porch swing and holding a glass of iced tea for him. He accepted it gratefully. A dedicated American soldier had finally come home.

BOOK 3

ACADEMIC LIFE

THE FIRST RETIREMENT

ON HIS FIRST EVENING in retirement, General Sam symbolically returned to his roots by reversing his patriotic journey of 1940, walking from the courthouse in Farmville to his family home near Rice, where his sister, Virginia, still lived. It was also the beginning of what promised to be an opportunity to pursue a different sort of life from the one he had known in the military. He and Brenda lingered for a time with family who had gathered at the home place, and then they drove down the road to their own farm, affectionately named "Frog Hollow." It was late, and General Sam was exhausted from the festivities of the day, but he was also restless from the excitement and from his realization that a great weight of responsibility had been lifted from his shoulders.

As they pulled into the driveway, General Sam told Brenda that he thought fishing might be a good anecdote to his restlessness. One of his brothers had left him a bucket of minnows by the dock, and Sam hoped Brenda would give him a few minutes to put a few on some drop lines that he liked to tie to the bushes hanging over the lake. Sam knew that Brenda did not particularly like the idea of his fishing on his first evening home, but since he felt it would relieve some of the tension he felt, he took her smile and go-ahead nod as a chance to unwind for a while on the pond.

At that time, a dead tree stood eerily in the far corner of the lake at Frog Hollow, and in the dim moonlight, General Sam could see an owl in the high branches of the tree outlined against the starry sky. As General Sam reached down and pulled the basket of minnows onto the floorboards of the boat, he noticed out the corner of his eye that the solemn owl had left its perch and was gliding quietly toward him. He looked up in time to see the bird swoop over him and disappear into the darkness. An owl coming out of nowhere and flying at him struck General Sam as a spooky event, perhaps an omen of things to come.

Shaking off the strange experience, General Sam got into the john boat and started tying short, stout cords to overhanging bushes, and from the cords he dangled large hooks a few inches below the water's surface. He methodically made his way around the lake, as he had many times before, putting the lines in strategic spots. He was finishing the sixth line when he heard a tremendous crash and splashing near the branch where he had placed the second minnow. He rowed back quickly and shone the jack lantern on the area. The whole bush had been yanked all the way into the water. As Sam drew closer, the bush plunged all the way under water again. "This is a big one," General Sam crowed to himself.

He made his way to the spot and managed to get his net under a massive channel cat. The fish had a long scar along its side, beginning at about the gills and running towards its tail. It also had longer whiskers than General Sam had ever before seen on a catfish. He carefully worked the hook out of the fish's mouth, keeping his fingers clear of the trophy fish's mouth. Since he could not immediately put it on the stringer, he dropped the fish in the bottom of the boat. Confident that he was in for a fantastic night of fishing, General Sam proceeded to re-bait the drop line.

As he was putting another minnow on the hook, a slight breeze blew the boat away from shore. At this point, "Old Whiskers," as General Sam had already dubbed the huge catfish, began to flop crazily about the boat. Already in a situation that required careful concentration and balance as he held the jack lantern between his knees and tried to bait the hook, General Sam was distracted by the commotion from Old Whiskers. With all the baiting and balancing, he failed to notice that the breeze was pushing his boat further and further away from the shore and was causing the drop line to get precariously tighter and tilting the boat. All of a sudden, with a big *cawash*, the boat turned over and threw General Sam into the water. As he fell, the gunwale of the boat cut him across the forehead, stunning him momentarily.

Then followed one of the strangest experiences of General Sam's life. For a few seconds, he floated motionless beneath the capsized boat. There were golden lights shining in his face, and he could hear music from the band that had played at his retirement ceremony that afternoon. General Sam began to get a feeling of lassitude, but then, suddenly, he realized he was drowning. He made a lunge upward and broke the surface of the water. As he gulped fresh air, he became conscious that the light shining in his face was his lantern floating just below the surface of the lake. Old Whiskers was long gone, as were his tackle box and the rest of his gear. He was left choking on lake water and wondering how he was going to get out of the mess he had created.

He managed to swim the few feet necessary to get his hands on the overturned boat. Bracing himself, he was able to kick hard enough to propel it back in the direction of the dock. Once on shore, he pulled himself up onto a small, sandy beach he had been maintaining, crawled forward, and began to vomit lake water. He lay there until once again he could breathe easily. Finally, he pulled himself to his feet and staggered up the grassy incline to the basement of his house. When he opened the door, Brenda was standing at the top of the stairs berating him for staying so long at the pond on his very first night of retirement. Then she noticed that he was covered with blood. Her screaming continued, but in a different key. She grabbed a towel and stanched the blood on his forehead. Together, they bandaged his cut and thanked their lucky stars that his first adventurous night in retirement had not ended with a more serious outcome.

At first General Sam found it difficult to adjust to the laid-back lifestyle of the farm. His rigorous schedule in Washington began with his alarm clock ringing every morning at four, and for the past thirty-seven years, General Sam's days had rushed by as he dealt with the infinite tasks and unexpected assignments of a military career. At Frog Hollow, he found himself sitting on the front porch of his rustic home overlooking a small lake with no noise louder than cicadas buzzing and crows cawing. The unfamiliar sensation of peacefulness took some adjustment.

The morning after his evening encounter with Old Whiskers, General Sam awakened to the persistent ring of the telephone. After letting it ring numerous times, he sat upright in bed and loudly demanded, "Will somebody please answer the damned telephone."

"Uh-oh," he realized when no one was there to respond to him, "from here on in, I will have to answer that phone myself." It was only then that he became fully aware that he no longer had his own personal office with nine people to respond to his demands. He was on his own.

The call that jerked General Sam awake to reality on his first morning as a civilian was from the Director of Central Intelligence, Admiral Stansfield Turner. Admiral Turner apologized for calling so early, but he wanted to know if Sam could drive to Washington by ten o'clock the following morning for a meeting of the U.S. Intelligence Board. They were hoping to recognize his service on the occasion of his retirement. General Sam thought to himself,

"This is the first morning of my retirement and already I'm being called back to Washington."

Knowing how Brenda would feel about such a trip, he answered, "Admiral, I'm sorry. I really cannot make it today. It will have to be some other time."

"Well, Sam," concluded the Admiral, "what are we going to do with your Distinguished Intelligence Medal?"

"Well, Admiral," General Sam said, "we'll just have to handle that some other time."

Of course the admiral thought General Sam should have been easily persuaded when he learned he was to receive the Distinguished Intelligence Medal, but Sam had actually been awarded that medal previously in his career, and the admiral's ignorance of this fact seemed a bit strange. The second medal was a distinct honor, but not compelling enough to disrupt his first day at Frog Hollow.

General Sam wanted to concentrate his time on one major focus—attending to Brenda's health and happiness. He began making accommodations that eased her daily activities. She could no longer walk easily, so he purchased a golf cart and parked it under the extension of their downstairs porch. He began to develop trails through the woods so that he and Brenda could ride the golf cart through the woods and fields together. She had a wonderful eye for spotting wildflowers, ferns, and birds' nests on their forays into the forest, and together they really enjoyed those rides. Occasionally, he could lure her into the old john boat, and they would go fishing together. She also tended to a flower garden during the spring, summer, and early fall and a second garden of vegetables that furnished a bountiful supply of peas, carrots, corn, succotash, potatoes, tomatoes, and fruits. At harvest time, they would drive together to the Prince Edward County cannery and put up their produce to enjoy all winter. During those years Brenda cherished periodic visits from her family. Her older brother was especially faithful in coming from Alabama for regular stays, three or four days long. When family came, they fished, played cards, or just sat on the porch together.

The years after General Sam's retirement were a time of contentment for Brenda, though she still had to compete for Sam's time. He spent several hours a week preparing his lessons for Sunday school at Jamestown Presbyterian Church. Teaching Sunday school at Jamestown was good for Sam because it reconnected him with the old church in which he was born and raised, and he enjoyed preparing and presenting the classes. He also accepted numerous consultant jobs for the government.

Almost immediately following his retirement, Federal agencies and departments began seeking his consultant services. Foremost among the requests were those from the CIA and his friends from the DIA. The CIA wanted him to serve as a consultant for the Russian defector program, just the kind of work Sam had cut his teeth on, so he was not opposed to staying involved, and those assignments were valuable to him because they kept his security clearance active. Even in retirement, he could gain access to information about sensitive issues.

One of the earliest calls General Sam received was from a man whom Sam had met in 1972 while serving as the United States Defense Attaché in Moscow. His name was Earl "Frosty" Lockwood. At the time, Lockwood was working as a nuclear physicist for a defense consultant corporation called RCA. In 1978, the year following General Sam's retirement, Lockwood decided to strike out on his own and establish his own defense consultant firm. He invited General Sam to stop by his new office. "Look, I've established this little company," Lockwood told Sam. "I want to be useful to the United States. I need your help and advice, and I'd like you to work with me."

General Sam could not help but respond honestly, even at the expense of tact, "Man, I don't like defense contractors, and I don't have any desire to be one or to be associated with them."

Lockwood looked at him and said, "But Sam, it's me!"

It was true that they had become fairly close friends. Finally, General Sam

Frosty Lockwood and Sam Wilson, 2000.

agreed to work with Lockwood, but he made it clear that if Frosty ever lied to him or if he ever saw anything dishonest, he would walk away and make sure Frosty's business failed. Thus began a professional relationship for General Sam with Frosty Lockwood and a corporation known as BETAC, which Frosty laughingly described as a fancy Polish acronym meaning *nothing*.

The professional aspect of that relationship entailed General Sam's traveling to Washington once a month to offer advice and suggestions for BETAC. In 1991, Frosty Lockwood sold his corporation for millions of dollars and retired to a sprawling château in Prince Edward County. He became a member of the Hampden-Sydney College Board of Trustees and maintained a close friendship with General Sam.

In his retirement, General Sam continued to maintain an active relationship with two military educational institutions. One was the U.S. Army's John F. Kennedy Special Warfare School at Fort Bragg, North Carolina, the school at which General Sam had served in many capacities, including a stint as the Assistant Commandant in 1969-1970. The other school was the U.S. Air Force's Special Operations School at Hurlburt Airbase in the Florida Panhandle. Both schools periodically invited General Sam to visit and lecture to groups of soldiers, and they would send planes to Farmville to make the commute easier, a practice that caused a bit of a stir at the usually sleepy airport. Occasionally, General Sam would drive his car the two hundred miles to Fort Bragg, but the drive to Hurlburt Air Base in Florida took eleven hours, so Sam welcomed the Lockheed Executive Jet the Air Force sent to fly him from Richmond to the Gulf Coast, a fast hour-and-a-half haul.

As an instructor, General Sam could pull lessons and stories out of his experiences in special operations, unconventional warfare, psychological operations, and nation building. He relished sharing his experiences with young officers. For Brenda, the travel was tolerable because his commitments were brief, and she knew they meant so much to her husband. She enjoyed sharing in his preparations, especially when he told her tidbits of recently unclassified stories he was incorporating into his lectures.

General Sam's most significant project during this period was as the lead consultant for Delta Force. He had been involved in the development of the initial concept of Delta while he was at Fort Bragg and was well aware that this highly sensitive force's primary purpose was to combat terrorism. As part of a consulting commitment he formed with Delta Force, General Sam traveled to Fort Bragg once a month for more than two years after his retirement. He worked with the commander and the subordinate commanders of the newly created Delta Force to help strengthen it and to prepare it for operational requirements.

This consultation period for Delta Force climaxed with a ten-day exercise that Sam helped prepare as a way to test the Force and ensure its readiness for action. The maneuvers took place in the latter part of October 1979 and concluded successfully on Saturday, the third of November 1979. That evening, key commanders of the operation gathered in Sam's motel room in Savannah, Georgia, to celebrate their successful passing of the arduous series of tests. It was a celebratory night, and they all went to bed happy, albeit somewhat unsteady on their feet. It was also a date they would remember because early the next morning, they learned that the American embassy in Teheran had been overrun by a mob of angry Islamic militants, and all embassy personnel had been taken as prisoners by Iranian extremists.

For President Jimmy Carter, the Iran Hostage Crisis became one of the most vexing problems of his administration. He turned to the fledgling Delta Force to rescue the hostages from Iranian control, and in response, Delta Force began planning and preparing for a rescue operation. For nearly four months, from November until March, every aspect of a rescue attempt was envisioned, dissected, and practiced. On the night of April 24, 1980, Delta force set out to attempt a rescue. The operation ended in a fiery failure in central Iran, a place shown on American maps as "Desert One." A refueling helicopter collided with an Air Force C-130, and the deadly explosion that resulted ended any chances for Delta Force's successful mission. The Americans retreated with eight helicopters burning on the ground, eight American soldiers dead, and the hostages still under Iranian control. It was an inauspicious beginning for Delta Force, but it was truly a national calamity, and indeed, in the view of some, the demise of President Jimmy Carter's political future.

By order of President Carter, a review board was formed to investigate what had gone wrong and what could be learned from this disaster. General Sam was initially selected to be the group's chairman, but several senior officials suggested that the chairman should be someone with no prior connections to Delta. A retired four-star admiral was appointed chairman, and Sam the vice-chairman of the review group. They worked for some weeks before publishing their detailed findings. Although some members were uncomfortable with the idea, General Sam insisted that there be an unclassified version of their findings for public review. Initially, the administration feared that unclassified findings might cause serious repercussions among the media, but as Sam had hoped, when the facts were presented at a press conference, they were welcomed for the clear and accurate account they offered the American public. General Sam eventually received thanks from several of the men who opposed the public version, and with the insights gleaned from the review Delta Force strengthened its operational capabilities.

Throughout this period, General Sam was bombarded with requests to make speeches at what he called the "rubber chicken circuit." These events included ladies' clubs, civic organizations, luncheons, reserve officer associations, and National Guard meetings. Sam could have scheduled an appearance every day had he accepted each invitation he received to speak. His more serious engagements were on the lecture circuit at places like Brown University, Washington & Lee University, Hampden-Sydney College, and the service academies. He also made several quick trips to Europe to make speeches for military organizations and at schools under U.S.-European command.

Sam also began to involve himself in affairs concerning the Office of the Governor of the Commonwealth of Virginia. This commitment lasted some twenty years, beginning with a request by Governor Charles Robb that General Sam survey the Virginia National Guard and provide a list of recommendations for improvements to their training, administration, logistics, and operational capability. At the time, the Virginia National Guard was languishing. General Sam visited a number of guard organizations and made notes with which to brief the governor on his findings, including a recommendation to appoint a new National Guard Commander and State Adjutant General. Before Sam could finish his lengthy and comprehensive briefing, Governor Robb interrupted him and said, "I don't believe I need to hear any more, General Sam, and it's clear to me what I need to do. I would like you to be my new Adjutant General and commander of the Virginia National Guard."

Sam agreed to consider the offer, but before he accepted the proposal, he advised Governor Robb to test the opinion of the General Assembly on the matter. General Sam knew that certain Assembly members were also in the National Guard and would be very interested in the position, and he realized that many political considerations accompanied any new appointment. As Sam had guessed, when Governor Robb floated his suggestion in the General Assembly, he encountered some resistance to General Sam's assuming this post over several other well-connected candidates who eyed the job. A quick appointment would not have been well-received by that body, and Robb invited General Sam to Richmond to discuss the matter. It was clear to

General Sam that the Governor was having second thoughts, but Robb was a man of integrity and was ready to stand by it, despite political backlash that was sure to follow.

At that point Sam decided to forego the appointment and return to his farm. It was too controversial a position for him, and he did not want to commit to a responsibility that would impede his giving Brenda the care and attention that she had deserved for so long.

On the heels of this development came a separate and equally complex decision. In the fall of 1980, the Commonwealth of Virginia was slated to elect a new Senator. The Virginia Democratic Party had selected U.S. Congressman Owen B. Pickett to run as their candidate against Republican Paul Trible, but Pickett withdrew from the primary in late April 1980, leaving the Democratic Party with no candidate for the election that was to take place in less than six months. Governor Robb turned again to General Sam and asked him if would agree, if asked, to be the Democratic candidate for the Senate race.

General Sam was flattered but hesitant. He told Governor Robb that he would have to consult with his wife, and when he did, he was surprised that Brenda was enthusiastic about the idea. Though General Sam wondered whether she fully realized how time-consuming such a job would be, her response was that, as a Senator, his absences would be neither as lengthy nor as dangerous as his military missions had been.

Conversation between Governor Robb and General Sam took place in secret, but news of their deliberations were leaked the news to the press, and articles began to appear in Richmond newspapers. General Sam was besieged at Frog Hollow by a parade of reporters trying to get a bead on Sam Wilson and his views. One of the key questions for the media was how the African-American constituents of the Virginia Democratic Party would respond to Wilson. Indeed, it was Douglas Wilder, the African-American head of the black caucus of Virginia and later governor of Virginia, whose remark to the press spelled the end of any political aspirations General Sam harbored. When asked for his comments on Sam's projected candidacy to run as the Democratic nominee for the Senate in 1980, Wilder said "General Who? From a Prince Edward County cabbage patch?"

That was about all it took for General Sam, who had not entirely convinced himself that he wanted to run, to withdraw his name. He and Wilder had never met, and it was obvious that Wilder did not realize that during General Sam's military career he had earned a reputation as one of the most moderate of all commanders concerning race relations. He had served on a number of panels and boards that addressed problems of race relations in the military and he had achieved a reputation for defending fairness, especially for African-Americans. Wilder's remarks were as offensive for their lack of information as for their insulting tone. When General Sam expressed his reservations to Robb, the governor accepted his withdrawal but asked him to at least give the keynote address at the Democratic State Convention in the first week in June.

General Sam agreed and enjoyed an evening at the convention in Roanoke, where he gave his talk, which seemed to be well-received, respectfully bowed out of the Senatorial race, and returned to Frog Hollow and his family. The party then chose Lieutenant Governor Richard Davis to run as the Democratic contender, a candidate who ran a close race but lost to Republican Paul Trible.

As far as General Sam was concerned, his political career was over, and that remained true for nearly a decade. Then in 1990, state Senator Douglas Wilder, by this point a candidate running for the governorship of Virginia, called Sam to ask if he would agree to be his co-chairman for military veterans. Sam politely declined by saying, "General Who? From a Prince Edward County cabbage patch?"

Wilder's rejoinder was hardly apologetic, "Oh Sam, that was just politics. You know that."

In early 1978, Brenda's elderly cousin in Washington, Helen Newton, who by this time was a semi-invalid and diabetic amputee, was preparing to move from her Washington condominium while the building was being renovated. Construction was projected to take a year or longer, after which she could return, but she called Sam in hopes that with retirement he might have time to help her. Sam spent a few days checking out possible accommodations for her in the Washington area and took her to inspect several options, but none of them seemed appropriate. He finally suggested, "Why don't you come down and live with Brenda and me at the farm? You can put your things in storage, and we'll take care of you. We'll give you the whole ground floor of Frog Hollow and set it up however you want."

Helen Newton accepted and soon moved to Frog Hollow, where she settled into her first floor quarters. General Sam began devoting much of his time to the elderly lady who had been so generous to him during his time in Washington. Taking care of Helen was not necessarily easy. She was less tolerant than Brenda of General Sam's temporary absences, but when he was at home, she enjoyed his attention and thoughtful kindness. About two months after moving to Frog Hollow, Helen developed complications and underwent several operations. Already an amputee, she began having trouble with blood poisoning in her good leg, and her condition deteriorated until she passed away on June 11, 1979. Sam saw that she was buried in Rock Creek Park Cemetery, just over the knoll from the spot in which he had buried Aldan.

In January 1979, there was an unusually heavy snowfall in Southside Virginia that left Frog Hollow completely snowed in and without electric power. The only thing working—and only intermittently—at the house was the telephone, which was on battery power. About midmorning, there came a rapping at the front entrance to the house and, surprised, General Sam looked out to see that a state police cruiser was parked in his driveway with its lights flashing. Hooded and booted against the cold, the policeman had trudged from his car through the snow and was knocking on the door.

Sam hurried to greet the man. The policeman reported that his office in Appomattox had received a radio message from the White House for General Sam. President Joseph Broz Tito of Yugoslavia was dead, and a Presidential delegation, headed by Ambassador Averill Harriman, was departing the next day for Belgrade to represent the U.S. at Tito's funeral. The Yugoslavs had requested that General Sam be a member of the ambassador's delegation. Sam knew that he had received such special consideration because he had had a close association with Yugoslav intelligence that served the interests of both Yugoslavia and the United States during the Cold War. It was a distinct honor to be invited to join the delegation, but he was not certain that he could navigate through the snow to Washington.

To the police officer, he said, "Well, I will try to go. I am not sure that I can, but tell them that the message has been delivered and that I will be in touch with them immediately." As they were talking, the off-and-on-again telephone in the kitchen began to ring. It was the Deputy National Security Advisor, who repeated the information that had just been delivered by the state trooper. Then the Security Advisor mentioned that by coincidence he had a close associate of General Sam's on the other line and he hoped General Sam would talk to this man.

"Who is it?" asked Sam.

"It's Bull Simon. You've got to help us deal with him."

General Sam had earlier been briefed on the circumstances: two key employees of Ross Perot's Electronic Data Systems, Inc. (EDS) who were working in Iran had been arrested and imprisoned by the Iranian secret police. All efforts on the part of the Perot company and the U.S. government to obtain their release had been of no avail. The prisoners remained in Teheran. In a new attempt to resolve the situation, Ross Perot had hired a recently retired Special Forces legend, Colonel Arthur D. "Bull" Simon.

Bull Simon was a tremendously capable officer. A man of fierce demeanor, he tended to be quite aggressive, and often he could be abrupt almost to the point of being antagonistic. He was also a legend in special operations for his many exploits in difficult situations. Loaded with plenty of Mr. Perot's money, Colonel Simon had gone to Teheran and hired people to create a demonstration in the streets that eventually turned into a rioting mob. Encouraged by Colonel Simon's Iranian agents, the mob broke into the Gazre Prison and freed all the political prisoners in the complex, and as they released several thousand political prisoners, the two EDS employees had also been freed.

Colonel Simon was holed up in a hotel room in downtown Teheran with the two EDS employees, and the ambassador was trying to persuade him to release the prisoners to U.S. embassy care. However, Simon worried that the embassy could not provide appropriate protection. In fact, he was so insistent that he should be the one to safeguard the men that he warned, "The first guy who sticks his head through the door will get blown in half. Get the U.S. government off my back."

Bull remained barricaded in the hotel room, trying to figure out how, on his own, to exfiltrate the EDS employees from the middle of hostile territory. When the White House staffer connected Bull Simon on the phone with General Sam, Bull was sitting on the bed of an Iranian hotel room, covering the door with a sawed off shotgun in one hand and holding a satellite phone in the other. He had been talking to the Deputy National Security Advisor in the White House, who was working two telephones, the second one connected to Sam Wilson at Frog Hollow.

When General Sam heard the Security Advisor link him to Bull Simon, he gave a cautious greeting. Bull gruffly responded by demanding, "Who in the hell is this?"

"Bull, this is Sam Wilson," was the measured response.

"What are you talking to me for?" replied an exasperated Bull Simon. General Sam did not really know.

"These guys have called me, I don't know why. I guess to persuade you that the U.S. government will help you get out of the country with your charges."

"Screw them," barked Simon angrily. "I've seen what they can do. I'll be better off getting out of here on my own."

"I understand you, Bull," Sam answered, unconvinced that he should be distracting Simon from his mission. "God bless you and good luck."

Later, Sam would learn that on the night after their conversation, Bull Simon had commandeered a pickup truck and headed towards the Turkish border with the Iranian secret police on his heels. He safely made the 450-mile trip to the border with the freed EDS employees. The Americans made their way safely home, and Bull Simon added another notch to his belt of audacious exploits.

Meanwhile Sam, in his Southside Virginia home, weighed the decision of whether or not he should travel to Yugoslavia for Tito's funeral ceremonies. He was snowed in, and even if he could dig out, he had his wife and an invalid cousin to consider. The trip would require lengthy travel, and he worried about leaving the farm for so long, especially in light of the storm. Regretfully, he decided to send written condolences and to decline the invitation. He sent his respectful greetings to Yugoslavia and set about preparing Frog Hollow to survive a few days buried in the snow.

During this period, a number of newspaper journalists and authors were asking to visit Frog Hollow to write about General Sam's adventures, but General Sam had no interest in those sorts of projects. There was, however one writer whom General Sam considered meeting. His name was James K. Pollock and he already had visited Fort Bragg and talked to Special Forces personnel there. Additionally, Pollock had recently completed a successful book, *Mission MIA,* about an operation to search for and rescue a prisoner captured by the Viet Cong. *Mission MIA* had sold well and then was turned into a movie. For his book, Pollock had interviewed a former prisoner of the Viet Cong, a man whom General Sam had met and remembered only by his first name, Danny.

General Sam met Danny, a Green Beret Master Sergeant and recovering POW, while the man was suffering severely from Post-Traumatic Stress Syndrome at Fort Bragg. Danny was resisting going back to the hospital, so General Sam, who then was in command of a Special Forces group, had asked his commanding general to assign Danny to him as a personal assistant. In that capacity, Danny accompanied General Sam on inspections of the unit area, helped him on various projects, and ran with him every morning. For a time, General Sam took the boy under his wing, and during his service as personal assistant, Danny began healing, eventually achieving a full recuperation.

When Pollock interviewed Danny, the young man had continuously talked about General Sam as a brilliant Special Forces commander and as an individual whose daily focused attention had been instrumental in his recovery. Sometime later, General Sam's phone rang, and Pollock introduced himself and asked if he could come to Frog Hollow for a series of interviews. At first Sam declined and cited his decision not to grant interviews. But when Pollock mentioned that Danny had described Sam as one of the best commanders in the history of the Special Forces, Sam reconsidered.

Danny had insisted that Sam was *the* man to see for a true picture of the Special Forces, and in the light of the young man's lavish introductions, it seemed only fair to meet Pollock. In a series of meetings at Frog Hollow, General Sam talked with Pollock and provided background information for a sequence of three books, one of which, *Crossfire,* proved quite successful. General Sam essentially composed two of the chapters in *Crossfire,* so the book's acceptance was especially gratifying. Pollock, however, remains the only professional writer whom General Sam ever assisted in any substantive way. He was always too busy with the here and now to devote his days to past history.

In May 1979, Sam was caught by surprise when on an early Sunday morning, he received a telephone call from the President of Hampden-Sydney College, Josiah Bunting III, saying that the Board of Trustees requested his presence at the upcoming commencement exercises, during which they wanted to present him with an Honorary Doctorate of Laws. General Sam was overwhelmed by the gesture, especially because he still had no college degree. He had earned a high school diploma, certificates of completion from a number of different schools and courses, and numerous hours of coursework on undergraduate and graduate work at several international institutions, including the Sorbonne, the Free University of West Berlin, and Moscow State University at Lenin Hills. He had accumulated somewhere in excess of two hundred academic credit hours, but they were not sufficiently connected to fulfill requirements for a final degree.

The award of an honorary degree from the college for which he had so much respect overwhelmed Sam. That diploma would be framed and hung in his office alongside the citation which accompanied it. In later years, he would receive an honorary degree in literature from Longwood University, and sixty years after his initial attempts to matriculate in 1940, Sam was awarded an undergraduate degree as a member of the class of 2000 at Hampden-Sydney College. That final degree came at General Sam's last commencement ceremony as President of what finally became his *alma mater.*

PURSUING INTERESTS

BY THE FALL OF 1982, after a restless half-decade of retirement, General Sam had settled into his new, more relaxed life, situated near his birthplace and surrounded by family. Not long after General Sam returned to Rice, his siblings began to relocate their homes to neighboring plots of land along the same country road that Frog Hollow fronted. His sister, Virginia, had long lived in the old farmhouse where they had all been born and raised. Bill, who had been the pastor of Norfolk's Royster Memorial Presbyterian Church for eighteen years, retired to a farm across the road from General Sam. John, who owned and operated radio station WFLO in Farmville, owned a home a few miles down the road and he also bought property adjoining the family farm and built a pond and a cabin. General Sam's youngest brother, Jim, sold his two veterinary hospitals in Northern Virginia and used the proceeds to buy land nearby. The siblings had been congenial when they were children, but they were even closer in semi-retirement. They saw each other often and were in constant communication. They rode on each other's trails, hunted in each

The Wilson siblings in 1992: Jim, Billy, Virginia, Sam, and John

other's woods, and fished in each other's lakes. There were two things they carefully avoided—cutting down a tree on a sibling's property or plowing land that belonged to one of the others. The thriving relationships with his family helped ease General Sam's transition back to the farm and deepened his contentment while he was there.

Over the years, Sam conducted lectures to groups and classes at nearby Hampden-Sydney College, but in 1982, he received a formal invitation from President Josiah Bunting III to join the faculty. Bunting's letter offered General Sam the title of Visiting Distinguished Professor of Political Science, an appointment that tremendously pleased General Sam. He realized that the events of his life had taken a circuitous route to furnish him an appropriate background for teaching at the college. He learned how to be an effective instructor while he was still a young noncommissioned officer when he spent a year at Fort Benning under the tutelage of the best teachers the government could enlist. Sam experienced a second dose of Fort Benning instruction in 1945, when he worked in the leadership program there for two years. While he was in the intelligence business, he was constantly asked to brief notables and government dignitaries, sometimes even presidents of foreign countries. Schooled for so long by practical experience, General Sam could hardly have been better prepared to stand in front of a group of twenty students.

The first course that General Sam taught at Hampden-Sydney College was titled "United States Foreign Policy and National Security, 1982-Present: Threats, Issues, and Responses" and included lectures which he had already been giving for several years as an unofficial, visiting professor. The course boasted a rather pretentious title, for which General Sam made no apologies. The material drew from his thirty-seven years in the military and in the intelligence arena, particularly under the auspices of the CIA. He drew on observations and extrapolations from his experience developing American foreign policy in posts around the world. He also included lessons from the extended periods he spent in Washington working at national policy levels in the Executive and Congressional branches.

Given the depth and variety of his experience, the course was not difficult for General Sam to teach. He could draw from countless stories to illustrate major contemporary issues in foreign policy and national security. Students were enthusiastic and eager, in part because class discussions, though supported by textbook material, were rooted in real life and focused on a future that would affect all of them. General Sam taught the class in Morton 119, a long seminar room on the first floor of Hampden-Sydney's main liberal arts classroom building where, every Tuesday night, about twenty students crowded around a big table. At first General Sam tried to limit the class size to fifteen, but he expanded because of the number of young men who tried to register. Interest was so strong that the course was divided into two separate sections, one focusing on foreign policy and national security, and the other concentrating particularly on U.S. national intelligence. The intelligence course became even more popular than the one on foreign policy and national security, perhaps because it evoked more of the colorful stories from General Sam's career. General Sam's courses were rigorous, but the young men never seemed to mind.

Each class met in the evenings once a week for three hours, and General Sam kept the classroom atmosphere relaxed. He tended to wear old button-down shirts and jeans, and he allowed the students to drink sodas and eat snacks during the long evening classes, though he put his foot down at smoking.

He took advantage of the blackboards that lined the perimeter of the classroom. As he gave his lecture, he would start writing notes on the first blackboard and wind up writing his way around the room. His handwriting was barely legible, but students followed his progress and knew that the evening session was about over when he filled the last blackboard.

In the class on foreign policy and national security, General Sam's favorite assignment was appointing each student as a television news correspondent. Everyone in the class was "stationed" in a particular area of the world where the U.S. had significant interest. Moscow, Beijing, Tokyo, Mexico City, London, and other important cities were all represented. He required the students to consider themselves on call to deliver a three-minute newscast of the events of the day in their region at any time. At the beginning of each class, he might call on the "CBS News correspondent in Moscow" or the "NBC correspondent in Jakarta." This exercise forced each student to familiarize himself with the geography, economy, government, people, and issues of his assigned territory. Students grew to become "at home" in their adopted country's capital city. They were expected to respond to his questions and inform the rest of the class about issues evolving in the area. He warned students to be prepared to talk as if they had a camera in their faces, and he expected them to become proficient at providing an informative news bite under pressure. General Sam knew that the requirements would force his students to get in the habit of following world news, and in the process he hoped to make "news junkies" out of every one of them.

After the first meeting of the foreign policy class, General Sam realized that there was not enough time to get a weekly report from every student, so he started choosing students at random, making sure that each one gave a report at least three times during the semester. They were required to be ready at all times, and at the second meeting of the class, with no advance warning, he brought an old jack-lantern and an inert microphone. When report time came, he called on his "ABC correspondent in Berlin" to give a report. As the student cautiously started his news bite, General Sam cut him short. "No, no, young man, stand up."

He shoved the lantern and microphone right in the boy's face. The student froze. General Sam let him sit down, whirled, and called on the "Correspondent from South Africa." When he put the mike in front of him and shone the light in his face, that student froze as well. General Sam laughed. Everyone worried that he would be next. General Sam paused before saying, "Gents, you gotta be ready for these things. What I'm going to do is this: I'm going to bring a camera in here and record you guys giving these presentations." At their next meeting, the students surprised him by all showing up in coat and tie, prepared for the bright light and microphone that would accompany their news bites.

In addition to immersing students in a particular geographic area and making that knowledge available to the rest of the class, the foreign policy course assignments gave students practice in speaking on their feet with confidence. General Sam wanted them to be aware of how it felt to speak cogently to a camera audience with someone raising complicated questions in a brief time period. After a bit of practice, the students enjoyed the multipurpose assignment. They watched each other attentively, and there was a feeling of competition. Sometimes very bright students who did well on exams would find themselves tongue-tied in front of the camera while less accomplished students excelled in the spotlight. All of them improved their speaking skills, and in later years General Sam received letters from a number of them who shared how valuable the experience proved to be in their careers.

In the intelligence course, rather than having his students play the roles of news correspondents, General Sam assigned them roles of intelligence officers working under cover for the CIA. In lieu of giving a TV news report, each student delivered a three-minute briefing. Once again, the students responded well to his challenge. They developed cover stories, complete with phony names, backgrounds, and documentation to explain how they would exfiltrate from their area if they ever found themselves in danger of being apprehended. They were learning, but creatively.

General Sam continued to teach these two courses, one in the fall, one in the spring, for ten years, and his students always knew that they were going to learn and the class would never be dull. He was renowned for using all kinds of props to keep classes lively, and he gained a reputation for his unconventional techniques that were both effective and fair. He expected attention and participation from each individual, and he had little trouble meeting those goals. One of his students, a star wide receiver on the football team, would often have to rush to class from football practice, and nearly as soon as he sat down, he would fall asleep. Actually, he was not the only young man who would occasionally doze in the late evening class. To combat this problem, General Sam made any student he caught nodding stand against the back wall for the rest of the class. Students quickly learned that if they were drowsy, they would likely be taking their notes standing up. The sleepy football player good-naturedly began skipping his chair entirely and spending the whole class against the wall.

Before their semester ended, students always became a tight group. They laughed a lot and worked hard together. Some of the students came out to the farm from time to time, and General Sam spent leisurely time conversing with them. He enjoyed the classes and the young men who participated with him every week, and he carefully planned his schedule so that Tuesdays and Thursdays were spent preparing notes during the day for classes those evening. For the years he taught, no other priority every outweighed his course commitments.

With her husband nearly always at home, Brenda appreciated the relaxed life at Frog Hollow. Her health stabilized, and she was able to tend her flower and vegetable gardens. She and General Sam often enjoyed fish, fresh from the lake, for dinner. Their black lab, Rip-the-Wonder-Dog, was very affectionate towards Brenda, and there was also a gray tomcat that was named "Jubal Anderson Early" after the great Confederate General from Lynchburg. One day a mongrel wandered up and established herself as the final member of the family. She was quickly dubbed "Spunky." Brenda had a special relationship with all the animals, even the deer that roamed the property. One day, General Sam watched from the porch as Brenda went around a corner in the yard and came face to face with a large doe. They looked at each other, and then Brenda turned and walked away softly. The deer, however, instead of running away, followed behind her, watching her every step, somehow unthreatened and curious about this lady.

In the early 1980s, General Sam was able to have his daughter, Susan, accepted at Innisfree Village, a model facility for the brain-damaged and handicapped. Located nearby, about eighteen miles west of Charlottesville, Innisfree Village was a place where patients could live together in alpine-style houses, each with its own garden. The facility had a building for weaving, a woodworking shop, gardens, and workstations for the patients, who were referred to as "volunteers." In addition to structured activities, each volunteer was assigned regular tasks and routines. Susan's condition stabilized greatly at Innisfree Village, and when she eventually returned home, she was much stronger.

In 1984, General Sam was appointed by Virginia Governor Jerry Baliles to a four-year term as a member of the Board of Visitors of Longwood College (now Longwood University). He was subsequently elected by the Board to the position of Vice-Rector. In this position, General Sam had the opportunity to participate in the inner-workings of an institution which was founded in 1839 by a group that included several of his relatives. It was also the college many of the women in his life had attended, including his mother, two of her sisters, and his father's mother, and it played an important role in his own early life as he courted young ladies there.

Additionally, General Sam's association with Earl F. "Frosty" Lockwood and Lockwood's BETAC Corporation continued to develop. Sam spent about three days a month in Washington working on policy, management, and special projects, and in return BETAC paid a handsome sum that was a valuable supplement to Sam's retirement pay. In the 1980s, Sam signed a consulting contract with the CIA to work in its Directorate of Operations. His commitment to the CIA involved about two days a month, frequently during the same trips to Washington that he was making for BETAC. The CIA contract allowed General Sam to maintain his security clearances and return to the operations arenas, and in the post he was able to use his linguistic abilities as well as apply his past experience to current operations.

Meanwhile, General Sam continued to serve as a military advisor for the Commonwealth, during the tenures of both Governor Robb and Governor Baliles, and he chaired the Virginia Korean/Vietnam War History Commission for six years. Additionally, he continued to speak at universities and military institutions around the country, traveled to Europe for presentations to members of the 10th Special Forces Group in Germany, and lectured at his former Detachment R school, which had been renamed "The Institute for East European and Slavic Studies."

Between 1982 and 1992, General Sam accepted several significant military obligations. He consulted with Army Special Operations, and he undertook projects with the Green Berets, the Special Warfare School, and Delta Force. Contacts from the Special Operations community frequently visited General Sam at Frog Hollow, largely for consultation purposes. A little fishing might be thrown in on the side.

During the mid-1980s, Congressman Dan Daniels from Virginia's Fifth Congressional District began to develop an interest in the role and mission of U.S. Special Operations Forces. Because of General Sam's background in that arena, Congressman Daniels turned to him for advice. He eventually began stopping in Farmville when he was traveling from Washington to his home in Danville so that he and General Sam could discuss Special Operations over dinner and drinks at the Hotel Weyanoke in Farmville. These sessions culminated in Sam's working from Congressman Daniels' Washington office as an informal consultant to the Senate's Armed Services Committee and the House's Armed Services Committee.

Sam worked with Daniels on an amendment to the Goldwater-Nichols Act of 1986, legislation that became known as the Nunn-Cohen Amendment. This important document resolved controversy within the U.S. Armed Services about how the nation's elite forces, called "Special Operations Forces," should be organized and employed.

When General Sam started working for Congressman Daniels, the House's and the Senate's Armed Services Committees were working on their own suggestions and had each drafted their own legislative solution to the problems in the Goldwater-Nichols Act. Sam had been tracking the competing legislation from Rice, so when Daniels asked him to help resolve the situation, he was well aware that he would be walking into a deadlocked situation. His task was to act as a negotiator to both sides. After several meetings, the two committees were finally able to draft legislation which was acceptable, and it was that compromise which became the Nunn-Cohen Amendment. Among other things, the amendment established a new joint command called the U.S. Special Operations Command, led by a new Four-Star General's position and located at MacDill Air Force Base in Tampa, Florida. The new commander would take charge of all U.S. Army Special Forces and other Special Operations assets, including the renowned Green Berets and the Army Rangers; all Naval Special Operations assets, including the Navy's vaunted Seals; and all U.S. Air Force Special Operations assets, including the descendants of the famous World War II "Air Commandos."

Combining all of these assets under a single command significantly improved the country's Special Operations Forces. Shortly after this new legislation was implemented, the United States could successfully undertake an operation like Desert One, that had failed so miserably six years earlier in Iran. For the U.S. Armed Forces, the Goldwater-Nichols Act and its Nunn-Cohen Amendment became one of the most significant pieces of military legislation from the second half of the twentieth century.

One provision of the Nunn-Cohen Amendment established the post of Assistant Secretary of Defense for Special Operations and Low Intensity Conflict (SOLIC). One of General Sam's friends, a senior Senate staffer for the Senate Armed Service Committee, James R. Locher, III, was named to the SOLIC position. To help the Secretary of Defense implement the Nunn-Cohen Amendment to the Goldwater-Nichols Act, Secretary Locher and General Sam set up a Special Operations Policy Advisory Group (SOPAG) of retired highly talented and experienced U.S. policy makers. This group helped fast-track the legislation through the Executive Branch down to the Department of Defense, and then they ensured that it was properly implemented. After implementation, the group continued to consider issues of importance to the Special Operations community and developed advice and suggestions on these issues for the Secretary of Defense.

Sam was named chairman of SOPAG, a position he could not have held had he still been on active duty, nor would he have had the latitude and the elbow room to talk with people in Washington whom he leveraged on behalf of the group. During his six Washington tours, he had learned how to run a meeting efficiently, but General Sam was careful to remain mission-oriented, sincere, frank, candid, and respectful as group leader. Some of the senior members of SOPAG were old friends of General Sam's, including former CIA Director William Colby and retired Army Four-Star General Richard Stillwell, and he sometimes leaned on them to help convince the rest of the group to follow his lead. He found that the group generally cooperated with him because they realized that the project was producing positive results for the military. General Sam once overheard one of the SOPAG members telling the Joint Chiefs of Staff Chairman, Colin Powell, that "Sam has whipped us into shape. He really moves in these meetings. He covers a lot of ground, and we are making some real headway with the Secretary of Defense." The chairmanship of SOPAG represented the most significant military undertaking of Sam's entire career.

One of the primary initiatives of the SOPAG was lobbying to install a

Special Operations Commander at the General Officer level under each military theater's Commander-in-Chief. Then as now, Congress was very reluctant to create additional general-level military positions. In order to prove the necessity of their request, SOPAG asked Secretary of Defense Dick Cheney if it could invite the theater Commander-in-Chiefs to brief them on their theater's Special Operations Forces, by now simply referred to as SOF. General Sam and Secretary Locher thought that this process would encourage the commanders to review carefully their SOF situations and might convince them of the need to centralize the leadership of this program.

The first to brief SOPAG was the Commander-in-Chief of the Pacific Theater, a four-star admiral by the name of Charles Larson. When Admiral Larson received the request from SOPAG to provide a comprehensive briefing on his Special Operation units, he logged thousands of miles visiting each SOF outpost in the Pacific to become familiar with his forces' status. He brought a photographer along with him to take illustrative pictures. After he had gathered all his information, Larson appeared before SOPAG and eloquently delivered a three-hour presentation—without using any notes or visuals except photographic slides. Larson had been deeply impressed by his SOF capabilities and was ready to recommend the commander be given the status of general. Ultimately SOPAG was able to sell the concept of a General Flag Officer for each of the SOF theater's commander positions.

General Sam and SOPAG then asked Secretary Cheney if they could be briefed by the Chief of Staff of each military service on their domestic SOF units. These briefings were equally successful and again put a spotlight on U.S. Special Operations Forces. The successful results in the Panama Operation of 1989 and the results of the Gulf War in 1991 showed the advantages of effective organization within these forces. With each military service's SOF capabilities working together, the U.S. had a far more effective force than had ever been seen before.

Although General Sam was busy with a number of time-consuming activities during this period, he still managed to schedule time alone with Brenda. He had been told in 1977 that she might live another two years, but the tranquil, stress-free atmosphere of song birds, trees, flowers, and rocking chairs on a long porch overlooking a small lake full of fish, all coupled with love from her family, had been a soothing tonic for Brenda. For a time, the condition of her health had actually improved, but almost ten years after his retirement, General Sam realized that her health was again failing. On May 25, 1987, she was hospitalized at Southside Community Hospital in

Farmville, and on Tuesday morning, June 9, 1987, Brenda died in Sam's arms. Even though his wife's passing had long been anticipated, Brenda's death was a traumatic event for Sam. The severe blow caused him to review once again his professional military career and the long periods of absence from her and from their children. As he had many times before, he wondered whether or not he had made the right choices with the direction of his life.

A few weeks after the death of General Sam's wife, Longwood University's presidency became unexpectedly vacant. Several prominent figures in the Longwood family approached General Sam about accepting the vacated position. Sam gave the prospect very serious consideration. He knew that Longwood was and had long been particularly well situated as one of Virginia's prominent teacher colleges. At one time, there was hardly a person in the Commonwealth of Virginia who had not had some exposure to a teacher who had graduated from Longwood. Sam went so far as to develop some concepts to promote his case for the presidency, but he narrowly missed the appointment. The negative outcome may well have been for the best. Since General Sam had been passed over for the Longwood position, he would be available when Hampden-Sydney College's presidency became available several years later.

About the time that Longwood University's Presidential search was coming to an end, Sam received an important telephone call. It was a repeat of a call he had been receiving every two years for the last fourteen to sixteen years from his friend Congressman Daniel. Every election year, Congressman Daniel asked Sam if he were ready to run for office. In the weeks following Brenda's death, Congressman Daniel had called and said, "Sam, I'm going to pull out. It's your time now."

This time the Congressman phoned and said, without any prelude, "This is Dan. Are you ready?"

Noise in the local paper, news radio, and even the *Richmond Times-Dispatch* had been suggesting that General Sam might replace Dan Daniel as the Democratic candidate from the Fifth Congressional District. Several months before the election, Daniel called General Sam once more. He left a message that said, "Sam, I'm not well. I'm running out of gas. I ought to go home and get in bed, but I've made a promise that I'd be in Bedford tomorrow night to give a talk. A promise is a promise, but you know what? I'd sooner die than go to Bedford."

That night, Daniel went to Bedford, gave his talk, and passed away in his sleep. Sam kept the tape cartridge from his voicemail machine as an audio memory of his long-time friend.

The Congressional seat was vacant, and General Sam felt pressure from various entities to take Daniels' place. Still, he realized that he had time-consuming responsibilities to his handicapped daughter and other important demands that took precedence over his political ambitions. Firmly, he informed the press that he was not going to seek the Congressional seat and threw his support to L.F. Payne, a local businessman who successfully ran for the office. It was the last time that active participation in politics would surface in Sam's life.

In April 1988, Sam traveled to the Special Warfare School at Fort Bragg to deliver a series of lectures. While walking down a hallway of the school building, he was greeted by a familiar looking female officer. She said, "General Wilson, my name is Susi Howton Tennis. I'm Harry Howton's daughter. I believe you'll remember me."

Air Force Colonel Harry Howton had been the commandant of the U.S. Air Force's Special Operations School at Hurlburt Air Base in Florida at the same time General Sam had been running the Army's Special Warfare School at Fort Bragg. General Sam had been to Colonel Howton's home several times during the '50s and '60s and had met his wife and two daughters. The older girl, Virginia, nicknamed "Susi," had struck him as bright and vivacious. As she re-introduced herself, he remembered that Army First Lieutenant Susi Howton had been the Assistant Protocol Officer responsible for organizing social events for the Commanding General of the Eighteenth Airborne Corps and the Commanding General of Fort Bragg almost twenty years earlier, in 1969 and 1970. Here they were again in the spring of 1988. Of course he remembered her.

They had lunch together while he was on that visit to Fort Bragg. He found that she had been married and now had two children but was in the process of obtaining a divorce. She was only called to active duty occasionally, so it was a fortunate circumstance that allowed them to cross paths on base. Sam and Susi began writing one another and then telephoning. In the summer of 1989, nearly three years after Brenda's death, General Sam and Susi Howton married.

After the wedding ceremony, they brought Susi's daughter Gwinn and son William to Frog Hollow for the summer. In the evenings, General Sam would regale them with his adventures. Together, they fished, rode trails, and played all sorts of games. He considered Susi Wilson his stalwart friend, supporter, and inspiration.

Just as he was settling into his new life with Susi, the unexpected happened again, as it so often did for General Sam. Hampden-Sydney College had begun to falter and lose its way. The feeling of community and unity was diminishing. The twenty-first President had been fired before he could complete his first year in office, and Hampden-Sydney was looking for a new President for the third time in three years. The Board of Trustees invited General Sam to assume the position, and he accepted. On July 29, 1992, General Sam was approved as the twenty-second President of the College.

That afternoon, the Chairman of the Board of Trustees drove with Sam from Richmond to the College's campus, where he had called ahead and assembled the community to greet the new leader of the academic village. As he finished his welcoming remarks to the assembly, the chairman turned to Sam and said, "Mr. President, say something."

Sam was momentarily caught off-guard. Pausing briefly, he said, "Well, as some of you already know, this is home for me. Hampden-Sydney College has been in my blood since I was a small boy. I am overwhelmed with delight to be here. And I have no particular message other than to note my primary conviction as far as the mission of this College is concerned. It is that the most important person walking the grassy knolls of this campus is the student. He is followed closely, almost lockstep, by the second most important person, the teacher. And the most important event transpiring on this campus is the colloquy between that student and that teacher. All else is secondary and supporting. That's the direction in which I'm headed, folks, and I hope you'll be with me."

Thus began what General Sam regarded as the most important assignment of his life.

THE HAMPDEN-SYDNEY YEARS I:
EARLY ACTION AND BUILDING ENTHUSIASM

THE NEW PRESIDENT had a long history with the college. As he was growing up on a farm twelve miles northeast of campus, he had heard his family referring to the College in almost reverential tones. Even before he saw the place for the first time as a small boy, young Sam could clearly imagine it as an old-fashioned village nestled in the woods on a hill and shrouded in the mists of history and tradition. Whenever young Sam expressed frustration with school or speculated to grownups about what he wanted to be, he would repeatedly be told, "Be good, do good, and you might just get to Hampden-Sydney someday."

The highest respect for Hampden-Sydney had been firmly implanted in his mind since his youth. Sam visited Hampden-Sydney's campus for the first time in the early 1930s, when he was eight or nine years old. Together with members of youth groups from fellow churches in the West Hanover Presbytery, his Sunday school class gathered at Hampden-Sydney for a summer retreat. General Sam vividly recalled the beauty of the campus, the stately buildings, and the overall atmosphere. He sensed the almost palpable feeling of history in the air.

Assuming the top administrative post at Hampden-Sydney also held great meaning for General Sam because of the extensive family connections he had with the College, going back to its inception. The first planning meetings for the establishment of Hampden-Sydney were held in the plantation office of General Sam's four times great-grandfather, Nathaniel Venable. That small white-frame building, which is now known as "The Birthplace," has been relocated and presently sits behind Atkinson Hall, about forty feet from the president's office.

Since that first meeting in 1775, every Board of Trustees of the College has included at least one of General Sam's kinsmen among its members, and through the years other relatives were associated with the administration of the college. General Sam's sister, Virginia Wilson Druen, worked from 1963 to 1988 as the executive secretary to three consecutive Presidents of Hampden-Sydney. Many of his relatives attended the school, including General Sam's older brother, William Lockett Wilson, who graduated *summa cum laude* in 1949 and went on to become a Presbyterian minister. William also was awarded an honorary Doctorate of Laws by the school in 1963. One of General Sam's younger brothers, John Dennis Wilson, was originally a member of the same class as William, but he left college early to attend the National School of Radio Broadcasting. General Sam's first cousin, James W. Wilson, Jr., was valedictorian for the class of 1941, and a number of General Sam's other cousins attended Hampden-Sydney over the years.

By the spring of 1940, although he already held an alternate appointment to West Point from Congressman Pat Drewry, Sam was taking steps to matriculate at Hampden-Sydney College. At the same time, however, the period of false peace that lasted from the fall of 1939 through the winter of 1940 had ended, and the Germans were smashing through West European lowlands and into France. They had driven the French First Army and the British Expeditionary Forces into the English Channel at the small coastal village of Dunkirk. World War II had begun in earnest.

As he listened to a radio rebroadcast of Churchill's speech to the House of Commons on the heels of the Dunkirk disaster, Sam had been unable to stand idly by. He joined the Virginia National Guard shortly thereafter and marched off to war instead of going to college. Hampden-Sydney disappeared from his personal horizon for more than four decades, but he eagerly accepted the second chance to choose Hampden-Sydney College.

Since he had been teaching in the Political Science department for fifteen years, General Sam already felt at home at the school. He still held deeply idealized and romantic feelings toward the College, so assuming the presidency felt like a natural progression. He also had a strong sense that every task he had faced since he took that opposite fork in the road from the one leading to Hampden-Sydney had all been a part of his preparation for the presidency of the college. Those feelings gave him confidence. The job, in General Sam's mind, was arguably the greatest challenge he would ever face, but he was well prepared for such a challenge and eager to tackle the responsibility.

With his idealized notions about the place, General Sam quickly faced a rude awakening. On July 29, 1992, he walked out from Crawley Forum at the end of his introduction as President to the Hampden-Sydney community and immediately began his first walk around the campus in that position. Meanwhile, unbeknownst to General Sam, Susi had pulled her station wagon around to the driveway of Middlecourt, the President's house. In the back of the station wagon were two hundred ears of fresh corn that she had just picked from her garden at Frog Hollow. Perched on the tailgate, she flagged people down as they came by and handed out the corn. General Sam was told later that Susi's down-to-earth generosity created a buzz around campus that was audible to everyone. People were saying to each other, "Maybe we've got a winning team this time."

The academic community was ready for a season of positive change. The College was in the midst of a leadership crisis, with four Presidents in three years, and the tumultuous period of leadership heightened other serious difficulties. Indeed, some people wondered whether the illustrious history of

Sam and Susi Wilson, as the new President and First Lady, 1992

Hampden-Sydney College was coming to an end. Enrollment was dropping, donations were diminishing, and morale was at an all-time low. There was significant friction among the various offices and departments on campus. Lateral communication had broken down, and all kinds of recriminations were being voiced by various constituencies of the College. There was criticism of the Board of Trustees for attempting to formulate faulty policies. General Sam's predecessor had been removed from his position after only ten months on the job, and even members of the President's own office were pitted against each other.

General Sam, however, saw more visible signs of strain as he meandered around the campus that afternoon. The sun was almost setting when he reached Fraternity Circle. He looked around and his jaw dropped in amazement. The area reminded him of the aftermath of urban combat. The class of 1992 had graduated on Mother's Day, as was customary, and though General Sam stood in the gathering twilight of a July evening three months later, nothing had yet been done to clean up what appeared to be a graduation rampage around Fraternity Circle. The scene was painful for Sam to witness. Some of the doors were broken off their hinges and were rotting in the front yards of the houses. Many windows had been shattered, and broken glass lay everywhere. Overstuffed furniture had been thrown out of the houses into the yards. Someone had clearly gone around with a knife ripping the stuffing out of chairs and sofas, and it was still blowing in the breeze like tumbleweeds. Broken bottles, beer cans, and all kinds of debris littered the lawns.

When General Sam entered the first house, he saw that banisters had been torn from the stairway and thrown to the middle of the common room. In other houses, mantles had been pried from the fireplaces and walls and were lying, shattered and broken, in the middle of the floor. Graffiti of all kinds, some obscene, defaced the walls. In one of the fraternity basements, five little piles of human excrement lay evenly spaced on the floor. Uneaten food rotted in sinks and on counters. Many of the refrigerators were still running with their doors hanging open. Ice had melted and water was dripping onto the floor. There were flies and other vermin everywhere. As General Sam left the last house, he began to itch and scratch as though bugs had invaded his clothes, and he could not be sure if it were a physiological or a psychological reaction he was having to the destruction he had just witnessed. His first night in Middlecourt found General Sam deeply disturbed.

That very evening, General Sam called each member of his senior cabinet and asked them to meet him in his office the following morning at 7:30. At the appointed hour, he led them along the same route that he had followed when he visited the Circle the previous evening. When they finished the tour, they returned to the office, and General Sam asked them for recommendations. From the various proposals that surfaced that day, Sam formulated a drastic course of action, one that was going to require the full support of the Board of Trustees.

It was clear that none of the fraternity houses belonged to the college, and in only one instance did the College actually own the ground on which a house stood. After painful discussion, the Board and administration agreed that Hampden-Sydney would assume the deeds to each fraternity house and all fraternity land on campus. The College would then renovate the houses to the standards of the best residence halls and academic buildings. Further, the College would construct new features, including a replacement for each fraternity's party room. Each would be equipped with a "party bunker," larger than the existing party rooms and built in accordance with established penitentiary standards so the walls would be impervious to puncture. The party bunkers would be walled off and independent from the rest of the house. Plans also called for significantly larger deck space for outdoor parties. Restroom facilities would be built near each party bunker so that visitors would not have to go through the living quarters of the house in order to get to a bathroom. Part of the reasoning behind this design concept was that visitors who had no sense of responsibility for the house caused much of the damage. Building thick, rock-hard walls and isolating the parties was one way of reducing damage by inebriated, irresponsible visitors.

The only provision that the College administration offered to national fraternity organizations in return for the deed transfers was a promise that in ten years, after necessary resources had been invested and the fraternity houses had been upgraded to acceptable standards, the fraternities could repurchase their houses and the lots on which they resided by paying the actual costs of the completed renovations, which approached three-quarters of a million dollars apiece. Buying a house back would be an expensive proposition, so General Sam was not concerned that the fraternities would want to repossess their houses.

The first fraternity renovated was Lambda Chi. When the other fraternities saw what a striking improvement the changes gave to the Lambda Chi house, they began to vie with each other to be the next in line to receive an upgrade. The process of rebuilding and renovation was expensive and time-consuming, and work on the last fraternity house was completed only a few weeks before

General Sam left office in 2000. While minor vandalism and damages still occur, there has never been a repeat of the kind of thoughtless wrecking of these fine houses that so horrified General Sam as he began his Presidency.

Despite the inauspicious start, General Sam spent a great deal of his time with the fraternities while he was President of Hampden-Sydney. Every fall, he would invite the chapter presidents to Middlecourt for a casual evening of drinks and talking about the idea of fun on the Circle. While the College President and the students did not agree on everything, the fact that their President invited them to his home and listened to their opinions had a profound effect on the young men. In fact, when one year's gathering broke up at about 10 o'clock, one of them said, "Hey, General Sam, we have a party over at our house. We'd love for you to come down."

General Sam walked down to the house that night, and the partygoers were thrilled that the President of their College would join them. He showed off his dancing skills and mingled with the group for about an hour. But the next morning, when the bugle blew for work, Sam was at his desk, and he expected the boys to be equally ready to work with "bright eyes and bushy tails."

During the school year, General Sam would occasionally sit in on fraternity meetings and allow the brothers to question him. After he had answered their questions and heard their comments, he would leave and allow them to continue their meeting without him. Opening the lines of communication was an important link in breaking the impasse that had developed between the administration and the fraternities. It was just one of the many steps in General Sam's determined effort to take a firmer approach without overstepping into hostility.

One Sunday morning following a tumultuous Greek Week evening, when loud music and carousing shouts had been heard throughout the night, General Sam was concerned about possible damage on Fraternity Circle. There were many visitors on campus that week, and the partying had lasted several nights—generally a recipe for problems. Just before sunrise, General Sam splashed his face with cold water, drank half a cup of coffee, and took a walk around Fraternity Circle to check out the situation. There was litter and trash, all of which could and would be cleared that morning, but there was no destruction and no real damage in any of the houses.

After home football games, General Sam would often go down to the Circle and walk from deck to deck where the fraternities were hosting parties. In an experience that reminded him of his time with the Russians, the fraternity boys would thrust beers in his hand and toast his good health. As soon as he put one down, another was offered, and he could not possibly finish each one handed to him. General Sam had to be careful not to drink too much, and he was careful not to walk from one fraternity to another with a drink in his hand. But while in the social atmosphere, he enjoyed meeting girlfriends, parents, and siblings, and the students did not hesitate to introduce him. He enjoyed the opportunity to be with the young men in the relaxed atmosphere of a Hampden-Sydney weekend. General Sam loved creative fun and found that externalizing internal tensions with singing, laughing, joking, and playing games was a healthy way to offset the stress of a pressure-filled week. He believed that social release is very important for people who are studying or working hard, though he never dismissed the importance of self-control.

There was no shortage of demands on the new College President, and on his first day in office, he began to identify and prioritize them. In writing, he listed the central players in the Hampden-Sydney community. General Sam noted nine constituent groups. Students were obviously the first group, and the second was the faculty, as he had assured them during his introduction the day before at Crawley Forum. The third group, he decided, was the trustees, as they were the final authority of the College. Then, not necessarily in order of importance, but maybe nearly so, followed the administration/administrative staff and the alumni. The sixth place included non-alumni friends, supporters, and donors. He penciled the media in at number seven. As number eight, he slotted the local community and the surrounding neighborhood, including Farmville, Prince Edward County, surrounding towns and villages, and local churches. In the final position, he listed sister colleges and universities, including associations such as the Virginia Foundation for Independent Colleges (VFIC) and the Council of Independent Colleges in Virginia (CICV), two organizations that would require a great deal of his attention. After prioritizing his commitments, General Sam then tried to decide what his obligations were to each of these constituent groups and how he might best go about fulfilling these obligations.

A few days later, a former President of the College stopped in the office. General Sam asked him if he had any advice on priorities and the former president responded, "Sam, it's very simple. You just keep the trustees happy and everything will be all right."

General Sam thanked him politely and did not reveal that he disagreed with the advice. He believed that establishing the Trustees as the number-one priority neglected the core reason for the College's existence: "The forming of good men and good citizens in an atmosphere of sound learning." As General Sam began the enormous challenge of assuming the Presidency, he labored to keep that goal his primary motivator.

Early on, General Sam visited every square inch of the campus. He was determined that no one would ever refer to a place at Hampden-Sydney that he had not seen with his own eyes. He went into basements, closets, attics, and barracks in each building. He also walked the campus boundaries. Reviewing the school's physical space required a significant investment of time and energy early in his presidency, but General Sam found that the investment paid off in many ways. It communicated a message that there was nothing going on that was not of interest to him and that he was determined to know about everything. He did his homework early so no one could fool him later, and in the process he began to understand the essence of the school.

As General Sam learned, you can come across all kinds of interesting things while poking around a campus as old as Hampden-Sydney's. In his inspections, General Sam discovered many leaky pipes, dripping faucets, and holes in roofs. In the quarter century before his arrival, the College had invested little in preventive maintenance and upkeep, so he was forced to initiate a costly program of extensive repairs. Several of the major buildings required renovation, including Cushing Hall, the oldest and most iconic building on campus.

While exploring Cushing Hall's basement, General Sam came across a hole in the floor covered by a small, square section about the size of a street manhole. He went over and kicked the handle, but he could not budge the door by himself. He called two students who were doing summer work on campus, and the three of them managed to pry it open with a crowbar. Sam looked down into a dark pit. "Anybody got a flashlight?" he asked. "Is there anything in there?"

There was a long silence. The two students looked at each other, then at the Building & Grounds worker, who had joined them but was also unwilling to answer. Sam sensed something was afoot. "Anything anywhere down there?" he repeated.

"Well, yes, sir."

"What is it?" It was like pulling teeth to get an answer.

Finally, one of the students said, "Well, Sir, a cat."

"A cat? What's he doing down there?"

"Nothing, sir."

"What do you mean? Down there and not doing anything? Where is he?

Is he dead?"

"Well, in a way, Sir."

"What do you mean 'in a way'? What happened to him?"

"He's hung, Sir."

"You mean he's down there hanging by his neck?"

"Yes Sir."

"Been there a long time?"

"A long, long time, Sir. He doesn't even smell anymore."

Sam ordered the top put back down. Later, when Cushing was being renovated, he watched as the construction workers pulled out the desiccated remains of the cat. All that revealed the creature's original identity was a bit of fur and a skeleton.

One of the early difficulties that General Sam faced as Chief Executive Officer of the small, all-male, liberal arts college in Southside Virginia was that a number of people in various departments on campus had developed the practice of bypassing the College President and going directly to trustees with their requests and concerns. Sam found this practice unsatisfactory. He established proper reporting channels, a task that proved more difficult than he had initially surmised. Indeed, some of the trustees enjoyed the opportunity to micromanage affairs at Hampden-Sydney without consulting the Chairman of the Board or the President. Fortunately, after some careful explanations and a few unpleasant raps on the knuckles of the most grievous offenders, the problem began to disappear.

In a related focus, General Sam worked to restore communication within the faculty and administration. The various entities of the College staff had become separate and protective of their turf. Not only were they no longer working together, in some cases they were not even talking to each other. Early in his term, General Sam realized that this communication breakdown had to be addressed, and as a first step to allay the problem, he scheduled regular Monday morning cabinet meetings. Every individual who reported directly to General Sam was expected to attend those meetings, including the College Chaplain, Reverend Willy Thompson. At these meetings, General Sam encouraged an exchange of information across different departments. The attendees reviewed any significant events of the previous week as a group, and then the administrators established priorities for the upcoming week and checked on the progress of longer term projects. Sam insisted that any information covered in the meetings be passed on to subordinates and, from time to time, he quietly checked to ensure that these lines of communication were indeed open.

In an effort to include the faculty, he asked them to nominate one of their own to be their representative at these regular meetings. Sam believed that the faculty liaison officer would make the Dean of the Faculty's job easier and establishing the position would reassure the faculty that their President intended everything the cabinet did to be completely transparent. As he tried to rebuild trust between the faculty and the cabinet, General Sam realized that transparency was an essential element. Opening the lines of communication reduced faculty gossip, misconceptions, or speculation about what the administration was planning, and the reassurances that they were "in the know" allowed faculty members to concentrate on teaching, the most important activity at any college.

As a rule, General Sam disdained meetings, but he also realized that a good meeting could accomplish useful things. He realized that it was essential that the topics they covered were interesting and directly related to the College's mission. He had learned over the years to run efficient, effective meetings, and he insisted that participants spoke succinctly so they did not drag. His aim was that everyone became involved, and he scheduled follow-ups to ensure that ideas generated during the sessions were implemented. While he realized that some meetings would be more productive than others, at the very least, he hoped to use Monday mornings to pull his team together and invigorate the group. His approach worked. People grew used to the weekly meetings, learned how to be prepared, and eventually began to look forward to them.

General Sam appointed the Dean of the Faculty, Scott Colley, to be his principal deputy, and he initiated a policy that left Dean Colley in charge when he had to be absent from campus. General Sam would stick his head in the Dean's door and say, "You've got the control," and wave goodbye, confident that the College would be in good hands during his absence. If there were decisions that had to be made while General Sam was gone, Dean Colley made them, and General Sam never quibbled with any of the dean's decisions in front of other people. He considered it vital to share authority so that people who walked into the President's office in Atkinson Hall looking for a decision could obtain one and walk out satisfied, even if the President were away. In similar fashion, General Sam told his special assistant, Paul Baker, that his responsibilities would be comparable to a Chief of Staff. While Dean Colley was the principal deputy and could make decisions in his own name, as "acting President," when General Sam was out of town, in similar situations, Dr. Baker could make decisions in the name of President Wilson.

These divisions of authority mirrored the distinctions General Sam had known in the bureaucracy of military organizations, and they worked well for him at the college. People had confidence that they could always obtain answers from the President's office.

General Sam realized when he assumed the job at Hampden-Sydney that he did not have a background in many of the activities that were taking place under his jurisdiction. He knew very little about admissions or the recruitment of students, and he knew even less about the task of raising money. In these and a myriad other areas where he had no experience, General Sam selected three of the College's most capable senior staff to be his advisory council. Once again, he turned to Scott Colley, the Dean of the Faculty, Paul Baker, an administrative wiz, and Norman Krueger, the Vice President for Business Affairs. If the matter under discussion concerned admissions, the group would invite Anita Garland, the Dean of Admissions, to join them. If the matter had to do with students, they would invite Lewis Drew, the Dean of Students, to participate. If it had to do with institutional advancement and development, they would invite the chief officer from that office to discuss the issue. In that way, advisory council numbers would fluctuate depending on the topic under discussion. General Sam borrowed the concept for this committee from a practice he had employed as the Deputy Director of Estimates for the DIA, which was essentially a think-tank job that required maximum intellectual talent and energy. To help answer any thorny problems that General Sam could not solve himself, his "three wise men," as he casually referred to Culley, Baker, and Krueger, would meet to brainstorm possible solutions.

General Sam officially called his Hampden-Sydney advisory council "The Advisory Group." They met once a week in Dean Colley's office to consider topics General Sam had requested and some topics that they had identified as areas needing to be considered. Typically, they discussed issues through a process of evaluation, with all the pros and cons considered and all the factors weighed. The Advisory Group provided General Sam with valuable insights, and it provided a boost of confidence when he lacked experience.

At the same time he was working to open communication channels among his employees at the college, General Sam was also working to ensure that the Board of Trustees also knew of all important decisions and activities. To that end, General Sam set aside Sunday evenings for a telephone conference with the Chairman of the Board of Trustees, Mr. W. Sydnor Settle. At nine o'clock each Sunday evening, Sam walked down College Road from Middlecourt to his office in Atkinson, reviewed the notes he had been preparing during the week, and made the call precisely at 9:30. For his part, the Board Chairman would be standing by, waiting for his phone to ring. These telephone calls frequently lasted for two hours, but General Sam carefully and concisely outlined all events, happenings, and projections from the previous week. He would then respond to Mr. Settle's questions or comments. General Sam was confident that keeping the Board informed as an essential element in the smooth operations of the college.

For his part, the Board Chairman loved the sessions and he referred to them as "Sammy-grams." The fact that General Sam worked hard to ensure that the Board was informed also gave Sydnor Settle a feeling of greater trust and confidence in Sam. The communication was especially appreciated because the College's situation remained somewhat precarious and the Board of Trustees had taken a chance on a man who did not have experience in academic administration. This weekly telephone call was General Sam's way of reassuring the Board Chairman and the trustees.

Throughout his presidency, General Sam continued to teach classes in the evenings, one on Tuesday evening on foreign policy and national security and another on Thursday evening on intelligence. The demands of his new job soon made it clear that two evenings a week were too many, and he reduced his load to one class in the fall and another in the spring. In addition to his academic responsibilities, he began teaching a Sunday school class in College Church. His style was to facilitate a freewheeling sort of discussion on moral and spiritual issues without attempting to convert people or proselytize. He simply tried to lead the young men who attended to confront their own mortality and their own destiny as it pertained to God. He would wake up at four o'clock on Sunday mornings to prepare the lesson for the students who attended. The early hour was made easier because Susi also was up by 3:30 on Sunday mornings, preparing a big lunch spread for the students who attended General Sam's class.

Susi typically spent six or seven hours preparing what came to be known as "Mis' Susi's Sunday Country Dinner." Her feasts invariably included hams, roasts, turkey, chicken, a medley of vegetables, fresh fruit salads, and a variety of cakes and pies. The long table at Middlecourt groaned from the weight of the dishes she prepared and served herself. General Sam's class generally finished at about 10:30 before worship services began at eleven. After the worship service, all the students knew that they were invited to lunch at Middlecourt. But somehow, between the 9:30 class and lunch time, the number of students would swell from the twenty-five who actually attended

Sunday school to seventy-five or eighty, some with their girlfriends in tow. They were all welcomed, and at Middlecourt, they shared not just lunch, but laughter, conversation, and friendship. Frequently someone played the piano while others at the party sang or danced. After the students finished off Mis' Susi's main course, they stuffed themselves on homemade pies and cakes— lemon meringue pie and strawberry shortcake among the favorites. Those "Sunday Country Dinners" became an institution for some of the students, and General Sam always loved hearing from graduates who described them with the same pleasure as he and Susi recalled.

During General Sam's tenure as President, Susi maintained her own demanding routine. In addition to her Sunday dinners, she participated in countless campus events and initiated programs that benefited the Hampden-Sydney campus and community. One of the traditions that she organized was the campus wives providing exam packets for students at the end of every academic semester. Susi and her team of college community ladies would fill dozens of packages full of fruits, nuts, candies, cookies, and brownies for students who were cramming for exams. The packages were sold for twenty-five dollars apiece, and they sold rapidly. In fact, during the days leading up to exam periods, Susi received checks in the mail almost daily from parents who wanted to provide a box for their sons. All the checks were donated to the Hampden-Sydney College Fire Department's drive to buy a new fire truck. One year, over ten thousand dollars was raised.

From the onset General Sam sought means by which Hampden-Sydney could become a "happening" place. He was determined to set the College on the national map. He talked in terms of "bringing the world to Hampden-Sydney." He recognized that some "children of concrete and asphalt," as he described them, were not programmed to enjoy the bucolic atmosphere of "the Hill," and unless there were something interesting happening on campus, something that captured their attention, they would escape for urban pleasures whenever they could. General Sam figured that the College had sufficient resources to persuade interesting people to visit, and since he still was involved with Washington matters, he had connections that helped in this endeavor. People of national and international reputation owed him a few favors and were willing to give lectures or participate in conferences and symposia. As timely and engaging speakers began to be scheduled in events at Hampden-Sydney, media attention grew and the campus was abuzz with activity, all of which created a sense of anticipation and excitement, not only on campus but also within the surrounding community, among the Trustees, and with prominent alumni.

These undertakings, particularly the substantive conferences and symposia which sometimes lasted from three days to a week, severely stretched the members of the administrative staff, and some resented the extra responsibilities and long hours. General Sam was accustomed to a strenuous work style, but his staff's reluctance to orchestrate complicated events sometimes limited his ability to schedule all the venues he envisioned. Working with the constraints of a limited budget and an over-extended staff, General Sam still scheduled numerous special lecturers, academic conferences, and symposia.

In 1991, even before he had taken office as President, General Sam arranged a campus event that featured a panel of high-profile media figures addressing the issue of protecting national secrets in a free society. He managed to procure commitments from the senior editor of *Time* magazine, the head of National Public Radio, the international editor of CNN, the *New York Times* military correspondent, the Director of the Defense Intelligence Agency, and a recently retired Lieutenant General, Tom Kelly, who had been the Pentagon's spokesman on the Gulf War. Sam was so persuasive that General Kelly agreed to fly down from Washington and participate in the Hampden-Sydney discussion on the evening of the very day that he retired from his Pentagon job. The eminence of the participants ensured that the symposium was well received and helped to raise the reputation of Hampden-Sydney College as a prominent place of learning.

Probably the most extensive and comprehensive symposium that General Sam was able to organize during his eight years as President of Hampden-Sydney College was entitled "Vietnam Twenty Years After: Voices of the War." This week-long event was conducted in September 1993, a little more than twenty years after American ground combat forces withdrew from Vietnam in April 1973. Sam enticed notables from all aspects of the conflict to participate in the Hampden-Sydney event. The program began with a comprehensive presentation from Dr. Walt Whitman Rostow, the National Security Advisor to the President during the early years of the war, followed by a detailed description of military operations from General William C. Westmoreland, Commander of U.S. forces during a major part of the war (1964-68). Pacification operations, the so-called "other war in Vietnam," were discussed by Ambassador William E. Colby, Director of Civil Operations in Vietnam and later the Director of the CIA.

In addition to soldiers and government officials, General Sam convinced the most prominent representatives of the public media involved in the Vietnam experience to talk about the role of the media in the conflict. Students were excited to meet and even sit at lunch with such well known public figures as television correspondents Peter Arnett and Morley Safer, filmmaker Oliver Stone, and famous authors like Neal Sheehan of *The Bright and Shining Lie.* The public media discussion was followed by a three-hour session called "Vietnam, the Soldier in the Field." Participating in this event were two retired four-star generals, including General Sam's close friend, Robert C. Kingston. Also in the group was Colonel "Charging" Charlie Beckwith, a Green Beret in Vietnam, who had just left his position as the original Delta Force commander. The individuals taking part in this particular event ranged from four-star General Kingston down to Private First Class Oliver Stone. Each talked about the war as it looked and felt from his particular vantage point and, not surprisingly, they were not always in agreement.

To ensure that the Vietnam War was considered from every angle, General Sam also included notable protestors, including former Senator George McGovern, former Senator Eugene McCarthy, and the former president of Vietnam Veterans Against the War. Their audience listened attentively and asked questions of these men, who explained their stance on the war in Vietnam and the reasons for the positions they had championed.

When General Sam had been in charge of recruiting scouts for the 82nd's reconnaissance company, he had recruited men for that company who could sing, thus ensuring that the recon scouts could double as the 82nd Airborne Division Chorus. General Sam still had good friends from the 82nd Airborne Division Chorus, and they performed on campus to a standing-room only

Sam Wilson at the Vietnam Symposium with General William Westmoreland (left) and reporter Peter Arnett.

Sam Wilson at the Prince Edward Story Symposium with actor James Earl Jones.

crowd. It was a memorable evening during a symposium that abounded with superlatives. The program was capped by musical entertainment entitled, "Vietnam: the Soldier's Songs," performed by Vietnam veterans who were accomplished musicians—pickers, players, and singers, nearly all of whom had written their own songs about Vietnam. These talented individuals rendered an artistic interpretation of the war experience.

The symposium was an overwhelming success. The front page of the State section of the *Richmond Times-Dispatch* featured each event as it occurred. Statewide television and radio stations also covered the multi-faceted symposium, and some of the programs were even highlighted by national magazines. Farmville radio station WFLO-FM covered the proceedings in detail. During the week of the program, the College housed a large number of famous guests on campus, many of whom ate at Settle Hall with students. Students were thrilled to call home and divulge the names of famous figures they had met in the cafeteria.

During General Sam's final year in office, he orchestrated another remarkable symposium called "Race in America: the Prince Edward Story." The program addressed a topic that remained very sensitive and controversial in Virginia. During the desegregation era, Prince Edward County was the only county in the country that chose to close schools rather than to integrate. A number of prominent supporters of Hampden-Sydney, including Trustees and donors, called, wired, wrote, and visited General Sam in their efforts to dissuade him from confronting the topic of race. One prominent donor called and said, "Sam, if you pull this thing off, I'll never give the college another dime."

Sam simply replied, "I have to do it. We have considered it very carefully. We are going to be as controlled and non-emotional as we can be, but we are going to do it."

In spite of the opposition, the College hosted a week-long symposium which examined the events in Prince Edward County, why they happened, and how they affected the present. General Sam and his staff avowed that the goal was to provide improved understanding and reconciliation within the community, a lofty aim which some called a pipe dream. Despite the naysayers, the skeptics, and the opponents, the symposium, which provided a platform for dialogue, was received very favorably by the community and local media.

In 1994, the College also hosted a Senatorial election debate among former White House staffer Oliver North, then-Senator Charles Robb, Douglas

Wilder, who later became the Governor of Virginia, and former State Attorney General Marshall Coleman. This sell-out program, held in Fleet Gymnasium, received national coverage on CSPAN and was moderated by Judy Woodruff of CNN.

Despite the strain they forced on organizers, these stellar programs involved Hampden-Sydney in the wider academic community and in the political conversation. Before he left office, General Sam organized nine symposia, an achievement that many considered impossible, given the lack of staff and facilities. Students were recruited to act as assistants, but even with the extra hands, everyone was stretched to the limit. In the aftermath of the Vietnam symposium, General Sam recalls mentioning that they should attempt a similar gathering to discuss the Gulf War. One of his senior subordinates quickly responded, "Not me, General. If you pull another one of these, I'll quit. If I don't quit, my wife will leave me."

In conjunction with raising the College's profile, General Sam believed that it was fundamental to Hampden-Sydney's future that its academic level be strengthened. A first step required improving the level of incoming students, and General Sam worked with the admissions office to raise the bar for new recruits. He traveled to high schools and private academies throughout the Southeast to attract promising students, and he expanded the program for honors scholars. When General Sam took office, the College had about twenty-eight honors scholars, a number he hoped to boost to one hundred. On spring weekends when prospective merit scholars were invited to campus, Susi spent the entire day Saturday baking treats for these special guests, though she had to be careful to hide these pies and cakes from the regular Sunday school crowd. After the lunch crowd had dissolved on the given Sundays, General Sam and Susi would set out another batch of cakes, pies, and soft drinks for Dean Garland, members of her admissions staff, and prospective merit scholars who gathered in the relaxed atmosphere of the Wilson's home. There, as everyone enjoyed Mis' Susi's reception, the President could extol Hampden-Sydney's qualities and encourage the young men to attend. The number of merit scholars began climbing steadily and, by the time of General Sam's retirement from office, had exceeded eighty.

With the support of an overwhelming majority of its members, the faculty approached the Board of Trustees to request that Hampden-Sydney become co-educational. When the administration polled the student body, the overwhelming majority of the young men were staunchly opposed to the prospect. Thus, the College faced a situation in which over three-quarters of the faculty were adamant that Hampden-Sydney should be co-ed while close to ninety-five percent of students took the opposite view. Outsiders weighed in on the matter as well, including some prominent politicians. The question was a complex one. While adding women to the student body would require costly adjustments and additions to facilities, it would also double the available applicant pool, thereby raising academic standards almost immediately. Based on General Sam's recommendation to the chairman of the Board of Trustees, a full year was spent considering the issue in a number of forums and debates, and the President attempted to ensure that anyone who had a view was heard and, more importantly, that each individual knew his or her opinion had been considered. In August of 1996, the Board of Trustees met in special session at the conference room of the Richmond International Airport to give the matter final consideration. A majority vote mandated that the College remain all-male. Following the decision, Chairman William Boinest and General Sam went together to a nearby conference room and met with a crowd of media to announce the outcome of the vote.

Susi Wilson waited outside for her husband, and when the press conference was over, General Sam walked from the building just in time to see a *Richmond Times-Dispatch* photographer snap a picture of a bumper sticker that Susi's son had slapped on the bumper of her car. It read "Hampden-Sydney, where men are men and women are guests."

Next morning, the picture ran on the front page of the *Times-Dispatch*. In an attempt to maintain good taste, Sam removed the sticker and asked the College bookstore to remove all the remaining stickers from its retail stacks. He felt it was inappropriate to flaunt the Board's decision in the face of those who had supported co-education.

With the decision to remain all-male, the Board members and President were aware that they would be subject to criticism for asserting masculinity and belittling feminism. To combat this perception, General Sam made special efforts to strengthen the relationship of Hampden-Sydney with the four women's colleges in Virginia at that time: Hollins University, Sweet Briar College, Randolph-Macon Women's College, and Mary Baldwin College. General Sam contacted the Presidents of these four women's colleges and suggested that they could improve all their institutions if they worked together to broaden the options offered to students, both academically and socially.

When the other Presidents agreed, they began meeting on a monthly basis as a group of five. They established several exchange programs, one of which included five students from Randolph-Macon Women's College joining his intelligence course on Thursday nights. In another exchange agreement, Sweet Briar College invited Hampden-Sydney professors to attend a social gathering with faculty in their discipline from the women's colleges. With the departure of several key figures in later years, the practice of shared academic community faded, but for several years all five single-sex institutions in the Commonwealth of Virginia benefited from faculty cooperation.

THE HAMPDEN-SYDNEY YEARS II:
IMPROVEMENTS AND LEADERSHIP

ON THE THIRTIETH OF JULY 1992, his first morning on the job as the twenty-second President of Hampden-Sydney, General Sam arrived at work early and sat in his big red chair gazing out the office window. After reflecting on his notes, he called his secretary. It was the first time that they had talked since General Sam assumed his new position, and in the course of their conversation, she informed him in no uncertain terms that she was not really a secretary. General Sam's predecessor had appointed her as "Special Assistant to the President" and she intended to keep that title. She continued, "And, in that connection, I don't pour coffee."

Instead of responding that he knew of at least two other people in the former President's office who had been given that title, Sam tersely replied, "Well, Ma'am, if you tell me how you like your coffee, I'll be happy to pour you a cup every morning when I come in."

She blinked and said nothing. Despite his efforts to brush off the affront, the secretary's attitude stuck in General Sam's craw for the rest of the day and into the evening. He knew that members of his immediate office did not much like each other. The two secretaries, in fact, were not even on speaking terms. They had erected a barrier of filing cabinets to separate their work spaces so that they would not have to look at each other during the day. The earlier remark to General Sam about coffee struck him as one more symptom caused by the lack of consistent leadership from the President's office for the past couple of years.

That night he went home, sat at his desk, and wrote his secretary a letter on the importance of each one serving and being helpful to others in the office. Before he was finished, it was four pages long. The letter described his personal philosophy, and gave multiple examples of how he had tried to live that philosophy himself in his past assignments. He stated that he did not believe anyone could work together effectively while maintaining that attitude. He put the letter in his pocket, carried it with him to the office the next morning, and sat for a second day in the big red chair behind his desk.

As he was turning to call his secretary in and hand her the letter, she walked in with a cup of steaming hot coffee and a sweet bun on a tray.

She had understood his meaning the previous day, and so the letter went back into his coat pocket and later, into the trash. Thereafter, she worked with him as Executive Secretary to the President, and she proved herself to be extraordinarily capable in every way.

One of the cardinal rules of General Sam's management philosophy had always been to resolve issues in as frank and open a fashion as possible, giving everyone a chance to be heard and to contribute to a resolution. General Sam believed so strongly about making sure that all thoughts and ideas received a fair hearing that at times he worried about possibly over-venting a problem. Once all aspects of the subject had been considered and everyone heard, Sam made a final decision on his own and expected everyone to support it. There was no voting process. The final choice was his and his alone, and he was the one who lived with the consequences.

General Sam discovered in his early days at the helm of Hampden-Sydney that policy discussions often became more contentious than he preferred. Often, he sensed that the dueling sides were arguing about personal as well as professional interests. There seemed to be a distinct effort to protect bureaucratic turf. He soon found a question that quieted dissension. That question was, "What is truly in the best interest of Hampden-Sydney College and its mission?" By taking the focus away from personal preference, the emphasis shifted to the long-range, best interest of the College. Sam was sometimes surprised at how quickly his simple question stifled dissent and caused people to join together for a common goal.

Another rhetorical question that he also found to be helpful was, "How will this situation appear ten, twenty-five, or fifty years from now?" He used that question so regularly that often, when the cabinet was trying to make a decision, someone would ask the question for him, and it caused them all to see things with a greater sense of historical perspective. In addition to encouraging everyone to subjugate their egos, the use of those two rhetorical questions forced General Sam and his colleagues to lift their gaze and think philosophically about problems at hand.

Early on, General Sam established an open-door policy for all members of his organization. If someone really was bothered by an issue and the system were not responsive, he or she could feel free to schedule an appointment to see the President. He promised himself that he would listen with an open mind to everyone who worked for him. General Sam figured that in a college of one thousand students a president could afford to adopt this kind of open-door policy. It kept grievances from simmering, improved staff morale, and created a greater sense of responsibility in the management chain. As he had hoped, the College constituents took advantage of his policy, and he soon had to schedule specific times for such sessions.

Before establishing residence in the President's house on campus, Susi and General Sam decided that Middlecourt, at least the first and second floors, should be open to the public. Their personal quarters were on the third floor, and these remained off-limits to others, but students and alumni were encouraged to wander around the house, especially on the ground floor level, and always on celebratory occasions. Susi and General Sam wanted to make Middlecourt as interesting as possible, so with the capable assistance of Dr. Richard McClintock, they displayed many of Sam's old photographs, plaques, and citations. Each item had a story behind it, and with so many places to pause and tell stories, it could take as much as an hour for General Sam to escort a visitor through the basement. Students and guests enjoyed walking around the house even when he was not there to guide them.

Gradually the campus community became accustomed to the open-door policy that General Sam and Susi instituted at Middlecourt. On one occasion, a student remarked to a media representative that " . . . during my first two years here, I had never seen the interior of Middlecourt and didn't know what it looked like. Now, I think I could go in downstairs, lie down on

Miss Susi at Middlecourt, preparing lunch for Sunday School students.

one of the sofas, and take a nap in the mid-afternoon if I wanted to." Indeed, on more than one occasion, General Sam and Susi found that a student had done exactly that.

One night, as General Sam was sleeping soundly in his third floor bedroom at Middlecourt, he was suddenly jerked awake by the jarring sounds of the opening to Beethoven's Fifth Symphony echoing from the piano below. "BA BA BA BOOM, BA BA BA BOOM." He grabbed his flashlight and hurried downstairs to the second-floor grand piano. There he found a shaggy-haired student playing the piano with great gusto. General Sam recognized the young man as one of the frequent visitors to Mis' Susi's Sunday Dinner. When he asked the student what he was doing, the young man replied, "Oh hi, General Sam. Mis' Susi said I could come play this piano any time I wanted," as if he were doing nothing out of the ordinary.

It was apparent that the young man was drunk, but General Sam suppressed his urge to give him a piece of his mind. Rather, he asked him to stand and they had a short, pleasant conversation, much like one they could have had when they passed each other on the sidewalk during the day. The student eventually departed into the darkness, and General Sam walked back upstairs to return to sleep.

During the first home basketball game General Sam attended in the fall of 1992, he was surprised that the pep band consisted of one lonely student sitting high in the bleachers with a trumpet and occasionally blowing "CHARGE" to inspire the crowd. He decided then and there that Hampden-Sydney had to have a real pep band for home basketball games. General Sam persuaded a supportive Trustee to buy musical instruments, and he recruited a number of students who had studied music and were interested in playing. In short order, the College had an active and noisy pep band that contributed to athletic events, especially basketball in Fleet Gymnasium.

To General Sam, sports of all kinds were vital to the health of the College as an institution. He helped recruit capable athletes who had interest in Hampden-Sydney, he attended games whenever his schedule permitted, and he found occasions to mingle with the school's athletes.

He was still new to the office when he learned that the famed Hampden-Sydney Men's Chorus no longer existed and had not been active on campus since the death of Professor Ned Crawley in 1984. General Sam knew that for decades the chorus had been a prominent part of life at Hampden-Sydney, and he was determined to activate the group again. Such a commitment would necessitate locating and funding a capable director, and so Sam immediately began searching for a qualified individual to fill the job. In short order, a director was hired and the Men's Chorus was back in business. It has remained an important part of the campus and a contributor to college life since that time.

The dining hall complex now known as Settle Hall had just been completed in 1992 when General Sam was named President, but there were insufficient funds to take full advantage of the unfinished lower level. When General Sam walked through the building for the first time, the basement had a ceiling almost twenty feet high, the walls were ugly cinder block, and the floors were grey concrete, more like an abandoned World War II aircraft hangar than an inviting college space. Under Sam's watch, plans were made to transform the building into the finest student commons in the Commonwealth. General Sam and his staff visited private clubs and student facilities at other colleges and universities before finally developing their plan for what was to become the new Tiger Inn. The project took months of planning and a great deal of money, but with the considerable financial help of an anonymous trustee, the Tiger Inn came into being as a carefully designed space where students could bring their girlfriends for chicken fingers and a soda or relax with friends over a few beers and listen to music, throw darts, or shoot pool.

Originally, the new Tiger Inn opened onto a marshy swamp with the grandiose name of Lake Chalgrove. General Sam saw the swamp as an eyesore and proceeded to revamp the area from swampland into today's landscaped lake. From time to time, Sam would enjoy fishing there, and one afternoon when he had dropped his line, he was greatly surprised to see a flash of gold under the water's surface. Largemouth bass and pan fish were more in the realm of his expectations, but when he peered into the water, a golden shimmer materialized into a goldfish, about fifteen inches long, swimming slowly along the shoreline. At first, General Sam was puzzled that a goldfish was in the lake. Then he realized that students most likely were dropping their unwanted pet goldfish into the pond at the end of the school year. Gradually a thriving population had been established.

General Sam considered the Tiger Inn and Lake Chalgrove important improvements because they represented positive diversions for the students he was encouraging to work hard and play hard. He knew that, unless students could find innovative and socially acceptable ways to vent their energy, they would be tempted to externalize their tensions in ways that would get them into trouble. By offering options, he hoped the college might distract young men from harmful habits.

For that same reason, the Wilson trail system was established in the woods surrounding the buildings. Hampden-Sydney's campus occupied only a small portion of the total acreage belonging to the college. Beautiful woods and streams remained untapped resources for student use, so General Sam charted trails in the woods for bikers, runners, and walkers. The trail system soon became a favorite haunt for students as well as members of the local community.

One of General Sam's most difficult responsibilities was fundraising. He was uncomfortable asking people for money, and his past experience had given him minimal preparation for this vital part of his job. Extensive personnel turnovers had disrupted the Development Office and destroyed the continuity that was essential for maintaining healthy relationships with potential donors. Poor organization, unfocused guidance, and irregular supervision plagued the Development Office and left fundraising efforts ineffective. To motivate himself for fundraising, General Sam developed a formula in which he rationalized that the individuals he was approaching had more money than they needed for living and planned to give away some part of their money, either to Hampden-Sydney or to some other cause. Thinking of his donors in that light made it easier for the President to approach potential givers and convince them that Hampden-Sydney represented a quality investment.

When General Sam assumed the Presidency, the College's endowment measured $30 million. A capital campaign was already underway for an additional $35 million, but it was being sluggishly pursued. It was clear to General Sam that fundraising was a glaring weakness and had to be addressed. He initiated a considerable overhaul within the Development Office to assemble a team that would be capable of achieving high levels of growth. He then established a goal of endowment growth to $100 million before he left office, and according to the Fall 1999 edition of the *Hampden-Sydney Record,* "The Wilson Years," the College had reached an endowment of $118,000,000 when General Sam stepped down as President.

General Sam found that it was necessary for him to spend a great deal of time away from campus in the quest to recruit qualified students and to raise funds for the college. If he engaged and sustained the interest of alums in the College mission, then financial contributions would follow. While some cities had well organized alumni clubs with memberships that numbered in the hundreds, others had none at all. In concert with the Development Office, General Sam identified several target cities and organized local chapters through which members could enjoy activities and could feel a reciprocal sense of involvement in the college.

Midway through the eight years of his Presidency, one of the Trustees dropped by General Sam's office and as the two men talked, the Trustee informed General Sam that he had spent the previous night in Richmond. When General Sam asked if he had stayed in a hotel, the Trustee replied that his late mother had left him a nice condominium near the Fan district, and he found it convenient to stay in that apartment whenever he was in the area. He mused that he probably should get rid of the property because he used it so rarely. Immediately, General Sam responded with a gleam in his eye, "Well, Sir, if the price were right, the College might buy it for Hampden-Sydney. It would give us an advance base in Richmond, a city where we do a lot of business."

At that point, General Sam was interrupted by an important phone call, and when he returned to his visitor he received a surprising offer. "Sam," the man smiled, "why don't I give that apartment to Hampden-Sydney."

General Sam thanked the Trustee for his magnanimity and assured him that the college would use the gift advantageously. Such generosity lifted Sam's spirits and encouraged him to continue approaching other potential benefactors.

A sensitive subject of great personal interest to General Sam was the status of minority students, especially African-Americans, at Hampden-Sydney. Many of the College's African-American graduates had become remarkably successful in the outside world and returned from time to time to Hampden-Sydney to provide advice to current minority students. The college had also sponsored annual gatherings of African-American alumni since about 1990. General Sam was disappointed to realize, however, that despite the enormous gains that had been made in society overall, racial relations still posed a problem at Hampden-Sydney, and vestiges of racism still lingered on campus. General Sam was determined to do whatever he could to implement improvements, and under his watch, the number of minority students slowly increased from year to year. He was proud to realize that African-American students built on their experience at the College and achieved success after they graduated. His experiences in the military had reinforced General Sam's lifelong commitment to equality. In the Army, he recognized his troops as uniformed Americans, then by their rank, and only at that time would he notice skin color or race. He wanted that sort of color blindness to take hold at Hampden-Sydney.

General Sam greatly valued the College's Honor System and he considered the strength of the Honor Code to be a reflection of the strength of the institution. As he observed student leaders carrying out their responsibilities for administering and upholding the system on a day-to-day basis, he was, on occasion, deeply disappointed that some of them did not seem to take their responsibilities seriously enough or they lacked the knowledge and experience requisite for handling their offices on the Honor Court. Sam mused on the problem for some weeks, and then one evening he realized, "If you had run the 82nd Airborne Division this way, you'd have been fired."

In the 82nd Airborne Division he was constantly educating squad leaders, platoon sergeants, first sergeants, and master sergeants. There, the leadership of the organization was trained in depth and detail on their leadership responsibilities, yet at Hampden-Sydney, students were being appointed or elected to positions of sensitive responsibility, given perhaps a half-day workshop on their duties, and then released to fulfill them.

Out of that late-night observation in 1996, there developed the organization that is now known as the Society of '91, named after the distinguished Hampden-Sydney class of 1791. This program was designed to focus on the leadership responsibilities of the College's top forty student leaders. The students studied topics such as what leadership consists of, the role of leaders in American society, and the specific roles of student leaders at Hampden-Sydney College. General Sam delegated responsibility of the program to the Dean of Students, Lewis Drew, who in the President's view was one of the most capable small college Deans of Students in the country. Although General Sam tracked and advised the project until it was finalized, he left most of the responsibility with the Dean Drew and his capable associate, Dr. David Klein.

Even after leaving the Presidency, General Sam remained committed to leading two sessions of the Society of '91. One of these took place during the program's weekend retreat each fall. For this occasion, General Sam developed a three-hour long presentation that he called his "Ten Presidents Speech," in which he analyzed the role of ten Presidents of the United States, nine of whom he knew well enough to develop an appreciation for the man as a person. For his other session, General Sam revamped a presentation that he developed many years earlier to address the characteristics and qualities of a successful military leader. After revising it to fit his civilian audience, he tweaked a few details to address student-specific issues.

General Sam's vision was to embolden Hampden-Sydney College to become nationally known as America's leadership college. In its first fifty or sixty years, the College had represented a beacon of progress in the young nation. It had produced leaders at the local, state, and national level far out of proportion to the size of the College itself. General Sam's hoped to restore the College to its former position as an incubator of leaders for public and political service, and the Society of '91 was an initial step towards realizing that aim.

Another piece in the leadership effort at Hampden-Sydney came from an unexpected source, a Presbyterian minister named Ben Mathes. Mathes was undertaking expeditions on rivers around the world, especially in underdeveloped countries, where he worked to improve the quality of life of native peoples. General Sam recognized that Mathes was doing something very much in accord with the military civic action programs that General Ed Landsdale had espoused to Sam back in the 1950s.

On one of Mathes's campus visits, he attended General Sam's Sunday school class and then spoke to the congregation at College Church. Afterward, he joined students at Middlecourt for Mis' Susi's Sunday Dinner. While Mathes and some forty or fifty students and their girlfriends were relaxing and enjoying the afternoon, two young men came rushing into the dining room saying, "General Sam, General Sam! We've got a deer out here on your front lawn."

"Is he still alive?" General Sam asked.

"It isn't a he. It's a she. And she's dead."

"What is she doing dead?" General Sam was curious.

"Well, we accidentally drowned her," replied the boys.

"How'd you do that?"

"She was on thin ice at Lake Chalgrove. We tried to help her to safety, but she tried to run from us. She broke through the ice and drowned."

The two boys had dragged her up to General Sam's lawn and were desperate to do something about the deer. At that point Mathes turned to General Sam and asked, "You got a skinning knife?"

"No," General Sam said, "but I'll bet you've got one."

Mathes went to his Land Rover and brought back a tray of handsome knives. He selected one and then they went out on the lawn and hung the deer on a branch of the ancient Osage orange tree in the flower garden. Mathes spat on the blade and rubbed his thumb down the edge. Then he turned to the crowd, "Anybody here got a stopwatch?" He asked.

Associate Dean of Students Dean Klein agreed to time Mathes, and in precisely eight minutes the deer had been butchered and the venison was secured in General Sam's freezer.

Thus Mathes quickly became a figure who sparked imagination and a sense of adventure, and when he introduced overseas service projects as an option for Hampden-Sydney students, they were well received. To date, dozens of students have traveled with the overseas programs organized with Ben Mathes. Every year, participants provide needed services to underdeveloped countries and, in the process, gain enriching opportunities for leadership development.

As President, General Sam found that his role did not always involve big-picture goals for Hampden-Sydney. He had always enjoyed his personal relationships with the young men on campus, and sometimes his bond with those individuals provided the best platform to resolve student-related issues. One such opportunity presented itself in the fall of 1994 when General Sam was jarred by an unpleasant surprise.

In the spring of that year, a group of Hampden-Sydney freshman, acting under the orders of a tough pledge educator in one of the fraternities, had gone to Richmond to engage in shenanigans in Hollywood cemetery. Returning to campus along Highway 360 through Amelia County in the wee hours of the morning, they spotted a large plastic replica of a Guernsey cow. It seemed a fine idea to impress their pledge trainer by bringing the cow statue back to campus with them. They managed to unbolt the plastic cow and wrench it loose from its platform. Draping it over the roof of the station wagon, the pledges carried the cow back to their fraternity's off campus house, "The Ranch." General Sam first learned of the incident and the missing cow in the late summer of 1994, when the landlord of "The Ranch" discovered the plastic cow and reported its presence to the administration.

General Sam had noticed earlier in the summer that the cow was missing from its usual post, and he had subsequently learned that the owner of the dairy farm was still searching for his cow, but Sam had not given the situation much more attention until he discovered that Hampden-Sydney students were involved in the icon's disappearance. The crime had to be addressed, and he investigated further. The offense was a matter of concern not only for the reputation of the College but also as a possible violation of the Honor Code. At the very least, it was a breach of the rules of student conduct.

As word of the incident and investigation spread, the campus began to buzz. The pledge educator had graduated and was long gone from campus, but the pledges involved were soon identified as well-known members of the student body. Certain voices began to clamor for the administration to drop any possible charges.

As General Sam unraveled the specifics of the incident, tension grew. The dairy farm owner threatened to take the pledges to municipal court and charge them with stealing. Two prominent Hampden-Sydney alumni from Richmond, each of whom had a son implicated in the incident, attempted to persuade General Sam to drop charges that might stain the young men's permanent records. General Sam assured both sides that he would use his best judgment in working through the sensitive problem, and he advised everyone to withhold judgment until they had seen the outcome of the investigation.

Shortly after his visit from the fathers of the former pledges, General Sam received a telephone call from the pledge educator's father, a prominent lawyer in the Deep South. He informed General Sam in no uncertain terms who he was and that General Sam had better sort out the matter of Amelia's plastic cow quickly and in the best interest of the students involved, or he would come to Hampden-Sydney himself to do the job. General Sam informed the pugnacious man that of the College's thirty-five-man Board of Trustees, more than half were prominent lawyers. If this father chose to become involved, Sam recommended that he not come alone because he would be greeted by a platoon of some of the best lawyers in the United States. That aggressive defense subdued the lawyer, and General Sam never heard from him again.

Because the issue had become such a topic of concern to students, General Sam and Dean Drew felt it appropriate to accurately explain the situation in a town meeting. Parents and Friends Lounge was packed to standing room only, and the noisy gathering lasted better than two hours. The administration was honest with the students and told all the facts that had come to light. They did not, however, discuss what sort of punishment the young men involved could expect to face. General Sam emphasized his belief that people are always responsible for their actions, but also that justice invariably must be mingled with mercy. He believed in rehabilitation. As the administration assured students that it was proceeding in as balanced and judicious a manner as possible, the evening discussion diffused the anger of some irate members of the community and soothed the fears of unjustly severe retribution.

The College administration purposefully lengthened the investigation as a tactic to give the students time to ponder what punishment would be required, but when a final judgment was given, it was deemed fair by all parties. Each of the students involved received one semester of disciplinary probation. The students admitted their guilt, expressed their heartfelt apologies, wrote papers on what they had learned from the experience, and performed community service without complaint. As a final act, they met with General Sam in the basement of Middlecourt where they discussed the incident, and after the meeting, General Sam closed the case. Amelia's plastic cow was returned, and its owner took the extra precaution of filling it with concrete.

A year later, a separate troublesome incident transpired in a situation that came to be known as the "Student X" development. In the fall of 1995, a student wrote General Sam a disjointed, wandering, and plaintive note in which he expressed many things that were troubling him, before stating that he was going to commit suicide. He then signed the note *Student X*. General Sam and Dean Drew immediately began working to identify the student. They compiled a list of possible individuals and mobilized College resources to narrow the field, but they could not be sure exactly with whom they were dealing. From time to time, Student X would make a quick telephone call to General Sam, Dean Drew, or Reverend Willie Thompson, telling them that he was really about to end his life. Perhaps he was teasing and tantalizing them, but they had to take him seriously.

Finally, Student X told General Sam exactly which would be his suicide night. On that evening, General Sam set up shop with other administrators in the office of the Dean of Students. He positioned security officers and members of the student body all over campus, and the night proceeded quietly, with no word from the troubled student and no unusual incidents on campus. The next day, Student X called General Sam and was agitated that the President had shared his earlier call and revealed his plan. General Sam placated the young man and assured him that his best interests were at heart and that he was proud that these efforts had prevented a possible disaster.

After lengthy review, the administration identified which student was most likely Student X. Thereafter, whenever General Sam saw the young man, he made a point of showing interest in his life. Though he never revealed his suspicions, General Sam made an effort to cross paths with Student X quite often during the year. The young man attended General Sam's Sunday school class and often visited Middlecourt for Mis' Susi's dinners. General Sam even met the troubled young man's family. That May, Student X graduated, and when he came across the platform and the President handed him his diploma, General Sam said, "God bless you, Student X, you finally made it."

The young man looked at him, a little shocked. His eyes moistened, and he responded, "Thank you, Sir," before walking off the stage.

In 1999, after nearly eight years in the big red chair, General Sam felt as weary as he had before his retreat from Moscow in 1973. During his tenure as President of Hampden-Sydney College, he never once took a vacation, and he worked or was on call twenty-four hours a day, every day. Only occasionally would he take an afternoon to go fishing or to spend a little time with his family. Since Susi and he lived full time at Middlecourt, his only opportunity to return to his home at Frog Hollow was on late Sunday afternoons.

On those rare occasions of serenity, General Sam lapped up the luxury of relaxation. When it came time to douse the small fire and lock the farmhouse for the night, he would dawdle. It was hard to leave the cabin and return to Middlecourt. In his seventh year as president, the non-stop workload was affecting his health. He began waking up at two or three o'clock in the morning and finding himself unable to go back to sleep. He would walk downstairs and pour himself a cup of coffee, then wind up in the big red chair of his Atkinson Hall office well before anyone else had arrived. Even though he was fatigued by the time the regular workday started, he had to steel himself to face an onslaught of demands. In time, his insomnia developed into sleep apnea, and medical attention became necessary

In addition to sleep problems, General Sam's legs began to fail him. The deterioration, from peripheral neuropathy, was partially a result of hard landings on too many parachute jumps in his military career. In 1997, five years into General Sam's term as President, the chief neurologist at the Medical College of Virginia warned him that it was highly unlikely that he would be walking upright for another twelve months. In addition, he developed a heart murmur from an aortic stenosis, an ailment that resulted in extreme fatigue. General Sam realized that faced with his deteriorating health, he might not have the energy, drive, or the mental acuity to handle his position appropriately for an extended time. After nearly a decade addressing the various problems that surrounded the campus community, he was growing exhausted.

In the late fall of 1998, General Sam signaled to the Board of Trustees that he wished to retire from the Presidency at the end of June 2000, thereby allowing eighteen months to find his successor. Although several members of the Board expressed regret and suggested a sabbatical to regroup and restore his health, they could tell that his decision was firm. They appreciated that he allowed ample time for them to find a successful replacement, and at General Sam's request, the search began somewhat earlier than would normally be expected. He wanted no stone left unturned in their attempts to locate the best available candidate. General Sam deliberately stepped aside and did not try to influence the choice of his successor. When, after a long, exhausting, and successful search, Dr. Walter M. Bortz was selected, Sam realized that his second retirement would finally become a reality. On the appointed day,

Dr. Walter Bortz was sworn in as the twenty-third President of Hampden-Sydney College, and General Sam Wilson was appointed President *Emeritus* and additionally named the James C. Wheat Professor of Leadership.

At the end of his term in office, the College hosted a farewell evening in Settle Hall for General Sam. An orchestra played, speeches were made, awards were given, and a recently painted portrait of General Sam was unveiled. It now hangs in the rotunda of Settle Hall. A smaller version of the portrait was revealed at the end of the ceremony and given to General Sam's family. It hangs in the Wilson Center for Leadership.

When asked about his successes as President, General Sam quoted a favorite saying of Mrs. P.T. Atkinson, a long-time icon at the college, "If you don't care who gets the credit, you can do anything."

He maintained that throughout his tenure the administration worked as a team. General Sam may have been the quarterback, but he could have done little by himself. Making changes to an institution with a history that straddles four centuries was a delicate project. General Sam valued the College's important mission of creating good men and good citizens in an environment of sound learning, but he also realized the need of preserving essential values from the late 1700s and pairing them with advances of the twenty-first century. General Sam believed that Hampden-Sydney's focus on this dynamic assured the College's place as an important and thriving academic leader.

*The portrait of Sam Wilson painted at the end of his term
as President of Hampden-Sydney College.*

POST-PRESIDENTIAL PERIOD:
THE SECOND RETIREMENT

ON JUNE 30, 2000, GENERAL SAM officially retired from his post as President of Hampden-Sydney College and, with Susi by his side, he once again began to adjust to the slower-paced, peaceful lifestyle of retirement at Frog Hollow.

Sadly, in November 2000, General Sam's beloved sister, Virginia Wilson Druen, died of cancer. From the time General Sam had assumed the Presidency, in July of 1992, until he left the office eight years later, her advice and counsel to him in the performance of his Presidential duties had been invaluable. She was a wise woman and an astute observer who kept the secrets that were necessary for the office but was willing to share with her brother all that she had learned about the running of Hampden-Sydney over her quarter century of service as executive secretary to the president. Her advice gave him an edge in the performance of his duties that few small college Presidents could enjoy. As he sat at his desk in his new office, down Via Sacra from the big red chair in Atkinson Hall, he prepared himself to tackle the next phase of his life without the support and advice of his loyal sister.

He began holding his evening classes in a small seminar room directly across the hall from his new office. He dropped the course that he had begun in 1982 on Foreign Policy and National Security, but he continued teaching Introduction to Intelligence and initiated a new course that he called the Advanced Seminar on Leadership and Ethics. General Sam had been wanting to make this curricular change for several years, but only in his new position could he take the time to create a syllabus. The Leadership Seminar became the capstone of General Sam's attempts to develop the College's leadership education.

He had taken the first step in April 1992, when he proposed to then-President Ralph Rossum and to Dean of the Faculty, Scott Colley, that the College should establish a center for excellence in public service with a focus on preparing students for political life, military service, diplomatic service, and service with non-governmental charities. While both Rossum and Colley showed interest in the idea, no new program developed. Several years after becoming President, General Sam posed the idea once again, stressing also the importance of including a highly organized emphasis on internships both during summer vacation and during academic semesters. One of the College's most capable political science professors, Dr. David Marion, in pursuit of the same kinds of ideas, proceeded separately to develop a public service certificate program that incorporated much of General Sam's original proposal. Professor Marion's public service certificate program caught on with the student body, and thanks to his energy and imagination, became sufficiently institutionalized to gain College-wide support. Gradually the program evolved into what became known as the Center for Leadership in the Public Interest. Upon General Sam's retirement in 2000, the College, acting on Professor Marion's recommendation, affixed General Sam's name to the Center. The Wilson Center for Leadership in the Public Interest has become one of the College's trademark programs.

General Sam's new seminar on leadership and ethics provided advanced work for high-potential upperclassmen, and it gave an opportunity for those young men to become deeply involved in leadership subjects before leaving Hampden-Sydney. The seminar initially enrolled only ten students, whose selection was based on recommendations from faculty members, athletic coaches, key administrators, recent alumni, and General Sam himself. He endeavored to select young men who were high achievers, who carried strong grade-point averages, and who occupied leadership positions in the student body. Responding to student pressure, he expanded the seminar to fourteen students, but he refused to expand beyond that number because he believed that he could not maintain the integrity of the class if his audience became too large.

Of all the undertakings in which he had been engaged during his twenty-five years at Hampden-Sydney, this small seminar, which met from 2000 through the fall of 2006, was General Sam's personal favorite. Here he was able to utilize all his experiences that pertained to leadership. The reactions of the young men around that Thursday evening seminar table were not only highly receptive, they were electric. Sessions were totally candid, with the doors closed, no holds barred, and no subjects forbidden. The highlight of those seminars happened just before Thanksgiving in 2004, when the seminar was ending for the evening at about 10:30, and all the students stood up as a group. One of them addressed General Sam. "General Sam," the student paused, "we have a request."

Unsure whether some sort of joke was underway, he responded with a jest, but he was told quickly that the matter was serious. The spokesman continued, "We are about to wrap up this seminar for the fall, but we would like to continue it into the spring semester, for these same hours on Thursday evenings. All of us would like to meet you here, whether we get academic credit or not."

General Sam was deeply moved by this request and did not know quite how to respond except to say, "Count me in. I'll do it." And they did.

Probably the most useful and tangible result generated by these sessions was the organizing of the students in teams of two to impart leadership lessons to younger students. Each pair was assigned to visit the underclassmen in their dormitories and fraternity houses in order to convey to them the essence of what the seminar covered on the responsibilities of leadership, the role of ethics and morality in leadership and leading, and the history and traditions of leadership at Hampden-Sydney College. Evaluation sheets were handed out to the younger students participating in these evening sessions, and their responses were enthusiastic. They appreciated these conversations on leadership with the older students, many of whom they admired, and they accepted that advice from their older brothers more readily than they would have from representatives of the faculty or the College administration.

General Sam recognized that there is an overarching demand for effective leadership in the twenty-first century, and he determined that Hampden-Sydney would do its part in filling the need. General Sam wanted young men to have the tools to discover themselves and to determine their own potential for leading, and he hoped to help his students identify the characteristics, prerequisites, and qualifications for becoming a successful leader in any field.

One program General Sam undertook in retirement was organized with his oldest son and namesake, Sam Wilson, Jr., a retired Green Beret lieutenant colonel who was teaching in the regional Governor's School at Longwood University. Colonel Sam had immersed himself deeply in the details of the local battles at Saylor's Creek in April 1865, when Lee's Army of Northern Virginia was decisively defeated by Ulysses Grant's Army of the Potomac. The remnants of these armies stumbled on to Appomattox, where three days later the Confederates surrendered. Colonel Sam had developed a small-scale replica of the battlefield which could be laid out either on the floor or on a series of tables in a large room. He had also carefully painted tiny block-figure soldiers, artillery pieces, horses, wagons, and battle flags. He created the entire replication as a model through which students could actually re-fight the

General Sam in his Wilson Center office with a student.

battle. Historically, some forty Generals were involved in the three separate engagements at Sayler's Creek, which meant there was an identified role for forty students to play. For the subsequent replicated battles, Colonel Sam had devised all kinds of gimmicks and gadgets to make the entire model come to life. Students immersed themselves deeply in the war game, addressing each other as General Grant and General Lee, General Ewell, General Humphrey, General Wright, etc. To General Sam, it was a novel way to teach about leadership during this Civil War battle that took place so close to Hampden-Sydney, and his collaboration with his son became a popular offering.

Almost since he first began working at the college, General Sam had been actively involved with Hampden-Sydney's Alumni Summer College. Through the Summer College, alumni returned to campus for an extended weekend to hear lectures, participate in seminars, and reacquaint themselves with their *alma mater*. General Sam's most memorable involvement with the Alumni Summer College was in 2005, when he played the primary role in the weekend's program as the central character in the production of *The Spy Who Loved Us*. To help prepare himself for the role, General Sam grew a long, white beard and on the night of the performance, he put on a floppy black hat and the cape from his dress military uniform. The opening show began with background music from the James Bond film, *The Spy Who Loved Me*. As the house lights of Crawley Forum went out, a single spotlight focused on one of the entrances to the stage area. The door slowly began to open with clouds of fog streaming out into the hall. Then a white-bearded General Sam emerged through the billowing fog with his hat pulled down over his eyes and his body leaning heavily on his cane. He ambled down to greet the dignitaries in the front row of the audience, addressing them in a smattering of seven or eight languages, laughing and carrying on as if they could understand his words.

When he finally got up to the lectern and began talking, he said, "Ladies and gentlemen, for the next three hours, we shall . . . " and was interrupted by an unknown voice calling out from the back of the room, "How long did you say?"

"Three hours," was the reply.

"Not me, brother!" the anonymous voice complained.

Then, BANG! A shot rang out, followed by the sounds of a body falling down the stairs. At that point, bedlam exploded against a backdrop of blaring, weird music and continued through a series of disjointed, unexpected activity that ended with Sam bellowing, "It is never too late!"

At that point, General Sam walked back on stage and asked the crowd to describe to him what they had just witnessed. The answers were all different. Then General Sam explained the bottom-line teaching point from the mad scene: never trust the first intelligence report. Get at least three reports that seem to make sense and then understand that the truth is likely to reside somewhere in the middle of these three points. He explained further that the wild scene they had watched was a device he had first used in 1942 as an infantry school instructor at Fort Benning. He had employed the technique to teach soldiers how to observe enemy activity from observation posts or while on reconnaissance patrols and then how to report promptly and accurately on what had been seen. The approach was novel and the lessons were vividly obvious.

Throughout the years after his retirement in 2000, General Sam worked to stay in close touch with students who attended Hampden-Sydney. He enjoyed frequent visits to his office from alumni seeking consultation. He often agreed to write letters of recommendation and references for his former students, including many who graduated and moved on but were seeking a helping hand in some application. In fact, he wrote hundreds of such references. He made a special point of keeping in close touch with the Hampden-Sydney students who went into one form or another of public service, especially with those who entered military service, the U.S. Foreign Service, or the Peace Corps.

In December of 1999, six months before leaving office, Susi and General

Sam voluntarily moved out of Middlecourt and back to the farm so that the College would have plenty of time to renovate the President's quarters. Once back at Frog Hollow full time, General Sam and Susi began to involve themselves in the local community. General Sam accepted a position as an Elder at Jamestown Presbyterian Church and began teaching Sunday school there. He found himself regularly responding to invitations that began with "Sam, now that you've retired and don't have anything to do, you can certainly come help us." The truth was he had as much to do in his retirement as he ever had.

Since his military retirement in 1977, General Sam had maintained his relationship with U.S. Special Operations and the intelligence communities. In the spring of 1995, he was invited to be the guest of honor at a United States Special Operations community gala in Washington. At this banquet, he was presented with the U.S. Special Operations Distinguished Service Medal and a second, even more prestigious medal, the annual Arthur D. "Bull" Simon Award, viewed in military circles as something like the Special Operations' Heisman Trophy. The gathering was attended by a number of distinguished guests, including celebrated American war and spy novelist, Tom Clancy. General Sam was deeply moved by the awards, which now sit on the mantel of the fireplace in the lounge at the Wilson Center for Leadership in the Public Interest.

In the spring of 1996, General Sam was invited by senior figures in the U.S. intelligence community, both active and retired, to join them at another banquet in Washington, where he was honored by receiving the William Oliver Baker Award, the intelligence community's equivalent of the Special Operation Community's Bull Simon Award. General Sam was the only person to ever have received both of these prestigious honors.

In light of physical infirmities and a crowded schedule, General Sam tried hard to limit his participation in social affairs, but in 2004, his invitation to attend the annual Alfalfa Club gathering in Washington was one that could not be missed. He was invited by the Chairman of the Board of Media General, and the event was held at one of the largest, most prestigious hotels in Washington. The guest list included the President of the United States, George W. Bush, as well as his father, the former President—everyone who carried influence in Washington's political circles along with representatives from the corporate world, entertainment figures, and famous members of the public media. General Sam relished the opportunity to meet a number of his former bosses, including the former Secretary of State and the Secretary of Defense, as well as several former Chairmen of the Joint Chiefs of Staff. On that evening, he had the opportunity to shake hands and hold a brief conversation with President George W. Bush. He also shared time with both the former President Bush, Sr., and Mrs. Bush, with whom he had developed a friendship while still on active duty. The evening reminded him of times in his military career when he had been fortunate enough to rub elbows with crowned heads of state, prime ministers, cabinet members, dukes, and duchesses. In Southside Virginia, General Sam would quickly assume the demeanor of a good old country boy, so it was a bit heady to be in that rarified atmosphere for an evening and to socialize with ladies and gentlemen of international distinction. Truth be told, he realized that as invigorating as the evening proved to be, he was a great deal more comfortable at Frog Hollow.

The Wilson Center staff. Seated; Professor James Y. Simms and Sam Wilson.
Standing, from left: Professor David Marion, Professor Curt Smith,
General Gerald Boykin, and Rondi Arlton.

CONCLUSION

IN THE FALL OF 2005, when I proposed to General Sam that I would like to compile the highlights of his life into a written document, neither of us had a clear, long-term vision for the undertaking. Pulling together an active eighty-four-year-old man's entire life was too intimidating a task for him or me to consider. We decided to begin with an initial goal of identifying foundations for leadership and life lessons gleaned from a man of the World War II generation. It did not take long for me to realize that there were far too many interesting stories that General Sam lived over the years to include them all in a book without having it swell into a multi-volume encyclopedia. Picking a few of his interesting tales, ones that were the most applicable to our original goals, has been a difficult task. I also found that breaking down a complicated life into a series of discrete, neatly organized events strays from the reality of living.

To avoid locking ourselves into a task that lost its appeal for both of us, we approached the project one semester at a time. General Sam and I initially agreed to spend only the spring semester of 2006 meeting once a week at his office to review the first twenty-one years of his life. That assignment completed, we would consider our options for future work. Fortunately, both of us enjoyed our sessions that semester and found the final product valuable enough to merit another independent study the following spring, this time exploring General Sam's professional military life. At the end of that semester, having traversed the first two-thirds of General Sam's life, we realized that stopping there would fall short of our obligations to each other and to the project. Now, with our work on all three phases of his life complete, we are relieved to have this substantial narrative as the fruit of more than seven years of work.

General Sam has lived a full life. He achieved great things for the United States military and for Hampden-Sydney College. His leadership aided our country and the College at times when it was greatly needed, and his leadership style deserves to be studied. For those reasons, the working title for this book at one time was *The Makings of an American Leader*.

Now, as I reread the text, I cannot single out one approach or key to his leadership style that helped him to excel. Despite the value of what I have learned in Hampden-Sydney's Society of '91 leadership seminar or in General Sam's leadership class, I have come to the conclusion that leadership cannot be understood completely from bullet-pointed lectures. General Sam's leadership style is not something that can be reproduced and mass-distributed. Leadership does not function in that manner.

Each individual must work to find his or her own strengths and weaknesses and learn from them to fashion a leadership style. General Sam successfully did exactly that. Perhaps an undergraduate's attempt to capture the personality of a man who used his innate physical and intellectual resources to react effectively to the stressful problems that life threw at him offers a more complete picture of leadership in action than a series of PowerPoint slides. I am wagering that a complex narrative portrait of this man will teach us more and will affect us more deeply than a sequence of culled principles or reductive rules.

Having the opportunity to know and to help others know a man who was able to act effectively in morally complex circumstances has been a privilege for which I am grateful. The greatest value of my project has been the opportunity to come to know, appreciate, and perhaps, in some measure, dramatize for others the life and achievements of an honest and passionate man, a patriotic American, General Samuel Vaughan Wilson. For that I will be forever grateful to him.

From the forests and fields of Depression-era Southside Virginia to the swampy jungles of World War II Burma, from the pinstripe suits of the White House to the shadows and mirrors surrounding the Kremlin during the Cold War, this narrative describes the journey of a man who spent his whole life in service. He learned early that by putting one foot in front of another, much can be achieved, and in the face of daunting challenges, he accomplished with unwavering determination what lesser men would call impossible. His innate abilities as a leader shone equally in his varied military career, his role as an educator and college President, his contributions to his community, and his devotion to his family and to God. General Samuel Vaughan Wilson offers each of us a glimpse into our own potential—if we have the will to reach for it.

—AJP

Drew Prehmus (at right above, on the porch of the Wilson Center) and Gen. Sam Wilson wrote this book as part of an independent study class over Drew's final three years as a student at Hampden-Sydney College. After working as the Special Assistant to the President at Hampden-Sydney for three years, Drew enrolled in Duke University's Fuqua School of Business.

Made in the USA
Charleston, SC
13 August 2013